EUROPE IN TRANSITION: THE
STUDIES SERIES

Also by Bonnie N. Field

Spain's "Second Transition"? The Socialist Government of José Luis Rodríguez Zapatero (*editor*)

Democracy and Institutional Development: Spain in Comparative Theoretical Perspective (*coeditor with Kerstin Hamann*)

Also by Alfonso Botti

La Spagna e la crisi modernista

Cielo y dinero. El nacionalcatolicismo en España, 1881–1975

Romolo Murri e l'anticlericalismo negli anni de "La Voce"

La questione basca. Dalle origini allo scioglimento di Batasuna

Storia della Spagna democratica. Da Franco a Zapatero (*coauthor with Carmelo Adagio*)

Il Modernismo tra cristianità e secolarizzazione (*coeditor with Rocco Cerrato*)

Romolo Murri e i murrismi in Italia e in Europa cent'anni dopo (*coeditor with Rocco Cerrato and Ilaria Biagioli*)

Storia ed esperienza religosa (*editor*)

Le patrie degli spagnoli (*editor*)

L'Ultimo franchismo (*coeditor with Massimiliano Guderzo*)

Clero e guerre spagnole (1808–1939) (*editor*)

Luigi Sturzo e gli amici spagnoli. Carteggi 1924–1951 (*editor*)

Politics and Society in Contemporary Spain

From Zapatero to Rajoy

Editedb y
BonnieN. Fielda nd Alfonso Botti

palgrave
macmillan

POLITICS AND SOCIETY IN CONTEMPORARY SPAIN

Softcover reprint of the hardcover 1st edition 2013 978-1-137-30661-6

First published in 2013 by
PALGRAVE MACMILLAN®
in the United States—a division of St. Martin's Press LLC,
175 Fifth Avenue, New York, NY 10010.

Where this book is distributed in the UK, Europe and the rest of the world,
this is by Palgrave Macmillan, a division of Macmillan Publishers Limited,
registered in England, company number 785998, of Houndmills,
Basingstoke, Hampshire RG21 6XS.

Palgrave Macmillan is the global academic imprint of the above companies
and has companies and representatives throughout the world.

Palgrave® and Macmillan® are registered trademarks in the United States,
the United Kingdom, Europe and other countries.

ISBN 978-1-349-45515-7   ISBN 978-1-137-30662-3 (eBook)
DOI 10.1057/9781137306623

Acknowledge permission granted by Tirant lo Blanch to republish portions
of the following work in chapter 5 of this volume:
Excerpts from chapter 7: "El Estado autonómico: superando la resaca
estatutaria y capeando la crisis," pages 197–202, 205–207, 208–211.
Editors: César Colino and Ramón Cotarelo
Title of book: España en crisis. Balance de la segunda legislatura de
Rodríguez Zapatero.
ISBN/issue number: 978–84–15442–58–5
Publisher: Tirant lo Blanch, Valencia
Date of publication: May 2012

Library of Congress Cataloging-in-Publication Data is available from the
Library of Congress.

A catalogue record of the book is available from the British Library.

Design by Newgen Imaging Systems (P) Ltd., Chennai, India.

First edition: June 2013

10 9 8 7 6 5 4 3 2 1

Transferred to Digital Printing in 2013

For Angela—Bonnie Field

For my children: Giaime, Edoardo, and Leo—Alfonso Botti

Contents

Figuresand Tables

Figures

Tables

Contributors

Carmelo Adagio (PhD in contemporary history, La Sapienza University in Rome) is currently a primary and secondary school principal. His dissertation is on the church and the dictatorship of Primo de Rivera. In addition to numerous articles in journals and collective volumes, he published *Chiesa e nazione. La dittatura di Primo de Rivera in Spagna 1923–1930* (Unicopli, Milan, 2004) and, in collaboration with A. Botti, *Storia della Spagna democratica. Da Franco a Zapatero* (B. Mondadori, Milan, 2006). Along with S. Urso and R. Cerrato, he edited *Il lungo decennio. L'Italia prima del 68* (Cierre, Sommacampagna, 1999).

Mireno Berrettini (PhD in political science, Università Cattolica del Sacro Cuore) has been a fellow at the Italian Centro Nazionale delle Ricerche. He is currently a postdoctoral fellow at the Università Cattolica del Sacro Cuore (Milan). He collaborates with the journal *Spagna Contemporanea*. He is interested in issues related to the Spanish Catholic Church and Catholicism. His latest publications are "La formazione del clero castrense spagnolo nei primi trenta anni del XX secolo," in A. Botti (ed.), *Clero e guerre spagnole in età contemporaea (1808–1939)*; "A settant'anni dalla Carta Collettiva dell'Episcopato spagnolo: Jerarquía, martirio, memoria collettiva," in E. Acciai and G. Quaggio (eds.), *Un conflitto che non passa. Storia, memoria e rimozioni della Guerra Civile spagnola*.

Anna Bosco (PhD University of Florence) is associate professor of comparative politics at the University of Trieste (Italy) and editor (with Susannah Verney) of the journal *South European Society & Politics*. She has carried out research on political parties in Italy, Spain, Portugal, Greece, and East-Central Europe. Her most recent publications include *La España de Zapatero. Años de cambios 2004–2008* (edited with Ignacio Sánchez-Cuenca, 2009) and *From Berlusconi to Monti: Parties' Default?* (edited with Duncan McDonnell, 2012).

Alfonso Botti is full professor of contemporary history in the College of Letters and Philosophy at the University of Modena and Reggio Emilia (Italy). Codirector of the journal *Spagna contemporanea*, he is also on the scientific boards of several Spanish and Italian journals. His research trajectory is centered on the history of Catholicism, of the church, and of nationalisms in Spain. Most recently, he published *La questione basca* (B. Mondadori, Milan, 2003), *Storia della Spagna democratica. Da Franco a Zapatero* (B. Mondadori, Milan, 2006) with C. Adagio, *Cielo y dinero* (Alianza, Madrid, 2008), and edited *Le patrie degli spagnoli* (B. Mondadori, Milan, 2007), *L'Ultimo franchismo* (Rubbettino, Soveria Mannelli, 2009) with M. Guderzo, *Clero e guerre spagnole, 1808–1936* (Rubbettino, Soveria Mannelli, 2011), and *Luigi Sturzo e gli amici spagnoli, Carteggi 1924–1951* (Rubbettino, Soveria Mannelli, 2012).

César Colino is associate professor at the Department of Political Science and Public Administration at the Spanish National Distance-Learning University (UNED) in Madrid. He has taught at the University of Salamanca and the Autonomous University of Madrid and has been visiting researcher at the Max-Planck Institute for the Study of Society (*MPIfG*) in Cologne and research officer at the Institute for Research in Public Administration (*FöV*) in Speyer, Germany. More recently he has been visiting fellow at the Center for Federal Studies at the University of Kent (United Kingdom, 2008). His recent research and publications have revolved around comparative federalism, intergovernmental relations, and constitutional reform in federations. He has published in journals such as *Policy & Politics*, *Regional & Federal Studies*, and *Publius*.

Eloísa del Pino (PhD Universidad Complutense) is senior research fellow at Institute of Public Goods and Policies (IPP) in the Spanish National Research Council (CSIC) (Madrid, Spain). She has taught at several Universities in Madrid (1995–2012) and has been visiting researcher at the Centre d'Études et de la Recherche sur la Vie Locale (CNRS) and at the School of Social Policy and Social Research at the University of Kent. Her research and publications have dealt with the political conditions for change of the welfare state, the reform of public administration and public policies, citizen participation and citizens' attitudes toward the state and welfare policies. She is editor of *Los Estados de Bienestar en la Encrucijada. Políticas Sociales en Perspectiva Comparada* (with María Josefa Rubio, 2013).

Bonnie N. Field (PhD in political science, University of California, Santa Barbara) is associate professor of global studies at Bentley University

(Massachusetts, United States). She is an Affiliate of the Minda de Gunzburg Center for European Studies at Harvard University. She has been a faculty fellow at the University of California, Irvine, visiting fellow at UCI's Center for the Study of Democracy, and Fulbright senior researcher in Spain. Her publications focus on regime democratization, political parties, and political institutions in Spain and Latin America. She is editor of *Spain's "Second Transition"? The Socialist Government of José Luis Rodríguez Zapatero* (2011) and *Democracy and Institutional Development: Spain in Comparative Theoretical Perspective* (with Kerstin Hamann, 2008). Her research has been published in *Comparative Political Studies, Comparative Politics, Democratization, Party Politics, PS: Political Science & Politics, Electoral Studies, South European Society & Politics, Revista Española de Ciencia Política*, and *Revista de las Cortes Generales*, and in several book chapters.

Alejandro Godino is a PhD student at the Institute for Labor Studies (IET) at the Universidad Autónoma de Barcelona. He holds a BA degree in sociology (University of Granada) and a master's degree in European labor studies. He has participated in the Seventh Framework Program funded project WALQING, focused on the quality of employment in new and growing sectors across Europe, and, currently, is involved in the "New strategies for immigration: requalification for a new labor market" project, funded by Agaur and Recercaixa, centered on trends and policies for unemployed immigrants. His PhD studies revolve around job quality in outsourced services. His research interests are workplace studies, collective bargaining, and organizational behavior.

Kerstin Hamann (PhD Washington University) is professor of political science at the University of Central Florida and editor of the *Journal of Political Science Education*. Her research focuses on Spanish politics, comparative political economy (especially trade unions) in Western Europe, and the scholarship of teaching and learning. Her books include *The Politics of Industrial Relations: Labor Unions in Spain* (2012), *Parties, Elections, and Policy Reforms in Western Europe: Voting for Social Pacts* (with John Kelly, 2011), *Assessment in Political Science* (coedited with Michelle Deardorff and John Ishiyama, 2009), and *Democracy and Institutional Development: Spain in Comparative Theoretical Perspective* (coedited with Bonnie N. Field, 2008). Her research has been published in journals such as *Comparative Political Studies, British Journal of Industrial Relations, European Journal of Industrial Relations, Publius, South European Society and Politics, Journal of Political Science*

Education, College Teaching, and *PS: Political Science & Politics*, as well as in numerous book chapters.

Óscar Molina lectures at the Institute for Labor Studies (IET), Universidad Autónoma de Barcelona. He holds a degree in economics from Pompeu Fabra University and a PhD in political and social sciences from the European University Institute, Florence, Italy. In 2005–2007 he was IRCHSS research fellow at the Industrial Relations and Human Resources Group, University College Dublin, and then junior ICREA researcher in the Centre d'Estudis Sociològics sobre la Vida Quotidiana I el Treball (QUIT). His research interests include comparative industrial relations, comparative political economy, labor market, corporatism, and varieties of capitalism.

Celia Valiente (PhD sociology, Universidad Autónoma de Madrid) is associate professor of sociology at the Department of Economic History and Institutions of the Universidad Carlos III de Madrid, Spain. Her main research interests are gender-equality policies and the women's movement in Spain from a comparative perspective. She has published articles in *Gender & Society*, *European Journal of Political Research*, *Politics & Gender*, and *South European Society & Politics*, among others. She is the author of *Gendering Spanish Democracy* (with Monica Trelfall and Christine Cousins, Routledge, 2005) and of numerous book chapters.

Acknowledgments

This project initiated with the Istituto Cattaneo in Bologna, Italy, which asked us to lead a project on Spain for their book series *Elezioni, governi, democrazia*. We then assembled an interdisciplinary group of international scholars who could shed light on the political, social, and economic developments in Spain. The collaboration led to the publication in Italian of *La Spagna di Rajoy* (Bologna: Il Mulino). We would like to warmly thank Gianfranco Baldini, Anna Bosco, and Stefania Profeti for their initiative and assistance, and express our gratitude for the financial support the Istituto Cattaneo provided to translate several chapters. We also thank the two translators who worked on the project, David Bull and Jeremy Carden.

Bonnie Field gratefully acknowledges the summer grant support provided by Bentley University. She also thanks her colleagues and friends at the Universitat Autònoma de Barcelona, particularly Joan Botella and Eva Ostergaard-Nielsen, for hosting her as an invited professor in June 2012, which allowed her to exchange ideas with a number of individuals that contributed greatly to her thinking on contemporary Spanish politics. Finally, she thanks the Center for European Studies at Harvard University for the invitation to participate in a roundtable on the 2011 Spanish elections, which also informed the analysis presented here.

BONNIE N. FIELD
ALFONSO BOTTI

CHAPTER 1

Introduction: Political Change in Spain, from Zapatero to Rajoy

Bonnie N. Field and Alfonso Botti

Spanish prime minister José Luis Rodríguez Zapatero was once a darling of European social democracy, and was and remains a villain for the Spanish political right. Leading the Socialist Party (PSOE) to a surprise electoral victory in 2004, following the Islamist terrorist attacks on the Madrid commuter train system, he enacted a striking set of progressive reforms (Bosco & Sánchez-Cuenca 2009; Field 2011).

He rapidly reoriented Spanish foreign policy by withdrawing Spanish troops from Iraq, reversing the support that his predecessor, the conservative José María Aznar of the Popular Party (PP), had given to the US-led war (Powell 2009). Parliament also passed a series of progressive social and civil rights laws, including an ambitious gender equality act and the legalization of same-sex marriage and adoption (Calvo 2009; Encarnación 2009). He placed particular emphasis on women's representation, appointing a cabinet that for the first time in the history of Spanish democracy included an equal number of women and men.

Rooted in the discovery of more than two hundred mass graves with the remains of the victims of Francoist and Falangist violence, Zapatero confronted Spain's divisive history of civil war, the Franco dictatorship, and human rights' violations more than any other Spanish leader since the transition to democracy in the mid-1970s (Aguilar 2009). He oversaw significant reforms of Spain's territorial institutions by expanding autonomy in several political regions (called autonomous communities) (Baldi & Baldini 2009; Muro 2009). Moreover, he strengthened

Spain's comparatively frail, at least in the Western European context, welfare state, especially with the passage of the dependency law, which committed the state to providing some care for those who cannot care for themselves. Nonetheless, it is important to note that various social policies initiated by Zapatero have been criticized for lack of resources, problems of implementation, and for the difficulties of actually meeting their stated goals (chapter 10 in this volume; Bernardi & Sarasa 2009; Calvo & Martin 2009).

The Zapatero government also began risky negotiations with the terrorist group ETA (Basque Homeland and Freedom) with the goal of ending the violence that the radical Basque independence group had been perpetrating since the later years of the Francoist dictatorship. The negotiations were supported by all of the parliamentary parties except the principal opposition party. The PP vehemently opposed the government's antiterrorist policies, and the subject formed part of the deep polarization (or *crispación*) that marked the relationship between the PSOE and PP (Field 2009; Sánchez-Cuenca 2009). The negotiations ended in failure and with a deadly bomb that ETA placed in terminal four of Madrid's Barajas airport in December 2006. It was undoubtedly a defeat for the government and a blow to Zapatero's leadership. But with ETA's declaration in October 2011 that it would definitively abandon violent activity, a month before Spain's general elections, some analysts stressed the contribution of the then failed peace process to the end of terrorism (Sánchez-Cuenca 2012, 55–65), or what the principal Socialist negotiator called a "tactical failure and a strategic win" (Eguiguren & Rodríguez Aizpeolea 2011, 247). Without doubt, the announced end of terrorist activity is a tremendous achievement of the Zapatero governments and for Spanish and Basque democracy more broadly (see chapter 5 in this volume).

Even though the Socialists under Zapatero's leadership had recognized the weaknesses of Spain's preexisting economic model based on consumption and construction, it is evident that the Zapatero government did not effectively reorient the economy or deflate the real estate bubble. This is in part due to the success of the Spanish economy during his first term. As Mulas-Granados (2009) notes, Zapatero preferred to prolong the period of economic expansion that he had inherited from his predecessors. Therefore, the more ambitious economic proposals contained in the 2004 Socialist Party electoral manifesto turned into timid fiscal and labor market reforms. According to Royo (2009a), Zapatero's economic team continued, in general, the economic policies of its predecessors, Felipe González (PSOE) and José María Aznar (PP), and according to López and Rodríguez (2011) Spain in broad strokes has continued to follow the same economic model adopted during the Francoist regime in the 1950s. The lack of effective action in times of economic expansion would end up being very costly when the international economic crisis began to explode after 2007 and to deeply impact Spain beginning in 2008.

Nonetheless, the government fulfilled much of the program with which the Socialist Party went to the polls in 2004. Despite the aggressive opposition of the PP, and other conservative groups such as the Catholic Church (see chapter 9 in this volume), to nearly their entire political agenda, the government's actions obtained substantial electoral support in 2008. Compared to 2004, the PSOE won more votes and increased its seats by five, with which it was able to continue governing again in minority (see chapter 4 this volume). However, it is important to note that the PP also increased its votes and seats, in fact more than the Socialists, producing the highest vote concentration in the two principal parties since the beginning of Spain's democracy.

Political scientists, historians, and other analysts all highlight the differences between Zapatero's first and second terms in office. The second term, inaugurated in 2008, was inescapably marked by the most severe economic crisis Spain has experienced in the past 80 years. This crisis has not only tested Spain, but, in its international dimensions, has indeed severely challenged the Euro and the European Union (EU). Accustomed to seeing itself (and to being seen) as the architect of a model transition to democracy and economic successes, in sharp contrast,[1] Spain is now at the center of international attention for its economic frailty, extremely high unemployment, and protest movements, such as the *indignados* (indignant).

Zapatero left office following the November 2011 elections, in which he did not compete, as an extremely unpopular figure, even among his prior base of supporters. With Alfredo Pérez Rubalcaba as the Socialist candidate for prime minister, the 2011 elections severely punished the PSOE, and together with the prior local and regional elections relegated the PSOE to its lowest quota of political power since the transition to democracy. This book provides the opportunity to reflect on Zapatero's legacy and to more broadly analyze contemporary Spain. The contributors to the book examine the major political, social, and economic events of Zapatero's second term in depth. They also contrast these developments with those of the first term in order to offer a comprehensive assessment. Last, they evaluate the challenges Spain and the new Popular Party government of Mariano Rajoy face. Before summarizing the chapters, this introduction first evaluates in more detail the economic and political crisis that exploded during Zapatero's second term and then analyzes the results of the November 20, 2011, elections.

An Economic and a Political Crisis

If Prime Minister Zapatero's first term in office is known for the extension of civil rights and liberties, among other reforms, the second term will surely be remembered for cuts in social benefits, reduction of labor rights, loss of jobs for many Spaniards, and reduction of economic prospects and living standards for many others. Moreover, the economic crisis and the adjustments to it have also provoked a severe political and institutional crisis that does not appear to have attenuated after the general elections of 2011.

We first provide a brief summary of some of the characteristics of the economic crisis. After a growth period from 1995 to 2007 characterized by a 3.6 percent average annual increase of gross domestic product (GDP), Spain entered a period of recession that reached −3.7 percent GDP growth in 2009, and −0.3 percent in 2010. After a timid recovery in 2011 (0.4 percent), the economy again, according to all estimates, experienced negative growth in 2012.[2] Simultaneously unemployment reached 24.4 percent of the active population in the first trimester of 2012.[3] Youth unemployment reached a dramatic 48.6 percent in 2011 (Fundación FOESSA and Cáritas 2012, 7). The evolution of the budget deficit as a percentage of GDP was 4.5 percent in 2008, 11.2 percent in 2009, 9.7 percent in 2010, and 9.4 percent in 2011,[4] while the government likely missed the 2012 deficit target of 6.3 percent of GDP (which had already been increased from a 5.3 percent target).[5]

The most revealing and at the same time distressing data are those provided by the report *Exclusión y desarrollo social* (exclusion and social development) (Fundación FOESSA and Cáritas 2012), which indicate that income per capita fell in real terms nearly 9 percent between 2007 and 2010 (p. 6), resulting in a rapid increase in inequality since the mid-1990s. The ratio of income corresponding to the wealthiest 20 percent of the population compared to the poorest 20 percent went from 5.3 in 2007 to 6.9 at the end of 2010 (p. 7); in fact this represents the greatest increase in the EU-27 countries. According to the study's estimates, the proportion of households that fell below the poverty line in 2011 was 21.8 percent, two points higher than in 2009—an increase without precedent in recent decades (pp. 10–11) and which places Spain among the countries with the most poverty in the EU-21, only surpassed by Romania and Lithuania (p. 13).

It is important to underscore some basic points about the economic and financial crisis in Spain. First, Spain was not Greece. Before the crisis exploded the government's accounts were healthy and in fact until 2007 there was a surplus. Spain indeed had been applauded for many years for being an example of economic success and the economy during Zapatero's first term exhibited very positive macroeconomic indicators (Royo 2009a,b). Second, the international crisis affected the Iberian country more punitively because of Spain's structural economic problems, such as low productivity and competitiveness, and a labor market divided between many with precarious jobs and others with permanent contracts and high job security (see chapters 6 and 7 in this volume; Royo 2009b; Salmon 2010), and due to its economic model that is based largely on construction and consumption, which produced an increase in unemployment without comparison in the rest of the EU. Spain has spent months on the edge of a cliff, over which Greece has already fallen, while Portugal dangerously approaches the abyss. Third, Spain's economic model did not originate in the Zapatero era and therefore responsibility for its failures lies with the PSOE and the PP, and the real estate policy in the prior decades is just one of the more obvious examples.

On the other hand, one can surely evaluate the Zapatero government for not having reoriented the economy as we mentioned earlier and for its response to the crisis. Zapatero has been harshly criticized for not reacting to the crisis in time and for denying or underestimating its magnitude. When the government began to respond at the end of 2008, initially its policies were Keynesian in nature, using moderate counter-cyclical fiscal stimulus measures. But, after May 2010, due to pressure from European institutions, the government's policies were completely reversed, and painful austerity-based adjustment policies were enacted. The government also liberalized the labor market, making firing easier and cheaper, against the fervent opposition of the unions (see chapter 7 in this volume), and with the argument that a more flexible labor market would facilitate employment. But, labor market reform did not create employment (Fishman 2012). The adjustment policies also did not resolve the economic crisis nor did they prevent the emergence of a sovereign debt crisis that persisted after Zapatero left office; many analysts also fear that the adjustment policies will not correct and may even worsen the structural problems of the Spanish economy and labor market (chapter 6 in this volume; Fishman 2012).

Let's consider the context within which the government developed its policies: it was and is an era dominated by neoliberalism; as part of the EU and the Eurozone Spain lacks the ability to devaluate a national currency; EU leaders insisted on austerity; and Spain was under tremendous pressure from the markets. These conditions certainly restricted the Zapatero government's options, but they did not determine the exact response. The government opted, perhaps because its leaders thought it was the best way to avoid the abyss, not only for austerity policies but also to concentrate on the reduction of spending, including social spending cuts and the reduction of public employees' salaries, and not on increasing government receipts through taxation particularly on the wealthy. It is often said that Zapatero focused on avoiding at any cost a formal bailout of the Spanish economy by European authorities; he succeeded but indeed at a very high cost.

It is in this context of severe economic crisis that support for the government and the Socialists eroded and political change occurred. The period that began in the summer of 2008 with the first effects of the international financial crisis in Spain was very different from Zapatero's first term. Nonetheless, the electorate, according to surveys of vote intention and to actual results in European and regional elections, did not immediately change its views as a result of the crisis itself, rather public opinion changed gradually and in response to the Socialist government's handling of the crisis. From this perspective, neither the regional elections in Galicia and the Basque Country in 2009, nor the European elections in the same year were decisive. In the former, the PP, with a small vote increase, recaptured its dominant position in the traditionally conservative region, putting an end to the first coalition government of the PSOE and the Galician nationalists of Galician Nationalist Block (BNG). In the Basque Country, the banning of the political party *Batasuna* from electoral competition, due to its association with the terrorist group ETA, and the Socialist government's political dialog with ETA permitted the Basque Socialists to govern and attain the premiership of the Basque government for the first time, though in minority with the external parliamentary support of the PP. In the European elections, the PP beat the PSOE but only by three percentage points, which can also be interpreted, at least in part, as a result of the abstention of the Socialist electorate.

Change began in May 2010 when Zapatero announced austerity measures under pressure from the European institutions. At this point Zapatero was reproached for a lack of leadership, the underestimation of the magnitude of the crisis, the delayed response, the drastic reduction of government spending, and the cuts to the welfare state (see chapter 11 in this volume). It was not by accident that it was only in October 2010 that PP leader Mariano Rajoy caught up with Zapatero in Spanish public opinion polls.[6] Simultaneously Rajoy, after experiencing the worst period of his political life in the aftermath of the 2008 election defeat and after having consolidating his leadership at the party convention in Valencia in 2008 by defeating the hawks within his own party, was able to trot out his triumph in the European elections the prior year (see chapter 3 in this volume).

In the Catalan regional elections in November 2010, the PP won four additional seats, and the decline of the Catalan Socialist Party (PSC-PSOE) and of the Republican Left of Catalonia (ERC) put an end to the tripartite government, which also included Initiative for Catalonia Greens (ICV). This was definitely an important symptom of public disaffection, but still not definitive proof that the electorate had shifted. The real change in the electorate's political orientation became evident with the remarkable defeat of the Socialists in the regional elections on May 22, 2011. This result combined with an economic situation that foreshadowed the adoption of even more drastic and unpopular economic measures that Zapatero no longer felt or no longer had the legitimacy to adopt or that he preferred to leave to his successor led Zapatero to call for early parliamentary elections.

The political and institutional crisis is deeper and more extensive than the defeat of the Socialists. Nonetheless there are few positive signs. The November 2011 elections were legitimately called by Prime Minister Zapatero, and the new parliament and the Rajoy government were the result of free elections. The traditional party system did not collapse in Spain, as had occurred in Greece in May 2012. Additionally, there are no significant xenophobic movements in Spain, as are present in almost all of Europe, in spite of the extremely high levels of unemployment and immigration, which we will explore in more depth in the concluding chapter.

However the political disaffection of Spanish citizens indicates grave problems for Spain's democracy. Among the citizenry, there is the palpable feeling that corruption permeates the political system and that it has increased in recent years (Villoria & Jiménez 2012, 431), especially polluting local and regional politics, often in connection with the urban development and construction "boom" (Jiménez 2009) that for the moment has particularly implicated the PP. Suspected corruption has reached as far as the royal family with investigations into the business dealings of Iñaki Urdangarin,[7] King Juan Carlos's son-in-law, and the Supreme Court with the resignation, without being indicted, in June 2012 of Carlos Dívar, president of the Supreme Court and of the General Council of Judicial Power, due to a scandal about trips paid for with public funds.[8] Between January and May 2012, an average of 10.2 percent of those surveyed identified "corruption and fraud" as among the "three main problems that currently exist in Spain."[9] While more of those surveyed indicated problems related to the economy, unemployment, and the "political class," this is the highest percentage since the mid-1990s when a series of scandals surrounding the Socialist governments of Felipe González erupted. Notably, the Zapatero governments enacted important anticorruption measures and corruption cases involving high-level officials in the central government were nearly nonexistent; nonetheless the perception persists that corruption also increased in central state politics (Villoria & Jiménez 2012). Villoria and Jiménez (2012) note the paradox that there is a "continuous increase in the perception of corruption precisely when the fight against it is greatest" (412) and that the perception of corruption does not correspond with "the objective reality of the phenomenon" (421).

Yet, as this volume was going to press, a severe corruption scandal exploded in late January 2013, involving purported illegal financing of the Popular Party and payments, above and beyond their official salaries, to its senior leaders. The documentation published by the newspaper *El País* is alleged to be secret accounting records of former party treasurer Luis Bárcenas. The names of many of the most significant figures of the Popular Party, including Mariano Rajoy, appear on the ledger as having received payments. While Rajoy and many others have denied allegations of impropriety and there are currently more questions than answers regarding this scandal, there is no doubt that it has profoundly shaken the citizens' trust in the Popular Party and in the government.

To the issue of corruption, we add the common belief, also prevalent in other democracies, that the existing democracy is not real, and that decisions are made in places far from the citizens and often against their interests. In this context we must analyze the *indignados*, a protest movement that emerged prior to the local and regional elections in May 2011 (see chapter 8 in this volume). This movement, in its initial stages dominated by young people who have in particular felt the consequences of the crisis but later heterogeneous, originated as a response to increased citizen malaise due to the economic crisis and to the Zapatero government's social spending cuts (Pastor Verdú 2012, 358). As Charnock et al. (2012, 5) indicate, the movement activists demand "real democracy" and reject the state institutions that they consider to be dominated by a corrupt political class controlled by bankers.[10] Their criticisms are directed at the system as a whole, and they express particular disdain for the political parties, which they see as undemocratic in their internal workings, as they also see the electoral system that reinforces the dominance of the two main parties. The broad support Spanish society gave to the movement is an indication that these sentiments resonate; in June 2011, 66 percent of those surveyed sympathized with the movement.[11]

Additionally, there is the prevalent view that public policies are imposed by technocrats of the European Union and by Germany, principally, and France, what was referred to as *Mercozy*, referring to the duo of Angela Merkel, chancellor of Germany, and Nicolas Sarkozy, president of France until 2012. The fact that the austerity measures imposed by the government concentrated on spending reductions, a reduction of social protection, and that public funds were used to save the banks reinforce the belief that politicians do not represent the people, which also helps explain the tremendous decline of support for the Socialist Party in the November 2011 elections.

The November 2011 Elections and the Victory of the Popular Party

After an election campaign that was notable for its lack of specificity on the policies that would be implemented to respond to the continuing economic crisis, the PP trounced the PSOE in the November 2011 parliamentary elections. The amount of institutional power the Popular Party obtained as a result is tremendous. On top of its absolute majority in parliament, it enjoys unprecedented power at the local and regional levels due to its gains in the local and regional elections in May 2011. Additionally, the principal party of the opposition, the PSOE, is in deep crisis because of its dramatic defeat.

The Socialist Party did not just lose the elections, it was nearly destroyed at the ballot box; it lost more than four million voters and attained its lowest vote share since the transition to democracy. Moreover, the party was left deeply divided between two weak leaderships, those of Alfredo Pérez Rubalcaba, the official leader, and Carmen Chacón. Even after being crushed at the polls, the party celebrated its thirty-eighth party convention without engaging in a serious analysis of the defeat or its causes, without new ideas for the future, and without the kind of analysis about the future of the welfare state and of social democracy that the circumstances demand (see chapter 2 in this volume). As much as the Socialists would like to characterize their new opposition strategy as "useful" (reclaiming one of the best and most productive slogans of Zapatero's era as leader of the opposition), the Socialists' opposition, due to the overwhelming majority that Spaniards gave the PP, risks being merely decorative.

Nonetheless it is necessary to analyze the details of the PP's victory to understand the political significance and implications (table 1.1). First, the PP, in particular, benefitted from the electoral system. With 44.6 percent of the national vote, the PP won 186 seats in the Congress of Deputies (53.1 percent of the seats), and therefore is able to govern alone with a comfortable absolute majority.[12] Also, vote shares can be misleading. The number of votes the PP won in this election (10,866,566) was actually lower than the number of votes the PSOE won in 2008

Table 1.1 Election results, Congress of Deputies, 2011 and 2008

| | 2011 | | | | 2008 | | | |
| | Votes | | Seats | | Votes | | Seats | |
	#	%	#	%	#	%	#	%
Popular Party (PP)	10,866,566	44.6	186	53.1	10,278,010	39.9	154	44.0
Socialist Party (PSOE)	7,003,511	28.8	110	31.4	11,289,335	43.9	169	48.3
United Left (IU)	1,685,991	6.9	11	3.1	969,946	3.8	2	0.6
Union, Progress and Democracy (UPD)	1,143,225	4.7	5	1.4	306,079	1.2	1	0.3
Convergence and Union (CiU)	1,015,691	4.2	16	4.6	779,425	3.0	10	2.9
Amaiur	334,498	1.4	7	2.0	–	–	–	–
Basque Nationalist Party (PNV)	324,498	1.4	5	1.4	306,128	1.2	6	1.7
Republican Left of Catalonia (ERC)	256,985	1.1	3	0.9	298,139	1.2	3	0.9
Galician Nationalist Block (BNG)	184,037	0.8	2	0.6	212,543	0.8	2	0.6
Canary Island Coalition (CC)*	143,881	0.6	2	0.6	174,629	0.7	2	0.6
Compromis-Q	125,306	0.5	1	0.3	–	–	–	–
Asturian Citizens Forum (FAC)	99,473	0.4	1	0.3	–	–	–	–
Navarra Yes (NA-BAI)	–	–	–	–	62,398	0.2	1	0.3
Yes to the Future (GBAI)	42,415	0.2	1	0.3	–	–	–	–
Others	1,122,760	4.6	–	–	1,058,231	4.1	–	–
Total	*24,348,837*	*100*	*350*	*100*	*25,734,863*	*100*	*350*	*100*

Notes: *Canary Island Coalition in alliance with New Canaries (NC) and Canary Nationalist Party (PNC) in 2011, and with PNC in 2008.

Source: Ministry of Interior, Spain.

(11,289,335) and 2004 (11,026,163), when it won the elections but several seats short of an absolute majority in parliament. Furthermore, the PP only increased its votes by approximately 588,000. Therefore a relatively moderate increase of support produced tremendous gains in terms of real political power.

Winning a majority of seats in the Congress without a majority of the vote is not unusual in Spanish politics. Of the ten postconstitutional parliamentary elections held since 1979, this is the fifth that has produced a single-party majority in parliament. None of these governing parties received an absolute majority of the vote. The closest was in 1982 when the PSOE won the elections with 48.1 percent of the vote. The PP's current win is the second highest vote share won by a political party since the transition. It is also the highest number of votes the PP has received in a general election. Single-party majorities have historically also been dependent on the support gap between the two largest parties. When competition between them is tight, minority governments tend to be produced; when there is a large gap, majority governments are the result. In this election, there was a 16-point gap between the PP and PSOE in terms of percentages of the vote.

The PP was not the only winner in these elections; in many cases the minor parties, a category that refers to all parties except the PP and PSOE, increased their votes, particularly the United Left (IU), Union, Progress and Democracy (UPD), the Catalan nationalist Convergence and Union (CiU), and the Basque nationalist coalition *Amaiur*. In general the minor parties did very well in this election. They gained double the number of seats compared to the last election—54 seats compared to 27 in 2008. They jointly captured 26.6 percent of the popular vote, the most since 1989. This result reverses a trend since that date of each successive election resulting in fewer votes for the minor parties, reaching a low of 16.2 percent in the 2008 election. Stated differently, it reverses the trend of vote concentration in the two largest parties. Though the smaller parties captured 27 percent of the vote, they jointly hold 15 percent of the seats, further highlighting the effects of the electoral system. Because of Spain's large number of districts and relatively small district magnitude (seats per district) the electoral system does not affect all minor parties in the same way. It particularly punishes IU and UPD, national parties that present candidates across the Spanish territory, rather than the regional or regional-nationalist parties that only present candidates and concentrate support in a small number of electoral districts.

Table 1.2 presents two rough indicators of proportionality. The first simply subtracts the national vote share from the national seat share.

Table 1.2 Proportionality indicators, Congress of Deputies, 2011 elections

	Votes		Seats		Seat share minus vote share*	Number of votes / number of seats
	#	%	#	%		
UPD	1,143,225	4.7	5	1.4	−3.3	228,645
IU	1,685,991	6.9	11	3.1	−3.8	153,272
Compromis-Q	125,306	0.5	1	0.3	−0.2	125,306
FAC	99,473	0.4	1	0.3	−0.1	99,473
BNG	184,037	0.8	2	0.6	−0.2	92,019
ERC	256,985	1.1	3	0.9	−0.2	85,662
CC	143,881	0.6	2	0.6	0.0	71,941
PNV	324,498	1.4	5	1.4	0.1	64,900
PSOE	7,003,511	28.8	110	31.4	2.7	63,668
CiU	1,015,691	4.2	16	4.6	0.4	63,481
PP	10,866,566	44.6	186	53.1	8.5	58,422
Amaiur	334,498	1.4	7	2.0	0.6	47,785
GBAI	42,415	0.2	1	0.3	0.1	42,415

Note: *Based on more precise percentages than those presented here.
Source: Ministry of the Interior, Spain. Authors' calculations.

Negative numbers indicate that the party is underrepresented vis-à-vis their national vote share in the Congress of Deputies. The second indicator takes the total number of votes the party received and divides it by the number of seats won. It generates a measure of the cost in votes of each seat. As can be seen in the table, UPD seats were the most costly in terms of votes (228,645), followed by IU (153,272) and *Compromís-Q* (125,306). The least costly seats were those won by Yes to the Future (GBAI; 42,415) and *Amaiur* (47,785), followed by the PP (58,422). Analyzed in terms of seat share versus vote share, IU is the party most harmed by the electoral system.

Nonetheless, the IU and UPD dramatically increased their representation in Congress. IU increased its vote share and seats, from the 2 won in 2008 to 11 seats, and was once again able to form a parliamentary group on its own. In the 2008 parliament, its two deputies (one in fact from ICV, which presented candidates jointly with IU in Catalonia) formed a parliamentary group with ERC. Though it has not returned to its historical highs of approximately 10 percent of the vote and 21 seats, IU certainly reversed a downward trend since the mid-1990s. It remains to be seen whether it is a temporary reversal.

The UPD experienced a striking increase. Its votes almost quadrupled (3.7 times) from 2008, the first time it competed in national elections. According to one estimate, the UPD won the votes of 450,000 prior

Socialist voters and of 350,000 prior PP voters.[13] In a few short years, the UPD has become the fourth largest party in terms of the number of votes. With 4.7 percent of the national vote and five deputies, it fell just short of the requirements to form a parliamentary group, which would require 5 percent of the national vote. However, due to the Asturian Citizens Forum (FAC) temporarily "lending" them a deputy it was able to form a parliamentary group.[14]

Given the importance of territorial politics in Spain, we provide a brief territorial vision of the election. It is crucial to note that the PP was the party that received the highest number of votes in every autonomous community except Catalonia and the Basque Country, which are often outliers due to strong nationalist sentiments and distinct party systems. PP won in 45 of Spain's 52 electoral districts—every district, except Sevilla and Barcelona (PSOE won); Girona, Lleida, and Tarragona (CiU won); Gipuzkoa (*Amaiur* won); and Bizkaia (Basque Nationalist Party/ PNV won). Except for Sevilla, the other districts are in the Catalan and Basque regions. Here we examine the results in these two regions, and for the Catalan and Basque nationalist parties, as these regional results are potentially the most significant and stand out from national dynamics.

The general election in the region of Catalonia produced a historic victory for the center-right, nationalist CiU (see table 1.3). It was the first time that CiU was the most voted-for list in Catalonia in a general election, surpassing the Socialist Party of Catalonia (PSC-PSOE), which is a party federated with the PSOE. CiU increased its representation in Congress from 10 to 16 seats, though this result still falls short of their high of 18 seats (achieved in 1989). Interestingly, CiU won despite the austerity measures implemented prior to the election by the CiU regional government. While the PP increased in votes and seats in Catalonia, it still placed third in Catalonia, a disappointing result for the party, with 21 percent of the vote, compared to 29 percent for CiU and 27 percent for PSC-PSOE. The decline of the PSC-PSOE in the region was dramatic, losing 11 of the 25 seats they attained in 2008. The left-green alliance of ICV-IU gained seats while ERC, ideologically on the left and proponent of Catalan independence, declined in votes even though it maintained the same number of seats.

Results from the Basque Country region also departed from national trends (see table 1.3). Because of ETA's October 2011 declaration that it would permanently abandon armed conflict, this was the first election without the threat of violence since the transition to democracy. Though participation in the Basque Country was slightly below the national average (68.9 percent), it increased three points from 2008 (from 64 percent

Table 1.3 Election results in Catalonia and the Basque Country, Congress of Deputies, 2011 and 2008

	2011			2008		
	Votes		Seats	Votes		Seats
	#	%	#	#	%	#
Catalonia						
CiU	1,015,691	29.4	16	779,425	20.9	10
PSC-PSOE	922,547	26.7	14	1,689,911	45.4	25
PP	716,371	20.7	11	610,473	16.4	8
ICV-IU	280,152	8.1	3	183,338	4.9	1
ERC	244,854	7.1	3	291,532	7.8	3
Basque Country						
Amaiur	285,290	24.1	6	–	–	–
PNV	324,317	27.4	5	306,128	27.1	6
PSOE	255,013	21.6	4	430,690	38.1	9
PP	210,797	17.8	3	209,244	18.5	3

Notes: PSC (Partit dels Socialistes de Catalunya); ICV (Iniciativa per Catalunya Verds).
Source: Ministry of the Interior, Spain.

to 67 percent). Participation did not increase in any other region; in fact national participation declined 4.9 percentage points. There was also a historic first in the Basque Country. It was the first time the national-ist parties received more support than the PP and PSOE combined in a general election.

Representation from the Basque Country is also more fragmented than before. While support for the PSOE plummeted, the PP did not increase its representation from the Basque provinces, maintaining three seats and a similar number of votes. The most significant development is that *Amaiur*, the new Basque nationalist, leftist coalition, placed second in percentage of votes in the Basque Country with 24.1 percent, behind the PNV (27.4 percent), but ahead of the PSOE (21.6 percent) and PP (17.8 percent). It placed first in terms of seats, winning one more seat than the PNV. *Amaiur* also won one seat in the Navarre region; therefore it holds seven seats in the Spanish Congress, more than the five attained by the centrist, nationalist PNV, whose votes and vote share remained fairly constant. The surge of *Amaiur* poses a serious challenge to the PNV, which has historically been the dominant representative of Basque nation-alism in the Spanish parliament, and indeed to the main national parties.

The PP majority did not allow *Amaiur* to form a parliamentary group in the Congress of Deputies. According to the parliamentary rules, there are two standards by which a parliamentary group can be formed: (1) with 15 deputies; or (2) with 5 deputies if the political formation(s) obtain a minimum of 15 percent of the votes in the districts where they presented candidates or 5 percent of the national total.[15] *Amaiur* met the 15 percent hurdle in the Basque Country districts, but it obtained only 14.86 percent in Navarre. While there is indeed a precedent of flexibility in the application of the parliamentary rules, the PP did not show any willingness to assist *Amaiur*. *Amaiur* has appealed the decision on its parliamentary group to the Constitutional Court, whose decision is still pending at the time of writing.

To conclude, Mariano Rajoy and the PP gained a tremendous amount of political power. Additionally, the 2011 parliament is more fragmented than the 2008 one. Mariano Rajoy faces an extremely weakened principal opposition party, and a large number of deputies from minor parties, in some cases reinforced by electoral improvements, and entirely new political formations. On the other hand, the minor parties, though reinforced electorally and in terms of seats, have seen their effective legislative power diminish vis-à-vis the 2008 parliament in which Prime Minister Rodríguez Zapatero did not have an absolute majority.

ChapterSummar y

This volume examines many of the recent political, economic, and social events in Spain. In the political sphere, chapter 2 by Anna Bosco analyzes the trajectory of the Spanish Socialist Party, making a comparison between the crisis of the second half of 1990s that led to Zapatero's leadership, and the most recent crisis that led to Alfredo Pérez Rubalcaba's ascent to the office of party general secretary. Without neglecting Zapatero's handling of the economic crisis, the chapter focuses on the generational battle between the "old guard" (close to former prime minister Felipe González) and the younger generation (Zapatero's) that divides the party. In chapter 3, Alfonso Botti presents the trajectory of the PP from its electoral failure in March 2004 to its triumph in 2011, highlighting the figure of Mariano Rajoy and his opponents within the party, and continuing until the first measures adopted by his government to combat the economic crisis.

Bonnie N. Field, in chapter 4, examines the dynamics of the Zapatero minority government, its parliamentary allies, and opponents. She also identifies and explains the change from a governing strategy based on shifting alliances to a more encompassing and stable agreement with minor parties. Chapter 5, written by César Colino, analyzes the developments with regard to territorial politics, concretely the changes in the "state of autonomies," as Spain's politico-territorial model is named. It highlights developments in Catalonia and the Basque Country, in particular the Constitutional Court ruling on the reformed Catalan regional charter (statute of autonomy) and ETA's declaration of the end of its violent activity.

Regarding economic developments, which are present in all of the chapters, Óscar Molina and Alejandro Godino in chapter 6 investigate the specific impact of the economic and financial crisis on the Iberian country, along with the structural problems of the Spanish economy, the measures the executive adopted to combat the crisis, and their effects. In chapter 7, Kerstin Hamann examines the relationship between the government and the labor unions, exploring the strategies of cooperation and conflict. She also underscores the problems of the labor market and unions' uneven access to policymaking.

In the social arena, Carmelo Adagio, in chapter 8, covers the youth protests through a chronicle of 15-M *indigando* demonstrations, examining the movement's use of social networks and the Internet, its organizational characteristics, and the social background of its members in order to identify the movement's principal characteristics and prior trajectory. It also evaluates the movement's influence on the 2011 general election results. In chapter 9, Mireno Berrettini studies the behavior of the Catholic Church and of different Catholics groups with respect to the secularizing policies of the Zapatero governments, specifically dealing with family, education, and bioethics. He provides a broad interpretive framework without which the ecclesiastic dynamics cannot be understood. Celia Valiente, in chapter 10, evaluates gender and equality policies. Her analysis not only focuses on the parliamentary agenda during Zapatero's second term, but also on the implementation of the ambitious signature laws of his first term. In chapter 11, Eloísa del Pino provides an overview of the development of Spain's welfare state and its challenges, and analyzes the recent changes in the context of the economic crisis, drawing attention to the shift from recalibration to retrenchment. In chapter 12, we conclude with some general thoughts about this new political juncture, and raise some questions about the future of the Iberian country.

Notes

1. The literature on this is extensive. For examples, see Noya and Prado (2011), and J. Noya, "Ni tanto ni tan poco," *El País*, June 1, 2012.

2. World Bank data. Available at: data.worldbank.org (last accessed on January 28, 2013).
3. Instituto Nacional de Estadística (INE), *Notas de prensa. Encuesta de población activa (EPA), Primer trimestre de 2012*, April 27, 2012, p. 1. Available at: http://www.ine.es/daco/daco42/daco4211/epa0112.pdf (last accessed on June 8, 2012).
4. Eurostat data. Available at: ec.europa.eu/eurostat (last accessed on January 28, 2013).
5. Spain likely missed its 2012 deficit-cutting goal," *Reuters*, January 22, 2013. Available at www.uk.reuters.com (last accessed January 28, 2013).
6. Rajoy surpasses Zapatero in January 2011. Data are taken from Centro de Investigaciones Sociológicas (CIS), studies 2847 (October 2010) and 2859 (January 2011). All CIS studies are available at: www.cis.es.
7. L. Gómez, A. Manresa, and M. Galaz, "Excelencia, le investigan," *El País*, November 12, 2011.
8. J. A. Hernández, "Dívar dimite sin conciencia de culpa y sintiéndose víctima de una campaña," *El País*, June 21, 2012.
9. CIS data, "Tres problemas principales que existen actualmente en España (Multirrespuesta %)." Available at: http://www.cis.es/cis/export/sites/default/-Archivos/Indicadores/documentos_html/TresProblemas.html (last accessed on July 2, 2012).
10. In fact an important group affiliated with the movement is *¡Democracia Real YA!* (Real Democracy Now!). See http://www.democraciarealya.org/.
11. J. Lobera, "El 15-M aumenta su apoyo ciudadano," *El País*, May 19, 2012.
12. All election results are from Spain's Ministry of the Interior. Available at: http://www.infoelectoral.mir.es/min/ (last accessed on May 10, 2012).
13. J. J. Toharia, J. P. Ferrándiz, and J. Lobera, "Fidelidad y fuga," *El País*, November 26, 2011.
14. There is a tradition of flexibility regarding the formation of parliamentary groups in the Spanish Congress. In some instances, parties or coalitions have "borrowed" deputies from other political formations temporarily in order to satisfy the parliamentary rules. In any case, the governing board of the Congress (the *Mesa*) is the body that approves the groups.
15. Reglamento del Congreso de los Diputados (Congress of Deputies Parliamentary Rules). See http://www.congreso.es/portal/page/portal/Congreso/Congreso/Hist_Normas/Norm.

WorksC ited

Aguilar, P. 2009. "Las políticas de la memoria." In Bosco and Sánchez-Cuenca, eds., *La España de Zapatero*, pp. 153–78.
Baldi, B., and G. Baldini. 2009. "La reforma del Estado de las Autonomías." In Bosco and Sánchez-Cuenca, eds., *La España de Zapatero*, pp. 101–28.

Bernardi, F., and S. Sarasa. 2009. "Las nuevas políticas sociales del Gobierno de Zapatero." In Bosco and Sánchez-Cuenca, eds., *La España de Zapatero*, pp. 227–48.

Bosco, A. and I. Sánchez-Cuenca, eds. 2009. *La España de Zapatero: Años de cambios, 2004–2008.* Madrid: Editorial Pablo Iglesias.

Calvo, K. 2009. "Calidad de la democracia, derechos civiles y reforma política." In Bosco and Sánchez-Cuenca, eds., *La España de Zapatero*, pp. 205–26.

Calvo, K., and I. Martín. 2009. "Ungrateful Citizens? Women's Rights Policies in Zapatero's Spain." *South European Society and Politics* 14(4): 487–502.

Charnock, G., T. Purcell, and R. Ribera-Fumaz. 2012. "¡Indígnate! The 2011 Popular Protests and the Limits to Democracy in Spain." *Capital & Class* 36(1): 3–11.

Eguiguren, J., and L. Rodríguez Aizpeolea. 2011. *ETA. Las claves de la paz: Confesiones del negociador.* Madrid: Aguilar.

Encarnación, O. 2009. "Spain's New Left Turn: Society Driven or Party Instigated." *South European Society and Politics* 14(4): 399–416.

Field, B. N. 2009. "A 'Second Transition' in Spain? Policy, Institutions and Interparty Politics under Zapatero (2004–8)." *South European Society and Politics* 14(4): 379–98.

———, ed. 2011. *Spain's "Second Transition"? The Socialist Government of José Luis Rodríguez Zapatero.* New York: Routledge.

Fishman, R. 2012. "Anomalies of Spain's Economy and Economic Policy-Making." *Contributions to Political Economy* 31(1): 67–76.

Fundación FOESSA and Cáritas. 2012. *Análisis y perspectivas 2012: exclusión y desarrollo social.* Madrid: Fundación FOESSA and Cáritas. Available at: http://www.foessa.es/publicaciones_compra.aspx?Id=4317&Idioma=1&Diocesis=42.

Jiménez, F. 2009. "Building Boom and Political Corruption in Spain." *South European Society and Politics* 14(3): 255–72.

López, I., and E. Rodríguez. 2011. "The Spanish Model." *New Left Review* 69(May–June): 5–28.

Mulas-Granados, C. 2009. "La economía española: del 'boom' a la crisis." In Bosco and Sánchez-Cuenca, eds., *La España de Zapatero*, pp. 179–203.

Muro, D. 2009. "Territorial Accommodation, Party Politics, and Statute Reform in Spain." *South European Society and Politics* 14(4): 453–68.

Noya, J., and F. Prado. 2011. "¿Cuánto ha empeorado la imagen de España?" *Análisis del Real Instituto Elcano* (ARI), no. 158/2011. Available at: http://www.realinstitutoelcano.org.

Pastor Verdú, J. 2012. "El movimiento 15-M y la política extraparlamentaria." In C. Colino and R. Cotarelo, eds., *España en crisis: Balance de la segunda legislatura de Rodríguez Zapatero.* Valencia: Tirant Humanidades, pp. 357–81.

Powell, C. 2009. "A Second Transition or More of the Same? Spanish Foreign Policy under Zapatero." *South European Society and Politics* 14(4): 519–36.

Royo, S. 2009a. "Reforms Betrayed? Zapatero and Continuities in Economic Policy." *South European Society and Politics* 14(4): 435–52.

———. 2009b. "After the Fiesta: The Spanish Economy Meets the Global Financial Crisis." *South European Society and Politics* 14(1): 19–34.

Salmon, K. 2010. "Boom to Bust—Reconstructing the Spanish Economy." *International Journal of Iberian Studies* 23(1): 39–52.

Sánchez-Cuenca, I. 2009. "ETA: del proceso de paz al regreso de la violencia." In Bosco and Sánchez-Cuenca, eds., *La España de Zapatero*, pp. 129–52.

———. 2012. *Años de cambios, años de crisis: Ocho años de gobiernos Socialistas, 2004–2011.* Madrid: Catarata.

Villoria, M., and F. Jiménez. 2012. "La paradoja de la corrupción: creciente percepción del fenómeno pese al impulso en las políticas anticorrupción." In Colino and Cotarelo, eds., *España en crisis*, pp. 411–31.

CHAPTER 2

The Long *Adiós*: The PSOE and the End of the Zapatero Era

Anna Bosco

In the general elections on November 20, 2011, the Socialist Party (PSOE) suffered a resounding defeat that marked a record low in its electoral fortunes. With just over seven million votes (28.8 percent of all valid votes), its performance was even worse than its 29.3 percent showing in the 1977 elections, the only previous occasion on which the party had fallen below one-third of the valid votes. Over four million votes fled from the PSOE (a 38 percent drop in votes from its support base compared to 2008), which won the smallest number of seats in the Congress since the country's return to democracy (110 compared to 169 in the previous parliament) (see table 1.1). If we add to this the fact that the PSOE had been trounced in the regional and municipal elections of May 22, 2011, which ousted it from regional and local government in much of the country; that the Popular Party (PP) went from being the opposition to the government with a very comfortable absolute majority; that the PSOE fought the electoral campaign with a candidate (Alfredo Pérez Rubalcaba) who was not the party general secretary and incumbent prime minister (José Luis Rodríguez Zapatero); and that in February 2012 Rubalcaba became the new PSOE secretary during a party convention marked by bitter internal conflict, one has a succinct but fairly complete picture of the difficulties facing the Socialists.

The events of 2011 recall the crisis the party went through in 2000, when, as in 2011, the PSOE had had to come to terms with a significant electoral defeat exacerbated by the fact that José María Aznar's PP won its first ever absolute majority. What's more, the PSOE went into the elections of March 2000 after a chaotic and unprecedented period of dual leadership (*bicefalia*) under the party secretary (Joaquín Almunia) and the candidate for prime minister (Josep Borrell). Defeat at the polls then produced divisions in the party, and as a consequence there were four candidates for the post of general secretary at the party's thirty-fifth federal convention. The convention sanctioned a change of leadership, with the election of Zapatero, and a profound reorganization of the party.

However, the events of 2000 and 2011 also differ in a number of important respects. In 2000, the PSOE's crisis stemmed from a lack of credibility because of a long series of scandals; while in 2011 the party paid the price for having been in government during the financial and economic crisis that hit southern Europe. Moreover, in 2000 the Socialists had already been out of government for four years, while in 2011 Zapatero was in his second consecutive term of office. Despite the different circumstances, however, the 2000 and 2011 defeats both marked a phase of internal crisis that led to change in the party.

In this essay, I will examine the two periods of crisis faced by the PSOE, highlighting the similarities and differences in the way the party responded to defeat and initiated change. The years 2011–12 concluded the era of Zapatero, who had become party leader in 2000 and prime minister in 2004. Although various appraisals have been made of the Zapatero governments,[1] an assessment of developments within the PSOE during the Zapatero era has yet to be attempted.

This chapter is divided into four sections. In the first, I briefly examine the party crisis during the second half of the 1990s, and the changes Zapatero introduced when he became leader. The second analyzes the impact on the PSOE of the economic and financial crisis that began in 2008, while the third traces the period of upheaval in which Zapatero was replaced as the head of government and of the party (April 2011–February 2012). Finally, in the last section, I will consider Zapatero's legacy for the PSOE and reflect on the way the party tackled the crises of 2000 and 2011.

Defeat, Crisis, and Change: Zapatero's Rise to Leadership

In the second half of the 1990s, the PSOE had to deal with a crisis that had various aspects in common with the 2011 one. It is therefore useful to recall some of its essential features and to piece together the way in which it was overcome.

In 1996, after having been in power uninterruptedly for 14 years, Felipe González, the PSOE's historic leader, had had to make way for

Aznar's PP government, which arrived at the Moncloa executive palace for the first time since the country's return to democracy, inaugurating the alternation between the center-left PSOE and center-right PP that has characterized Spanish political life ever since. The 1996 electoral defeat marked the beginning of a long period in opposition for the PSOE (until 2004) and a crisis that undermined the party's political credibility. There were so many problems to solve that the PSOE experienced further defeat at the polls (in 2000) and a complex period of leadership change before putting the crisis behind it.

The PSOE's loss of credibility in the mid-1990s was due to the scandals and corruption cases in which government and party members had become involved since the beginning of the decade. They included episodes of illicit party financing, kickbacks for public works commissioned by Socialist regional governments, the enrichment of political appointees through tax evasion and secret funds, as well as even more serious offences, such as the assassination of presumed collaborators of the terrorist group ETA (Basque Homeland and Freedom) by groups who were supported by the interior ministry (Pérez-Díaz 2003). Despite the gravity of the charges, however, the Socialist leadership decided to deny all the accusations leveled against it until the conclusion of the legal proceedings. This choice had two negative consequences. First, it created deep divisions within the party, where there were two clear camps: those who wanted to immediately acknowledge some responsibility, and those who thought that no one should be considered guilty before justice had taken its course. Second, the fact that the party failed to offer the electorate any explanations, not even to party members and supporters, ended up creating strong disaffection toward the PSOE and a lack of trust in its ability to run the country (Maravall 1996).

Mistrust and disaffection inevitably undermined the party's electoral performance, eroding a significant proportion of the bedrock electoral support it had enjoyed since 1982. Research by Barreiro has shown that those who abstained in the 1996 general elections came above all from the left of the political spectrum, a sign that many Socialists decided not to go to the polls rather than vote for a party implicated in an interminable series of scandals. What should be stressed, though, is that the PSOE then found it difficult to win back the voters who abstained. Indeed, abstention in Spain continued to affect the left-wing and center-left electorate much more than their counterparts on the right (Barreiro 2002, 2004; Sánchez-Cuenca 2009, 34). In-house PSOE documents estimate that of the 1,600,000 voters the party lost in 2000 with respect to 1996 at least one million abstained (Bosco 2005, 195). Thus, the crisis of credibility associated with the scandals in the 1990s had negative electoral consequences that the party urgently needed to address by rebuilding lost trust and remobilizing its electoral base.

The second aspect of the crisis was internal, and concerned the sensitive issue of who should succeed the party leader who had led the PSOE since the mid-1970s. When, after the 1996 election defeat, Felipe González announced his resignation as party secretary during the party's thirty-fourth federal convention (June 1997), he designated Joaquín Almunia to succeed him. However, this method of handpicking (*elegir a dedo*) his successor exacerbated the crisis rather than resolved it. On the one hand, grassroots Socialists felt disregarded by the decision of their (admittedly charismatic) outgoing leader. On the other, Almunia, who had held posts in the party and in government, was regarded as representing continuity with the past. He was therefore unable to put together an effective agenda for political renewal because he was in part controlled by the party *barones* (barons), the powerful presidents of the regions governed by the PSOE.

Almunia tried to redress this by holding, for the first time in the party's history, primaries (open to party members) to choose the party's candidate for the prime ministership. His aim was clearly to try to set himself apart from the old guard, earning legitimacy from the grassroots, and he counted on the fact that since 1977 the party secretary and the candidate for the prime ministership had always been the same person. But he had not taken account of the groundswell of feeling among party members: in the primaries, held in April 1998, the primary voters preferred Josep Borrell, a former minister whose main campaign strategy was to stress that he had nothing to do with the party apparatus, over Almunia.

Until May 1999—when Borrell resigned after some of his former aides also became embroiled in scandal—the PSOE had to deal with the unprecedented coexistence of a party secretary and a different candidate for prime minister. The party structure was ill-prepared for it, and the result was a chain of minor conflicts that only served to further damage its image.

The PSOE therefore went into the elections of 2000 without having regained political credibility and without a convincing leadership: in fact, after Borrell's resignation, the party could do no better than offer up Almunia. When the election results showed that the Socialists had lost further ground with respect to 1996, while the PP obtained an absolute majority, Almunia resigned along with the entire executive committee. It was in the months between the elections of March 12 and the party's thirty-fifth federal convention (July 21–23, 2000) that the crisis reached a peak, and the election defeat made change an absolute necessity.

At the start of the convention, the Socialists were disoriented and divided, as the number of candidates for the party's highest position showed. At one point there were as many as eight—an all-time first in the party's history—before the figure fell to four. The two candidates that attracted most attention were José Bono and José Luis Rodríguez Zapatero. The former, who had served five consecutive terms as president of Castile-La Mancha, had government experience and the support of the outgoing executive committee. Zapatero, who was about 10 years younger (he was only 39), came from the Congress of Deputies, where he had first been elected at the age of 26. His candidacy was supported by *Nueva Vía* (New Way), a group formed in the wake of the party's defeat and that brought together parliamentarians in their forties, officials from various party secretariates, and leading figures associated with the PSOE's excellent training school, Jaime Vera. *Nueva Vía* saw Almunia's resignation as marking the end of a political generation and the opportunity to begin a profound political and organizational overhaul of the party; it wished to make generational change but without breaking with the elite of the transition period, embodied by Felipe González, to whom *Nueva Vía* was thinking of offering the party presidency (López Alba 2002, 126–49 and 238–42).

Against all odds, Zapatero was elected party secretary, with just nine more votes than Bono. The young deputy's success was unexpected, in that he did not have the support of any of the party's historic sectors or families nor of the party apparatus. Nonetheless, he managed to give voice to the desire for change in the party. In the months following Zapatero's election, in fact, the PSOE embarked on a sweeping process of renewal that lasted at least until 2008, involving the updating of its program and political agenda and the modernization of the party.

It should be stressed that the party did not introduce a disjointed set of changes but rather carried out a fairly coherent operation designed to court and remobilize the left and center-left voters that the PSOE had lost since the second half of the 1990s. This was the pool of potential voters to whom Zapatero's party appealed with its program and with the policies implemented by its governments. And it was these voters that the PSOE tried, and managed, to turn away from abstention and get to back the party in the 2004 and 2008 elections. The role assigned to the party was essential to this task: it was reshaped into a more modern and attractive structure, endowed with fresh incentives, motivated and, above all, given the mission of mobilizing the electorate.

The party's new agenda and the policies implemented in Zapatero's first term (2004–2008), through which the prime minister pursued his so-called citizens' socialism, were all part of this framework. Without going into details, as many studies already exist on this topic (see note 1), it is worth recalling the modernization of civil rights; enhanced social rights for the disabled and elderly; measures to compensate Republican victims of the civil war and Francoism; the initiation of the reform of several regional statutes of autonomy; the launching of a peace process with the terrorist organization ETA; and clashes with the Catholic Church on reforms such as those related to divorce, abortion, same-sex marriages, and religious education. For the most part, these decisions and policies were introduced during Zapatero's first term, and the PSOE's electoral base responded positively. In 2008, in fact, almost 60 percent of the extreme left-wing electorate and 71 percent of the left (respectively, positions 1–2 and 3–4 on the left-right axis, where 1 corresponds to the far left and 10 to the far right) voted for the PSOE, a remarkable improvement on 2000, when just 41 percent of far left-wing voters and 48 percent of those on the left made the same choice (Sánchez-Cuenca 2009, 34).

If the program and policies were designed to appeal both to voters and party members, the reorganization of the party was directed at party members and activists, who had been sorely neglected by their leaders in the 1990s. Following the thirty-fifth party convention, in fact, the party on the ground, to use the well-known expression coined by Katz and Mair (1995), was revitalized and turned into an instrument of electoral mobilization. Various innovations went in this direction: the new magnetic strip membership card and the revamped party logo; the introduction of the figure of the party "sympathizer" (someone who had stopped paying the membership fee, but wanted to remain in contact with the party), and of theme-based party groups associated with specific issues; the possibility of member participation in primaries to select candidates for public office; and the technological modernization of the party's territorial branches.

The impetus for the renewal of the party came from the decision of the new party leadership to make the organization an instrument for electoral mobilization. As abstention in Spain mainly affected left-wing voters and hit the PSOE most of all, winning back abstaining Socialists was more important than attracting voters away from other political forces. Employing the party on the ground for this purpose proved to be an effective choice: members and sympathizers were a crucial resource in the drive to get the left and center-left electorate to vote. Sympathizers, in particular, were listed in a special registry, together with their phone numbers and email addresses. As they had expressed their consent to be contacted by the party, they could be rapidly mobilized and informed about campaigns launched by the PSOE.

Renewal of the party thus became an integral part of the plan to get the PSOE back into government. The objective of making the organization a tool for electoral mobilization was pursued actively in the electoral campaigns preceding the 2004 and 2008 elections. Far from traditional, it is reminiscent of the efforts run by the Democratic Party in the United States, where volunteers are mobilized to do door-to-door canvassing but also to work through social networks. In 2004, for example, some 30,000 PSOE volunteers went to strategic, competitive neighborhoods to distribute leaflets and talk to potential voters, while the 2008 campaign drew on the help of about 50,000 trained volunteers who were guided by electoral cartography programs that indicated areas with high percentages of abstentions and of undecided voters that were decisive for determining the outcome in terms of the allocation of seats. In both cases, the mobilization was considered a success.[2]

The PSOE in Times of Recession

In July 2000, delegates attending the PSOE's thirty-fifth party convention gave Zapatero a mandate to renew the party and return it to government. The ensuing changes included the transformation of the political agenda (citizens' socialism), the overhaul of the party organization, with great attention focused on the party on the ground, and the development of an electoral strategy designed to mobilize left-wing voters who had become abstainers. The profound renewal also involved the generational change pledged by Zapatero: the average age of the members of the new executive committee was 42 and it was made up almost exclusively of the secretary's closest allies (Bosco 2005, 170).

As demonstrated elsewhere in this volume in abundant detail, Zapatero's two terms in government were very different. A successful legislature (2004–2008), in which the government accomplished nearly all of its electoral promises,[3] was followed by another one in which the political agenda was monopolized by the economic crisis, which induced a U-turn in May 2010 when the expansionary policy employed until then was disavowed. The 2008 electoral pledge to make Spain one of the richest and most advanced nations in the Western world remained only on paper: the bursting of the real estate bubble, soaring unemployment, and the spending cuts begun in 2010, added to reform of the labor market and changes to the constitution to introduce a budget deficit cap, led to the incessant erosion of the party's electoral support won in 2008. In particular, there was a growing perception among voters that the PP was more capable of tackling the crisis and creating jobs than the PSOE, while progressive voters reproached the PSOE for a lack of coherence between the ideology it professed and the policies it implemented (Fundación Alternativas 2011, 2012).

The weakening of Socialist voters' faith in Zapatero is clearly charted by opinion polls carried out by the *Centro de Investigaciones Sociológicas* (CIS). Unlike the first term, when PSOE voters' faith in Zapatero grew year by year, reaching 73.5 percent in July 2007, during his second term the figure fell from 66.5 percent in July 2008 to 35.2 percent in July 2011. The deterioration in the leader's image due to his handling of the crisis was such that in the opinion of Socialist voters Zapatero gradually came to be likened to the PP leader, Mariano Rajoy. So, while in January 2009 three-quarters of PSOE voters (74.5 percent) had judged Zapatero's capacity to govern to be superior to that of Rajoy, in January 2011 just 50.4 percent felt the same way. In another survey question, 51.3 percent were convinced that Rajoy could do as well if not better than Zapatero, compared to only 32.7 percent in January 2009.[4]

The main charge leveled against Zapatero and his government was not his incapacity to solve the economic problems, but the way in which he faced up to them. The government's attitude toward the crisis—first denied, then played down, and finally suffered—was a big blow to the prime minister's credibility. Moreover, when, in May 2010, Zapatero decided to abandon the expansionary policies pursued until then in favor of austerity measures, he neglected to explain to the electorate in general, and to his own support base in particular, the meaning and significance of that decision. In fact, the prime minister announced the *ajuste* (adjustment) in the Congress of Deputies without giving his own parliamentary group prior warning of the steps he intended to take, and disregarding the recommendation made by his advisors to speak to the nation on television to clarify and explain the about-face in economic policy. The consequence of all this would prove devastating for the government's and Zapatero's popularity, in that it contributed to fostering the conviction that the PSOE had mishandled the crisis and betrayed the party's ideological principles (Ortega & Pascual-Ramsay 2012, 65 and 150–57). From 2010 onward, therefore, the PSOE, and Zapatero in particular, suffered from a credibility deficit that affected their relationship with the voters who had supported the party with the greatest enthusiasm in the

2008 elections, that is to say, voters on the far left and left of the political spectrum (Urquizu 2012).

The gravity of the economic crisis, reflected in the PSOE's successive drops in polls of voting intentions, obviously impacted on the party. The Socialists' internal difficulties surfaced on April, 2, 2011, when Zapatero announced that he would not be standing for a third term, and that the party would hold primaries to choose a candidate for the 2012 general elections following the regional and municipal elections of May 22. Zapatero's aim was to prevent the PP from turning the local elections into a referendum on the government's performance, and to improve the PSOE's prospects, given that the opinion polls were far from rosy.

However, the April 2 announcement did not have the desired effect: in fact, the PSOE suffered a crushing electoral defeat and embarked on a convoluted shake-up of the party leadership that concluded with the thirty-eighth party convention in February 2012. Electoral defeats are often associated with leadership succession processes in political parties, because the "challenge of the polls" makes it urgent, in the eyes of party officials and militants, to replace the incumbent leadership. In the case of the PSOE, this process was complicated by two factors. First of all, in 2011 the party had to come to terms with two dramatic defeats—the regional and local elections of May 22 and the early general elections of November 20—that demanded the party rethink its political direction and party model in addition to confronting a change of leadership. Second, a challenge of such proportions, following seven years in government, caused profound divisions in the party organization and called into question the party's internal equilibrium. These issues deserve closer attention.

The outcome of the May elections expelled the party from political power in much of Spain: the disastrous municipal elections, in which the PSOE lost key cities such as Barcelona and Seville, was combined with regional elections, where the party was defeated in all six communities in which it had previously governed, including strongholds such as Extremadura and Castile-La Mancha, where the Socialists had been in power since 1982. Analysis of the election results shows that the losses were across the board, irrespective of the level of approval for the Socialist municipal and regional governments; meanwhile the PP even gained support in regions in which its image had been tarnished by scandals and serious instances of misgovernment. In other words, despite Zapatero's decision to bow out, the party was castigated in the regional and local elections by voters' dissatisfaction with the national government. The PSOE was punished for the way it had handled the crisis and because of the widespread conviction among its prior supporters that the PP was better equipped to tackle the country's economic problems (Barreiro & Sánchez-Cuenca 2012).

The electoral defeat also triggered internal conflict, which upset the orderly plan for the choice of a new prime ministerial candidate. When Zapatero announced his decision not to seek a further term of office, the names of two possible candidates began to circulate—the ministers Carme Chacón and Alfredo Pérez Rubalcaba. Chacón, born in 1971 and an exponent of *Nueva Vía*, was a young Catalan politician very close to Zapatero, who had appointed her as defense minister (after serving as housing minister starting in 2007). Rubalcaba, born in 1951, was a seasoned politician, who had held various ministerial posts under both González and Zapatero. In October 2010 he had become one of the most powerful figures in democratic Spain, when, in addition to being interior minister—a post he had occupied since 2006, playing a key role in the fight against terrorism—he was also appointed as first deputy prime minister and government spokesperson.

Lined up behind Chacón and Rubalcaba were two strands of the party that had coexisted in equilibrium since 2004, when Zapatero had become prime minister. Zapatero's election had in fact prompted a kind of compromise between those who were closer to González (politicians who had participated in his long period of government), and those belonging to *Nueva Vía*, who had supported Zapatero's rise to power. The former group included ministers and deputy prime ministers such as María Teresa Fernández de la Vega, Pedro Solbes, Elena Salgado, and Rubalcaba himself; Zapatero's cabinet chief, José Enrique Serrano; and politicians destined for nongovernmental posts, such as Joaquín Almunia, who became European commissioner.

From the ranks of *Nueva Vía*, on the other hand, came ministers such as Carme Chacón, Jordi Sevilla, Jesús Caldera, and Juan Fernando López Aguilar, and powerful party officials who later entered government, such as José Blanco (the party secretary for organization before becoming infrastructure minister in 2009) and Trinidad Jiménez (the party secretary for international relations before entering the government as health minister in 2009). The two groups were distinguished by an evident generational fracture (*Nueva Vía* brought together Zapatero's peers, in their forties, and other younger politicians) and by their respective shared experience (such as the government experience of the González group in the 1980s and 1990s).

As long as the economy fared well and Zapatero reaped successes, the two groups got along without too much difficulty. Not all of the prime minister's first-term initiatives were supported by the *felipista* group, but they were accepted. This peaceful coexistence was reflected in the composition of the executive, where, until autumn 2010, the González camp had as many if not more cabinet members than that of *Nueva Vía*. However, while the *felipista* group remained united and increased its influence, *Nueva Vía* was unable to maintain its initial cohesion and, over time, lost some of its members, who either left the government or, as in the case of Blanco and Jiménez, moved into the González sphere (Sánchez-Cuenca 2012, 25–32).

The capacity of the two blocs to coexist crumbled with the worsening of the economic situation and the prospect of losing power. At that point the González-generation group, thanks in part to the fragility of *Nueva Vía*, managed to increase its control of the government and party. But it was when Zapatero decided not to run for office again that the fracture became evident, turning into open conflict for the party's leadership, with the González group supporting Rubalcaba, while Chacón could count on the backing of *Nueva Vía*. Although some politicians switched camps, the conflict remained intense and divided the party through to the thirty-eighth convention.[5]

The split became public in the week following the electoral disaster of May 22, when the *felipista* camp asked for the primaries to be called off, on the grounds that they were too divisive, and to move forward the date for the party convention. The idea was that holding the convention before the general election (and not after, as is the PSOE tradition) would enable a thorough discussion of the May defeat and the election of a new leadership. This would make primaries pointless. According to PSOE regulations, in fact, when the party is in government, primaries for the position of prime minister can only be called if requested by the majority of the federal committee. Otherwise it is taken for granted that the party's general secretary will be the candidate.[6] By contrast, Zapatero's plan, strongly supported by Chacón, was to call primaries immediately in order to choose a candidate to represent the party at the general election. The party convention would then be held after the end of the legislature, and only then would Zapatero be replaced by a new secretary.

The request to advance the date of the convention, which exploded like a bombshell in the party, was made by Patxi López, the general secretary of the Socialist Party in the Basque Country and the *lehendakari* (regional president) of the Basque autonomous community, regarded as being very close to Rubalcaba. In reality, the *felipista* gambit was to thwart the imminent primaries and Chacón's mobilization of supporters more than to bring forward the convention as such. The convention would in fact have led to the election of a new secretary and a new executive committee before the general elections, which, in May 2011, were still scheduled for spring 2012. This would have resulted in an unprecedented delegitimization of Zapatero and made it necessary to hold early elections, given that in Spain the prime minister is the leader of the largest party. Daunted by this prospect, Chacón decided to back down, even though she had already begun to prepare her candidacy.

The primaries were thus effectively interred and on May 28 the PSOE federal committee proposed Rubalcaba as the party's candidate. The challenge to Zapatero's authority by López and his camp was one of the most serious that the Socialist secretary had faced in over a decade as party leader, and a sign that no holds would be barred in the succession struggle after the general elections. Further proof that the Basque secretary's request was aimed at blocking the primaries, thus accelerating Rubalcaba's nomination, is the fact that the request to bring forward the party convention was soon dropped and the *felipista* group was content instead to hold a political conference, a different type of political gathering, in autumn 2011.

The Succession: Losing the Elections and Winning the Party Leadership

The 2011 election campaign was one of the most difficult ever run by the Spanish Socialist Party. For Rubalcaba, who stepped down from all his government posts in July 2011, it was the beginning of a complicated phase in which he had to distinguish himself from the government despite having long been part of it. Furthermore, the *bicefalia* at the head of the party limited the scope for maneuver both of the prime minister—forced to introduce austerity measures—and the Socialist candidate, who, in an effort to win back the progressive electorate, moved toward the left. In this context, the announcement on July 29 of early elections to be held on November 20, several months before the natural end of the legislature in March 2012, favored the Socialist campaign. Predictions of a further worsening of the economic situation, the popularity Rubalcaba initially seemed to enjoy in the opinion polls, and the deterioration of the political and social climate convinced Zapatero to make this decision.

In actual fact, it was a desperate effort at damage limitation. The campaign leading up to the elections on November 20 was all uphill for the PSOE, who had to deal with the daily growth in the state's borrowing costs, meansured in the spread between the cost of German and Spanish 10-year government bonds, and in unemployment figures, and with an economy more and more obviously in recession. In this situation, basing the campaign on an attempt to stir feelings and mobilize voters—the main slogan was *"pelea por lo que quieres"* ("Fight for what is important to you")—did not yield the desired results. In the face of the silence of the PP candidate, who revealed the bare minimum about his own program, Rubalcaba appealed for a vote to save the welfare state, proposed a tax on banks and the very wealthy in order to save jobs, announced plans to fight tax evasion, proposed cuts in the armed forces and the provincial government institutions (*diputaciones*), and championed some of the requests, including the call for electoral reform, aired by the *indignado* (indignant) social movement that, in May, had occupied the central squares of many Spanish cities. However, offering a more left-wing program than that of the government did not alter the PSOE's election prospects. Nor, for that matter, did ETA's historic announcement of an end to terrorism, in which Zapatero and Rubalcaba, as interior minister, had played an important role.

The CIS opinion polls clearly show how the gap between the PSOE and the PP widened inexorably from July 2009 onward. Just 1.2 percent in July 2009 (39 percent for the PSOE, 40.2 percent for the PP), the gap grew to a 16.7 point lead for the PP in October 2011, on the eve of the general election (29.9 percent versus 46.6 percent). The decision to run Rubalcaba had enabled the PSOE to improve a few points between April and July 2011 (from 33.4 percent to 36 percent), but it was a short-term boost that was not enough to swing the contest. With a 16.7-point gap a month before the election, the limits of the campaign were only too clear to the Socialist election committee, whose aim was, if possible, to prevent the PP from obtaining an absolute majority and in any case not sink below its showing in 2000, when the PSOE had won just 34.2 percent of the vote and 125 deputies.[7]

When the election polls showed that the party had fallen dramatically short of the 2000 results, with 28.8 percent and 110 deputies, the internal divisions reopened at the prospect of leadership succession. Although Rubalcaba and Chacón, insofar as they were ministers in the outgoing government, did not offer a break with the past, they were the only contenders for the party leadership. Backing them were the two generations that had been battling for control of the PSOE for months: *Nueva Vía*, which secured the support of a few *felipista* politicians like Fernández de la Vega and Cristina Narbona (who had helped to draw up Rubalcaba's electoral program); and the *felipista* generation, which had won the backing of some politicians previously aligned with Zapatero, such as Oscar López and Trinidad Jiménez.

On November 26 the PSOE's federal committee expressed some mild self-criticism—Zapatero admitted having made mistakes in explaining the crisis—and scheduled the thirty-eighth party convention for February 3–5, 2012, to elect the new executive bodies. The date of the convention and the location, Seville, were an effort to boost the Socialist Party of Andalusia, which had to defend its absolute majority in regional elections on March 25, 2012. But the imminence of this important electoral test prevented, in the preconvention debate, a frank examination of the errors and false steps that had led to the PSOE's defeats in May and November.

Chacón's attempt to base the discussion on a critical assessment of the Socialist government's performance (delay in acknowledging the crisis, spending cuts not accompanied by the fight against tax evasion and by higher taxes for higher income earners, little action in Europe) was rejected by Rubalcaba's supporters, who saw the move as being unfair to Zapatero, whose achievements they defended.[8] The two candidates differed both in the content of their proposals and in their personal style. Rubalcaba took a traditional social-democratic line in defense of the weaker sectors of society and of the middle classes; he promised constructive opposition in the interest of the country, rejected further steps forward in reform of the autonomous communities, proposed a vision of a participatory party that did not remain confined to local party branches, and supported open primaries for the choice of the prime ministerial candidate. Greater participation and the democratization of the party also distinguished Chacón's position. However, she took a more radical political stance in her fiscal and economic pledges, in her support for the antiright-wing social mobilization (the May 15 indignant movement), and a tougher tone when speaking against Spain's European partners.

But it was in their styles that the greatest differences emerged. Chacón exploited her age—she was 40—and enthusiasm to promise the dawn of a new era in the party's history. Rubalcaba, instead, used his experience, pragmatism, and rhetorical skills to explain how he intended to restore the PSOE's credibility and woo back disenchanted voters. In short, the generational divide was exploited by Chacón to symbolize change and by Rubalcaba to represent experience.

From the outset it was apparent that the contest played out in the federal convention in Seville in February 2012 would be among the most uncertain in the party's history, similar to the one in 2000 that ended with the surprise election of Zapatero. The episode of the aborted primaries, the unprecedented electoral defeat, and the entrenched positions of the *Nueva Vía* and *felipista* factions in the party's territorial federations created deep divisions among grassroots party members. In such a situation, the election of the secretary, by the personal and secret ballots of the delegates, was unpredictable because the party was divided, and the regional and provincial federations did not express a shared preference for one particular candidate. Chacón's and Rubalcaba's efforts to win over the 956 delegates continued right up to the eleventh hour, with many regional and provincial secretaries trying not to come out in favor of one candidate or the other, for fear of backing the losing candidate and being delegitimated by the convention.

The party's internal divisions became more and more evident as the convention neared. The solid support enjoyed by Chacón in Catalonia, her home region, was an isolated case. The party federations of Madrid, Andalusia, and Valencia, which provided almost half the delegates, were split, and Rubalcaba had substantially more support only in the center-north federations of Spain such as the Basque Country, Asturias, Galicia, and Castile-León.[9] The hunt for votes right up to the final day also brought the party's historic leaders into the limelight. While Zapatero remained neutral, as befitted the incumbent secretary, Felipe González, Javier Solana, José María Maravall, and Alfonso Guerra all publically supported Rubalcaba, while the former deputy prime minister, Fernández de la Vega, backed Chacón.[10] The prevailing uncertainty at the convention was finally dispelled on Saturday, February 4, when Rubalcaba was elected secretary by a 22-vote margin, with 487 votes (51.1 percent of valid votes) compared to the 465 obtained by Chacón. An indication of how the leadership battle had polarized the party is that, of the 956 delegates, only 4 did not support one of the two candidates (2 blank votes, 1 abstention, and 1 null vote).

Despite the slender margin of his victory, Rubalcaba decided to form an executive committee dominated by his closest allies, while Chacón's supporters were only a small minority (18.4 percent). When presented to the delegates for approval, 80.4 percent voted in favor of the new committee. This figure, which the *felipista* camp presented as indicating an increase in support for the new secretary, actually revealed the discontent of the excluded group. Not only did almost 20 percent of the delegates *not* support the new leadership, but in 2000, the executive committee chosen by Zapatero had won the backing of 90.2 percent of the delegates, almost 50 percent more than the 41.7 percent with which he had been elected secretary.[11]

Conclusions: Crisis and Change, or Just Crisis?

Rubalcaba's election marked the end of the long eleven-and-a-half-year period in which the party had been led by Zapatero. After Felipe González (general secretary, with just a brief interruption, from 1974 to 1997), Zapatero was the party's longest-serving leader and had significantly rejuvenated the party's program and organization. His citizens' socialism, hinging on a flexible, innovative state delivering quality services, and on the central role of freedoms and civil rights, had won back the progressive electorate disenchanted by the scandals of the 1990s. Moreover, the modernization of the party structure, with the increased attention directed at members and the formal establishment of the new figure of the party sympathizer, had enabled the new Socialist ruling elite to mobilize the party in elections, restoring a crucial party function. After his unexpected election as party secretary in 2000, when he was not yet 40, Zapatero had managed to pull the PSOE out of the quicksands in which it was mired and take it into government for two consecutive and very different terms of office.

After 2008, the poor handling of the economic crisis by the Socialist government eroded the credibility of the PSOE and its leader, causing a hemorrhaging of electoral support and internal crisis. This brought back to the fore a fracture that seemed to have been resolved, between the generation that had led the democratic transition and the first Socialist governments, and the generation that had taken over after the two successive defeats in 1996 and 2000.

The convention in February 2012 seemed to have resolved the 2011 crisis in the same way as the one in 2000, with the election of a new secretary ready to renew the party. And yet 2012 was not 2000, and the situation the party faced was different. The generational divide of 2000 was, in fact, also a contrast between continuity and a break with the past. Zapatero was outside the inner circle of the party, while Bono represented the party apparatus and the connection with the *felipista* generation. The 2012 contest was, at most, a clash between generations, as both Chacón and Rubalcaba had been in the government for years. Neither of them, then, represented discontinuity, as Zapatero had in 2000.

Having said this, careful observation shows that the crisis has not yet been resolved. Rubalcaba faces at least two challenges within the party. On the one hand, the new secretary will have to work to rebuild party unity. In fact, in many federations the local conventions—which, in the PSOE, are held after the federal one—have revealed the existence of divided parties. The loss of power in a large part of the Spanish territory after the May 2011 elections has weakened the old *barones* and created new appetites that are not easy to manage. The party leadership in Madrid will have to work hard to heal these divisions.

Second, Rubalcaba's leadership could be temporary. The thirty-eighth federal convention introduced the possibility to holding open primaries to choose a candidate for the prime ministership. Although the regulations have not yet been drawn up and therefore it is not clear whether they will be open only to sympathizers or to the electorate in general, the new system seems to point to the possibility that the PSOE general secretary will not automatically become the party's candidate to rule the country. Thus far Rubalcaba has avoided the issue of a second run as a candidate, and the name of Patxi López, the Basque *lehendakari* (born in 1959) and one of Rubalcaba's staunchest supporters in the succession struggle, has begun to circulate in various quarters. Discussion about the choice of the next Socialist candidate for the prime ministership is certainly premature, but the risk is that it will end up becoming entangled with other existing sources of conflict, delaying the recovery of Spain's main opposition party.

Notes

1. Works offering an appraisal of Zapatero's terms in office include: Bosco and Sánchez-Cuenca (2009); Colino and Cotarelo (2012); Field (2011); Pettit (2008); and Sánchez-Cuenca (2012).
2. For more about the 2004 and 2008 election campaigns and their outcomes, see Bosco (2005, 193–98); Bosco (2009); Cordero García and Martín Cortés (2010, 44).
3. For a detailed analysis of the implementation of the PSOE's 2004 electoral program, see Sánchez-Cuenca (2012, Chapter 3).
4. Opinion polls by the Centro de Investigaciones Sociológicas (CIS): October 2005 and July 2006, 2007, 2008, 2009, 2010, and 2011. Available at: www.cis.es.
5. Interview with PSOE politicians, Madrid, November 2011.
6. PSOE, *Normativa Reguladora de los Cargos Públicos*, 2005.
7. The importance of the 2000 election results as a measure for evaluating the ones in 2011 was confirmed by various PSOE politicians in interviews given in November 2011. Polling data taken from CIS.

8. See *Mucho PSOE por hacer*, a document posted on the web by Chacón's supporters on December 20, 2011, and the response from the Rubalcaba group, *Yo sí estuve allí*. Both available at: www.elpais.com.

9. A. Díez, "Ligera ventaja de Rubalcaba sobre Chacón tras los 'congresillos' del PSOE," *El País*, January 23, 2012; F. Garea, "La incertidumbre se apodera del PSOE," *El País*, January 22, 2012.

10. A. Díez, "Felipe González: 'Alfredo, creo en ti, mi compromiso es contigo,'" *El País*, January 23, 2012; L. R. Aizpeolea, "Sólido en tiempos de crisis," *El País*, February 4, 2012.

11. G. López Alba, "Rubalcaba se rodea de un equipo de fieles," *Público*, February 6, 2012.

WorksC ited

Barreiro, B. 2002. "La progresiva desmobilización de la izquierda en España: un análisis de la abstención en las elecciones generales de 1986 a 2000." *Revista Española de Ciencia Política* 6: 183–205.

———. 2004. "14-M: elecciones a la sombra del terrorismo." *Claves de Razón Práctica* 141: 14–22.

Barreiro, B., and I. Sánchez-Cuenca. 2012. "In the Whirlwind of the Economic Crisis: Local and Regional Elections in Spain, May 2011." *South European Society and Politics* 17 (2): 281–294.

Bosco, A. 2005. *Da Franco a Zapatero. La Spagna dalla periferia al cuore dell'Europa.* Bologna: Il Mulino.

———. 2009. "Buenas noches, y buena suerte. La seconda vittoria di Zapatero." In Bosco and Sánchez-Cuenca, eds., *La Spagna di Zapatero*, pp. 46–66.

Bosco, A., and I. Sánchez-Cuenca, eds. 2009. *La Spagna di Zapatero*. Bologna: Il Mulino.

Colino, C., and R. Cotarelo, eds. 2012. *España en crisis. Balance de la segunda legislatura de Zapatero*. Valencia: Tirant Humanidades.

Cordero García, G., and I. Martín Cortés. 2010. *¿Quiénes son y cómo votan los españoles "de izquierdas"?* Working Paper 164/2010. Madrid: Fundación Alternativas.

Field, B. N., ed. 2011. *Spain's "Second Transition"? The Socialist Government of José Luis Rodríguez Zapatero*. London: Routledge.

Fundación Alternativas. 2011. *Informe sobre la democracia en España 2011*. Madrid: Fundación Alternativas.

———. 2012. *Informe sobre la democracia en España 2012*. Madrid: Fundación Alternativas.

Katz, R. S., and P. Mair. 1995. "Changing Models of Party Organization and Party Democracy. The Emergence of the Cartel Party." *Party Politics* 1(1): 5–28.

López Alba, G. 2002. *El relevo. Crónica viva del camino hacia el II Suresnes del Psoe 1996–2000*. Madrid: Taurus.

Maravall, J. M. 1996. *Accountability and Manipulation*. Working Paper no. 92. Madrid: Centro de Estudios Avanzados en Ciencias Sociales.

Ortega, A., and A. Pascual-Ramsay. 2012. *¿Qué nos ha pasado? El fallo de un país.* Barcelona: Galaxia Gutenberg.

Pérez-Díaz, V. M. 2003. *La lezione spagnola. Società civile, politica e legalità.* Bologna: Il Mulino.

Pettit, P. 2008. *Examen a Zapatero.* Madrid: Temas de Hoy.

Sánchez-Cuenca, I. 2009. "Le elezioni del 2008: ideologia, crispación e leadership." In Bosco and Sánchez-Cuenca, eds., *La Spagna di Zapatero*, pp. 25–44.

———. 2012. *Años de cambios, años de crisis. Ocho años de gobiernos socialistas 2004–2011.* Madrid: Libros de la Catarata and Fundación Alternativas.

Urquizu, I. 2012. "Las elecciones de 2011." In *Informe sobre la democracia en España 2012.* Madrid: Fundación Alternativas, pp. 131–49.

CHAPTER 3

From Opposition to Government: The Popular Party of Mariano Rajoy

Alfonso Botti

The November 20, 2011, elections confirmed what by now appears to be a rule in Spanish democracy, namely that alternation of government is more the result of the failures of the governing parties than of the ability of the opposition to present alternative plans that appeal to the electorate. This is what happened in 1982 when Felipe González's Socialists were voted in to replace Adolfo Suárez's Union of the Democratic Center (UCD), which by then was in decline and in pieces; and in 1996 when the Socialist Party (PSOE), exhausted and undermined by scandals, was replaced by José María Aznar's Popular Party (PP). The same thing took place when Aznar was defeated in 2004 and then Zapatero in 2011, both caused by the poor handling, from a political and communications point of view, of events that had hit Spain from outside (the Islamist terrorist attacks in Madrid's Atocha train station and the eruption of the economic and financial crisis, respectively). It will suffice here to recall that Aznar and his minister of the interior had held back from pursuing the Islamic fundamentalist line of investigation into who was responsible for the attacks, in order to avoid paying an electoral price for Spain's involvement in the war in Iraq, instead stubbornly blaming the Basque terrorist group ETA (Basque Homeland and Freedom) for the massacre (Botti 2004a, b; Montero et al. 2008; Sampedro 2008) and that Zapatero, as late as the end of June 2008, in a long interview given to the newspaper *El País*, had considered it "questionable" to use the term "crisis" when faced with alarming statistics from all of the economic indicators.[1] Another parallel can be found in

Aznar's low level of popularity at the time of his election in 1996 and the equally low ratings from public opinion and the Spanish electorate that Mariano Rajoy received until very late in Zapatero's second term, as shown by a large number of opinion polls. Polls showed only a slow and late increase in support for the Popular Party leader, in spite of the dramatic fall in the level of support for the PSOE. Indeed, we should take note of the fact that, according to the figures released by the *Centro de Investigaciones Sociológicas* (CIS), it was not until October 2010 that Rajoy's popularity ratings were nearing Zapatero's,[2] and it was not until January 2011, as we shall see later, that the leader of the Popular Party actually surpassed the Socialist leader in the polls.

This search for similarities is not based on a predilection for looking for coincidences, but on the opportunity that they provide to reveal trends and tendencies that are deep-seated in Spanish society—the public's response to Aznar's and Zapatero's handling of their respective crises demonstrate that Spanish society does not tolerate being kept in the dark, mocked, or deceived by its politicians. The low popularity levels of both Aznar and Rajoy serve to remind us that it is the exercise of power and the ensuing media exposure that transform dull figures into leaders that command respect, even if they are somewhat lacking in charisma.

Having established this, the chapter is divided into six parts. The first traces Mariano Rajoy's political trajectory. The second analyzes the internal dynamics of the Popular Party and the battle against his leadership fought by the right wing until the sixteenth party convention. Part three looks at the PP's opposition style during Zapatero's second term. The fourth part deals with the electoral performances of the party in the intervening subnational and European elections, with special attention paid to the local and regional elections of May 2011. Part five focuses on the party's extraordinary electoral success in November 2011 and the new government team, whose main policies directed at combating the worsening economic situation will be considered in the final section.[3]

Who Is Mariano Rajoy?

But who is the current leader of the Spanish Popular Party and the new "president of the government" (prime minister) in Spain? Born in Santiago de Compostela in 1955, Mariano Rajoy studied in the Jesuit school in León until the age of 15, then in Pontevedra in a public school, before going on to study at the University of Santiago de Compostela, where he graduated with a degree in law. As a 23-year-old, he successfully competed to become a *registrador de la propiedad* (a type of property notary), a profession that he pursued for a short time in Villafranca del Bierzo (León), before being called to do his military service in Valencia. At the beginning of the 1980s, Rajoy took his first steps in politics in his home region of Galicia, becoming active among the ranks of Manuel Fraga's Popular Alliance (AP). Fraga, who died on January 15, 2012, had been a high-profile figure for at least half a century. Under the Franco regime, he was an influential minister of information and tourism and then ambassador in London; he led the *aperturista* (those that supported political opening) sector of the regime during the 1960s and then during the years of the democratic transition in the 1970s, before finally becoming the top leader of the post-Franco right. Fraga was responsible for refounding AP with the launch of the PP in 1989 (Adagio & Botti 2006, 82–85), and for the selection of Aznar to lead the party in 1990, the same year that Fraga was elected to lead the autonomous community of Galicia, a position that he held until 2005.

Rajoy was elected as a deputy in the first Galician parliament in 1981. He then became president of the provincial council (*diputación*) of Pontevedra in 1983, and subsequently a deputy in the Spanish parliament in 1986, but he resigned at the end of the year in order to take the position of vice president of the *Xunta*, the government of the autonomous community of Galicia, until the end of 1987 when the Galician government lost its majority. When this happened he left politics for a short while to go back to his professional work, which he carried out in Santa Pola (Alicante). The move that was to prove decisive was made in 1990 when he accepted the position of vice secretary general of the party, offered to him by Aznar, with responsibility for coordinating election campaigns, and he moved to Madrid (Rajoy 2011).

It is a well-known fact that Rajoy was never entirely on the same wavelength as Fraga, and that in fact relations between the two were always problematic. This is why it is probably no coincidence that Rajoy made a permanent move to the capital, while at the same time Fraga retreated to Galicia. After Aznar's victory in 1996, Rajoy took over the ministries of public administration (1996–99), and later education and culture (1999–2000); then, during Aznar's second term, he became first vice president (similar in function to a deputy prime minister) and minister of the presidency, with a short interval at the interior ministry (2001–2002), before returning to the ministry of the presidency where he also became official spokesman for the government while still retaining the position of first vice president (2002–2004). In September 2003, Aznar chose him as his successor and candidate for the presidency of the government from a shortlist of four possible contenders, preferring him to the more highly esteemed Rodrigo Rato.

As stated previously, it was not Rajoy who was responsible for losing the 2004 elections, but rather Aznar and his handling of the crisis, in political and communications terms, during the dramatic hours that passed between the bomb attacks and the opening of the polling stations.[4] This defeat took the PP four years to digest, that is, the entire legislature, as they insisted on arguing that ETA was involved in the attacks—a theory that was definitively refuted by the National Court (*Audiencia Nacional*) on October 31, 2007, in its judgment on those who actually carried out the atrocity, and which was largely confirmed by the judgment of the Supreme Court (*Tribunal Supremo*) dated July 17, 2008—while they also argued that the winner of the elections was not the legitimate winner (Avilés 2010). During these years, all of the opinion polls showed that Rajoy performed worse in the debates on the state of the nation held in the Congress of Deputies in 2009, 2010, and 2011.

In the 2009 debate, Rajoy's performance was given a negative or very negative assessment by 44.5 percent of those interviewed compared to 30.2 percent for Zapatero, while only 22.2 percent assessed Rajoy quite positively or very positively, compared with 41.5 percent for Zapatero.[5] In the 2010 debate, 56.4 percent of the interviewees assessed Rajoy's performance negatively or very negatively, whereas the portion was lower (44.4 percent) in Zapatero's case. These figures were mirrored by the positive assessments, with 19.6 percent of interviewees rating Rajoy's performance as quite positive or very positive, compared with 32 percent for Zapatero.[6] Yet again, following the debate on the state of the nation in 2011, the performance of the Popular Party leader was given negative or very negative assessments by 47.8 percent of those interviewed, compared with 43.1 percent for Zapatero, while on the positive side Rajoy received 22.5 percent as against 30.8 percent for the Socialist leader.[7] These opinions take into account the overall performance of the two leaders throughout the course of the debate, in which the president of the government intervenes on a number of occasions (introductory speech and two responses, first to the speech given by the leader of the opposition and then to each of the spokespersons for all of the parliamentary groups), while the leader of the opposition has fewer opportunities to speak. In fact the opinion of the interviewees changes when they are invited to express a view on the content of the two leaders' speeches, namely, whether they agree or disagree with them. When asked this question, 67.4 percent of them in 2009 stated that they agreed with few, almost none, or none of the things said by Rajoy, compared with 26.5 percent who agreed or largely agreed with most of what the Popular Party leader said, while 54.1 percent disagreed entirely or in part with Zapatero, with 39.9 percent in agreement or partial agreement with most of what the Socialist leader had to say.[8]

Although in 2010 there was a clear drop in the positive assessment of most of what Zapatero said (27.6 percent) and an equally marked rise in the negative ratings (67.2 percent), there was no corresponding shift of support toward his opponent. In fact, most of what Rajoy had to say appealed to 22 percent of the respondents, who stated that they agreed or partially agreed, while the joint percentage of those who partially or entirely disagreed rose to 71.9 percent.[9] It was not until the debate on the state of the nation in 2011 that a significant change took place. In fact, only 26.7 percent of respondents said that they agreed or partially agreed with most of what Zapatero said, as against 66.3 percent who shared few of his points, almost none, or none at all. On the other hand, 27.6 percent said they agreed or partially agreed with most of what Rajoy had to say, while 64.2 percent stated that they disagreed.[10] This shift was confirmed by the overall assessment of which of the two leaders had won the debate. While in 2009 37.6 percent stated that Zapatero had won, with only 14.4 percent giving the victory to Rajoy, the percentages moved to 26.1 percent for Zapatero and 19.8 for Rajoy in 2010. It was not until 2011 that Rajoy (27.2 percent) overtook Zapatero (18.7 percent).[11]

The Battle within the Party

Even earlier, the new Rajoy leadership had struggled to take off, both within the party and as leader of the opposition. The opposition had not appeared credible, because it seemed to be rigidly ideological and uninspired, strongly influenced by Aznar and the other party hawks: above all, the presidents of the autonomous communities of Valencia and Madrid, Eduardo Zaplana and Esperanza Aguirre, respectively, as well as the general secretary of the party from 2004 to 2008, Ángel Acebes. The opposition added fuel to the conspiracy theory by insisting beyond reason that ETA was supposedly involved in the March 11 attacks at Atocha and on the decisive influence of the attacks on bringing about the PSOE's election victory in 2004, and with the help of articles in the newspaper *El Mundo*, radio programs on the *Cadena COPE* network (which is owned by the Spanish Episcopal Conference and other church bodies), *Telemadrid* (the public TV channel run by the Madrid region, and therefore strongly linked to Esperanza Aguirre), and of the Association for the Victims of Terrorism. In 2008, the director of the newspaper *ABC*, José Antonio Zarzalejos, decided to distance himself from the PP's opposition as a result of disagreements over its aggressive approach (Zarzalejos 2010). The opposition, almost like a broken record, accused Zapatero of wanting to continue to hold talks with the Basque terrorist organization ETA, and accused the executive of wanting to destroy Spain by agreeing to the reform of the regional statutes for autonomy (Astudillo 2009).

Rajoy tried to free himself from the control of the party hawks, but did not manage to do so until the party's defeat in the March 9, 2008, elections that brought Zapatero another term in office, which for the reasons just mentioned was not entirely Rajoy's fault. It was at this point that Rajoy made full use of the knowledge of the party machinery he had gained and when he was best able to show his qualities as a dispassionate man, thoughtful, cautious, a good networker and negotiator, and above all his extraordinary ability to endure and resist. The months after the March 2008 elections turned out, in fact, to be the worst months of his political career.

Journalists and aggressive opinion-makers such as Jiménez Losantos and César Vidal continued to inveigh against him, criticizing him for lacking a fighting spirit, an inability to excite and to generate enthusiasm, and they labeled him a loser, incompetent. To stigmatize his formally polite relationship with Zapatero, they called him "minister of the opposition" (Malet 2008). These were crude accusations, made in such a vulgar fashion that we cannot rule out the possibility that they may have provoked sympathy for Rajoy among moderates and the polite, well-educated middle classes.

These attacks peaked in the months preceding the Popular Party's sixteenth party convention, when Rajoy's leadership was hotly debated by the right wing of the party, but it proved to be their final stand. Just over a month before the opening of the meeting, María San Gil, leader of the Basque PP—a close collaborator of Jaime Mayor Oreja and somewhat of a party symbol as a result of having witnessed the murder of Gregorio Ordóñez at the hands of ETA—in a demonstration of open dissent with Rajoy, whom she blamed for attempting to soften the PP's hard line as far as the demands of the nationalist parties were concerned, particularly Basques and Catalans, disassociated herself from the political report that would be presented at the convention, in spite of having contributed to writing it.[12] This move brought statements of support from Aznar's wife, Ana Botella, and from some of the party leaders, such as Ignacio Astarloa,[13] while Aznar, Esperanza Aguirre, and Acebes released statements distancing themselves from Rajoy.[14] A few days later, José Ortega Lara, a prison officer who was the victim of a kidnapping by ETA that lasted 532 days, announced his decision to leave the PP, within which he had been active for over 20 years.[15] The party hawks did not, however, have a figure, like Rajoy, capable of reaching out to all sections of the party and building support around him or herself. During the second half of May the possibility of an alternative candidate in the form of Juan Costa—the former minister of science and technology (2003–2004) and a close collaborator of Rodrigo Rato—emerged but fizzled out in the span of a few days.[16] At the same time, Rajoy, although defeated in the general elections, took credit for good results, an increase in votes (2.5 percent) and seats (seven), compared with lower gains for the Socialists. The final defeat for the right wing that pushed them to the margins came at the sixteenth PP convention that was held in Valencia from June 20 to 22. Rajoy was triumphantly reelected party president, while one of his close allies, María Dolores de Cospedal, became general secretary. From that moment, she was to be second-in-command in the party (and president of the region of Castile-La Mancha after the regional elections of May 22, 2011, which she won with over 48 percent of the votes). Alberto Ruiz-Gallardón, ex-president of the autonomous community of Madrid (1995–2003), then mayor of Spain's capital city, also rose to the high ranks of the party. He had become involved in politics as a very young man with high ambitions, and considered himself to be a representative of the more reformist and progressive wing of the Popular Party. He sought a national role, but Rajoy did not wish (or was not able) to put him forward as a candidate in the 2008 general elections, partly because of the determined opposition of Esperanza Aguirre. The time had come for Rajoy to reward him (and he did so later by appointing him to a ministerial role), co-opting him onto the party's executive committee, thereby putting into practice his declared intention to renew the party leadership.

From the sixteenth convention onward, Rajoy's leadership was no longer in danger, not even after the explosion of the Gürtel case in February 2009 (Gürtel means "belt" in German, as does the surname in Spanish of the person at the center of the drama, the entrepreneur Francisco Correa). This was one of the most serious scandals to hit Spanish democracy, as it involved party leaders (such as the party treasurer Luis Bárcenas) and also touched various high-level figures (Aznar, his wife, and their son-in-law Agag), but it was an issue (the network of corruption, tax evasion, and administrative wrongdoings) that Rajoy delayed dealing with (Palomo Cuesta 2011).

Once he was free of internal opponents, Rajoy began to lead a more united opposition and one on which he tried to put his mark, even in the tone it adopted when Zapatero's mishandling of the economic crisis began to clear the way for Rajoy to take over at the Moncloa executive palace.

An Ineffective, Ideological Opposition

One needs to carefully consider the fact that the main battlegrounds on which the PP based its opposition during Zapatero's first legislature, which we need to examine once again, did not bring the desired effects: neither the protests against the law that enabled people of the same sex to marry, in which various leading PP figures took to the streets on a number of occasions alongside some of the bishops; nor the campaign against the negotiations the PSOE carried out with ETA before the attack on Barajas airport on December 30, 2006; nor the campaign against the new Catalan statute of autonomy (that was ratified by Catalan citizens on June 18, 2006) and which continued with the appeal lodged with the Constitutional Court that decreed on July 28, 2010 that 14 articles were unconstitutional; nor the obstructionist tactics against the law that was inappropriately called the "historical memory law" approved on October 31, 2007 (Aguilar 2009); nor the constant derision of the Socialists' foreign policy, particularly on Europe (with Zapatero accused of carrying little weight and of being unable to get his way), but also concerning the ending of the embargo on Cuba and the Alliance of Civilizations initiative. These were all unconvincing lines of attack, even though some of them were very insistent, and they failed to persuade large swathes of the electorate, as proven by the fact that Zapatero was reelected to govern the country in 2008. One of the few exceptions to the party's opposition, as far as foreign policy is concerned, was the alignment of the PP with the government that came about on the approach to Kosovo; both the PP and Socialists feared the precedent that Kosovo's independence would represent for the demands made by the Basque nationalists. It is curious that the positions aligned on an issue on which Spain remained isolated on an international level (Molina 2011). Later the PP was to side with the Socialists on the ratification of the Lisbon Treaty (which received 322 votes in favor, 6 against, and 2 abstentions in the Congress of Deputies on June 26, 2008). In January 2010, agreement was reached on the appointment by the Senate of members of the Constitutional Court. In January 2011, the PP voted with the Socialists on the reform of the electoral law (Organic Law 3/2011),[17] which laid down the conditions for challenging the participation of political groups that justify terrorist violence.

In the early part of Zapatero's second term, Rajoy seemed to moderate the party's opposition style. On closer analysis, the tone was no less critical, but the targets were more specific. On June 1, 2010, the PP lodged an appeal with the Constitutional Court over the presumed unconstitutionality of various articles in the Organic Law 2/2010 of March 3, 2010, on sexual health, reproduction, and the voluntary termination of pregnancies, against which various Catholic organizations had already mobilized. The eruption of the economic crisis and the way in which it was tackled by the Socialist government offered an opportunity to the Popular Party to criticize the diagnosis and the remedies offered by the Socialists. But the PP did not chase down the government as doggedly as it had in the preceding legislature; it seemed to wait for it to make mistakes, convinced that these might lead to a hemorrhaging of support. The strategist behind this approach, which seems to fit well with Rajoy's character, was Pedro Arriola, former advisor to Aznar, who by this point had completely moved over to Rajoy serving as his right-hand man in the election campaign and as his ghostwriter, thereby being referred to in the media as a guru (Palomo Cuesta 2011).

As far as the trends among the electorate are concerned, however, things were beginning to change due to the economic crisis and the way the Socialists confronted it. In any event, it was a gradual change, as the intervening rounds of elections showed.

Intervening Regional and European Elections and Voting Trends

Elections were held on March 1, 2009, in Galicia and in the Basque Country. In Galicia the Popular Party increased its vote share slightly (from 45.3 percent in 2005 to 47.9 percent), and obtained an extra seat, and with it an absolute majority, which allowed them to regain control of the autonomous community, after a period of coalition government comprised of Socialists and nationalists from the Galician Nationalist Block (BNG). In the Basque Country, however, the PP lost in terms of votes, percentages, and seats, and, in spite of the slight gains for the Basque Nationalist Party (PNV) that gave it one more seat, it was the Socialists who gained most from the dialogue that Zapatero had begun with the nationalists, moving from 18 to 25 seats (with a percentage increase of over seven points), and for the first time they were able to take over governing the Basque region.[18]

The first sign of the change in voters' attitudes was seen in the European elections of June 9, 2009, when the PP overtook the PSOE in votes (6,670,377), vote share (42.1 percent), and seats (23) compared with the PSOE's 6,141,784 votes, 38.8 percent share, and 21 seats. But the message was still contradictory, given the high level of abstention (55.1 percent), which is an indication of apprehension from the Socialist electorate.

The Catalan elections of November 28, 2010, were a defeat for the Socialists and for Republican Left of Catalonia (ERC) and a victory for Convergence and Union (CiU), which regained power in the *Generalitat*, the Catalan regional government, with Artur Mas, while the PP gained four seats. Even this result can be interpreted as unique, and therefore not indicative of a more general trend.

In any event, it was in January 2011, according to the CIS data, that for the first time Rajoy overtook Zapatero in the opinion polls, with 19.2 percent of respondents stating that they were very or fairly confident in his abilities, as opposed to 18 percent for Zapatero.[19] A comparison with the results obtained the previous January shows that Zapatero had received very positive or fairly positive responses from 26.3 percent of those interviewed, compared to 19.8 percent for Rajoy.[20]

The electorate's change in attitude became clearer when the results came in for the local and regional elections of May 22, 2011. As predicted by all the opinion polls, the Socialist collapse came exactly as expected, just like the Spanish high-speed trains. In absolute terms, the Socialists lost around one and a half million votes, while the Popular Party gained around 600,000, beating their opponents by about 10 percentage points. In 13 of the 17 autonomous communities where voting took place (to which one needs to add the autonomous cities of Ceuta and Melilla in North Africa), the Popular Party won in 4 that were previously held by the Socialists (Aragon, Extremadura, Castile-La Mancha, and Cantabria); they increased their votes in the regions they already governed (Balearic Islands, Castile-León, La Rioja, the autonomous community of Madrid, Murcia, Valencia, to which Ceuta and Melilla should be added) and in the Canary Islands, where, however, they remained in the opposition, as was also the case in Navarre. The latter was a particular case, due to the fragmentation of the political spectrum, which was made up of parties that are well-established across the entire country (such as PP and PSOE), and nationalist and regionalist parties, and within which the rift between the Union of the Navarre People (UPN) and the PP, which had an agreement to join forces until 2008 (similar to the one that binds the CDU and the CSU in Germany), later led to the formation of a coalition government between UPN and the Navarre Socialists. Another special case was Asturias, where the defeat of the governing Socialists did not benefit the PP but instead the separate list of candidates presented by a former leader of the party, Francisco Álvarez Cascos, who went on to form a minority government. The victory of the PP in Castile-La Mancha was particularly significant because the Socialists had held power there since 1983. For different reasons, the case of Extremadura was also a significant one; although the PSOE won 33 seats, compared with 32 for the PP, it was unable to form a government due to the fact that the three regional deputies from the United Left (IU) abstained, thus allowing a PP president (José Antonio Monago) to govern. Cities such as Barcelona and Seville did not have a Socialist mayor for the first time in over 30 years, while Cordoba, the only provincial capital run by the IU, now had a mayor from the PP. Taking a more general view, the PP took power in 34 out of the 50 provincial capitals, which is 12 more than in the 2007 elections. There was no significant increase in the number of abstentions, which is normally high in Spanish elections, with a turnout of 66 percent, while there was a slight increase in the number of blank or spoiled voting ballots. There was widespread agreement among commentators: it was a political vote that punished the Socialist government, its contradictions, and its indecisive performance. It was more a case of the Socialists losing than the Popular Party winning.

The local and regional elections of May 22 marked the beginning of a new political phase and, after Zapatero's decision not to run again as a candidate in the 2012 elections, which he announced on April 2, launched a heated debate within the PSOE about the party's leadership, Mariano Rajoy immediately called for early elections. The Popular Party, however, not only had no credible alternative policies for rebuilding the economy or for bringing down unemployment, but they also still lacked the number of votes necessary to present a motion of censure in the *Cortes* (as the Spanish parliament is named), which, if it failed, might have had a boomerang effect. On July 29, Zapatero announced that early elections would be held on November 20, 2011. On September 2, following pressure from the International Monetary Fund, the European Commission, and the Central European Bank, Socialist and Popular Party deputies in the Congress approved a reform of article 135 of the Spanish constitution, which introduced the obligation to maintain a balanced budget. This was practically the last act of the legislature before the *Cortes* was dissolved.

General Elections and New Government

Thus this is the context in which the extraordinary but widely predicted and totally expected victory of the PP in the elections of November 20, 2011, took place, along with the spectacular collapse of the PSOE, which was greater than the most pessimistic forecasts. Rajoy's Popular Party secured an absolute majority in the Congress of Deputies with 186 seats, representing 44.6 percent of votes cast. Alfredo Pérez Rubalcaba's Socialists won just 110 seats, with 28.8 percent of the vote (see table 1.1). Leaving the Senate aside—as it only has a secondary role in the Spanish parliamentary system and where in any case the PP strengthened its position by moving from 101 to 136 seats while the Socialists dropped from 89 to 48—the Popular Party reached its highest point in the entire history of Spanish democracy in terms of votes, vote share, and seats, surpassing the triumphant reelection of Aznar in the general elections of 2000. The Socialists hit rock bottom in votes, vote share, and seats. Compared with the preceding general elections, the PP grew by nearly five points, with an increase of 32 seats. The PSOE lost more than 15 percentage points in terms of votes and 59 seats. In absolute terms, nearly 4,300,000 voters deserted them, with some of their votes going to IU, others to Union, Progress and Democracy (UPD), but some shifted directly from the Socialists to the Popular Party.

On December 20, Rajoy was officially elected in the Congress of Deputies with an absolute majority of 187 votes. In addition to the votes from the deputies from his own party, he also obtained the vote of the representative of the UPN and of the deputy from the Asturian Citizens Forum (FAC). Those voting against him included the Socialists, ERC, CiU, UPD, IU, and the Galician nationalists of BNG. There were 14 abstentions: PNV, Canary Island Coalition (CC), and the 7 Basque radical nationalist deputies from *Amaiur*. The following day, after being sworn in by the king, Rajoy announced his list of ministers.

Rajoy formed a streamlined government made up of 13 ministers, of whom only 4 were women, even though one of these, Soraya Sáenz de Santamaría, the youngest member of the team, held the important position of first vice president as well as spokesperson for the executive and minister of the presidency. Rajoy mainly chose people of his own generation, with legal or economic backgrounds, many of them with experience in government or in other state institutions, close collaborators or personal friends and people he could fully trust.[21] The most well-known members of the team were the new minister of the economy, Luis de Guindos, ex-secretary of state for the economy in the previous Aznar government and European advisor for Lehman Brothers; the justice minister, Alberto Ruiz Gallardón, the least conservative of the Popular Party leaders and long-standing mayor of Madrid, a position that he passed on to Ana Botella; and, for the opposite reasons, the surprise appointment was José Antonio Wert, an expert in the sociology of communication and a university professor.

Only two months had passed since the new government had been formed before the seventeenth party convention of the PP was held in Seville, from February 17 to 19, 2012. Rajoy was reelected president of the party with 97.5 percent of the votes. Cospedal, once again general secretary, strengthened her position in the party executive. The convention put out propaganda aimed more at the imminent regional elections in Andalusia and Asturias on March 12 than at the government's program. For this reason Rajoy decided to postpone presenting the state budget to the *Cortes* until after the elections, as he feared that the cuts might have a negative impact on the vote. When the elections took place, the results were disappointing for the PP, which had hoped to gain an absolute majority in Andalusia with its candidate Javier Arenas, and to see a crushing defeat of the Socialists and Álvarez Cascos's movement in Asturias in order to regain control of the principality.

In Andalusia, there was an increase of almost 10 percent in abstentions, which can certainly be attributed to a sense of disillusionment among Socialist voters. The PP advanced but not spectacularly, going from 47 to 50 seats. The PSOE vote fell, declining from 56 to 47 seats, but the left vote benefited IU, which doubled its seats, moving from 6 to 12. The number of seats needed to form a majority is 55, which the PP did not and could not achieve, but which the coalition between Socialists and IU could reach (even though within the IU this step could only be taken with a considerable degree of difficulty), and on May 3 the Socialist José Antonio Griñán was elected to the presidency of the Andalusian government.

In Asturias the PSOE gained two seats, going from 15 to 17, the PP stayed at 10, while the movement led by the Popular Party dissident Álvarez Cascos (Asturian Citizens Forum/FAC) dropped from 16 to 12 seats. The result for IU with the Greens confirmed the increase in the left vote, as they moved up from 4 to 5 seats, while UPD won 1 seat, having had no representation in the preceding Asturian legislative assembly. The majority needed amounted to 23, a threshold that was reached on May 26, when the Socialists, IU, and UPD elected the Socialist Javier Fernández Fernández to the presidency of the principality. It is too early to see in the Andalusian and Asturian votes the first symptom of a fall in confidence in the Popular Party leader, but it is certainly true that the failure to disperse the clouds caused by the economic crisis, along with the unpopular steps the leader of the government took in an attempt to tackle the crisis, above all on the reform of the labor market, against which the first general strike of his term in office took place on March 29, show that Rajoy's popularity had undoubtedly begun to fall. As an editorial in *El País* on April 29 put it, Rajoy is being criticized for his long silence, that is, his failure to respond to public opinion and his inability to hold a dialogue with the unions.[22] Moreover, drawing confidence from the strength of his majority, Rajoy turned down offers for a *pacto de estado* (broad-based agreement) that would make the opposition parties jointly responsible for the handling of the crisis.

The Economic Crisis and the Government's First Steps

Faced with a worsening economic crisis, Rajoy chose to continue on the path Zapatero had been forced to take as a result of the intervention of the European authorities in May 2010: cuts to bring the public deficit under control and structural reforms to encourage growth and employment. These were the same cuts and reforms that Rajoy and the PP had fought against when they were in opposition, by voting against the 15 billion budget cut launched by the Socialist government in May 2010 and against the reform of the pension system in June 2011, while they abstained on the reform of the financial system and of the labor market in March and September 2011, respectively. If we compare the path they had followed previously, the promises made during the election campaign and the PP's behavior since coming to government, the differences could not be greater.

The decree law containing urgent steps for the economy launched at the end of 2011, later approved by the Congress of Deputies in January, cut ministry spending by almost nine billion euros, while the spending of regional entities was cut by almost one billion. The government also announced the presentation of a law to reduce the funding of political parties, unions, and employers' organizations by 20 percent, and it froze the salaries of public servants and also limited the replacement of civil servants who retire (setting a limit of 10 percent for the police, army, health, and education). Furthermore, it increased the hours in a work week, delayed any increase in the number of potential beneficiaries of the law that provides support for dependent people (one of the pearls of Zapatero's welfare reforms) until January 1, 2013, and it raised income tax for 2012 and 2013 by between 0.75 and 7 percent, according to the different tax thresholds, and also raised taxes on income from savings from 2 to 6 percent. With the same objective in mind, the government proposed to set an upper expenditure limit for the autonomous communities. This plan had already created controversy with the communities, even though for the first time in the history of Spanish democracy the PP enjoyed almost complete control of the country, with all the main cities and nearly all the autonomous communities (with the exception of the Basque Country, Catalonia, the Canary Islands, and, after the elections of March 12, 2012, Andalusia and Asturias) under its control. Alongside these drastic measures, it ordered the revaluation of pensions by 1 percent from January 2012 and extended unemployment benefits of 400 euros for the long-term unemployed and retained other benefits.

The next step was the reform of the labor market that, after expressing a willingness to negotiate with unions on a number of occasions, Rajoy launched on February 10 making use of the solid majority his government held in parliament.[23] Both the Socialists and the unions opposed it, on the basis that the reform would only make firing easier and reduce benefits and safety nets.

At the beginning of March, Rajoy, without first consulting the European authorities, announced that the percentage of the deficit against GDP in 2012 would be 5.8 percent[24] instead of the 4.4 percent previously agreed; yet he finally succeeded in obtaining an agreement on 5.3 percent.

In the budget bill for 2012 that was presented to Congress on April 3 (to be voted on in the second half of May), Rajoy's government confirmed the policies of budget cuts (worth 27,300 million euros); an increase in taxes on companies, capital gains, and houses (from 4 to 10 percent on properties valued above the average); and an increase in the cost of electricity. Funds set aside for research were cut by 34 percent, while those for infrastructure projects were halved compared with 2010, not to mention funding for social policy, education, and the promised investment in suburban areas. It also proposed a tax amnesty (the third in the history of democratic Spain, after the ones in 1984 and 1991) in order to raise 25,000 million euros in lost revenues, with tax evaders being responsible for paying 10 percent of the amount owed. It should be noted that the PP had opposed a similar move by the Socialist government in 2010, when it also proposed introducing a tax amnesty.

Rajoy announced further cuts of around ten billion euros in health and in education on April 9, which received the support of the presidents of the autonomous communities run by the PP on April 14. He then turned to the EU for the cleaning up of the banking system, preferring to refer to the 100-billion-euro package as a "loan" rather than as a "bailout." Moreover, he even maintained that this intervention would not affect the public debt, although this was immediately refuted by Eurostat.

After the European Council meeting in Brussels on June 28 and 29, Rajoy made the most classic of "blood, sweat and tears" speeches to the Congress of Deputies on July 11, announcing a package of drastic cuts in public expenditure and of new income streams for the reduction of the deficit. The main cuts were as follows: a reduction in the number of public administration employees (with a cut in their vacation days and in time allowed for union-related activities); the suspension for all state employees, deputies, and senators of the thirteenth salary payment at Christmas time for 2012 (to be recovered after 2015 in the form of pension contributions); a reduction in the number of public companies and foundations; new cuts worth 600 million euros to the ministry budgets; confirmation for the 2013 budget of 20 percent cuts for political parties and unions already put in place in 2012; reduction in unemployment benefits after the sixth month from 60 to 50 percent for newly registered unemployed people; 30 percent reduction in the number of local councilors, with a requirement for mayors and council members to make their incomes public. As far as new income streams are concerned, Rajoy confirmed what had been feared, namely, that indirect taxes would increase, with value added taxes going up from 18 to 21 percent and from 8 to 10 percent, leaving essential goods at 4 percent, and the elimination of the tax reduction for first-time home buyers beginning in 2013. In total, if we include the new income and the reductions in expenditure, this was a 65 billion euro hit over the next two and a half years.[25] This type of bloodletting, added to the earlier ones, risks bringing about irreparable damage to the social fabric.

While Rajoy was presenting his new budget to the Congress, a few hundred meters away there was an explosion of anger from miners who had come to Madrid to demonstrate against cuts in subsidies to the coal industry, after a long march from the mining areas in the north of Spain. There were clashes with the police, with injuries on both sides, and a number of protestors were arrested. More protests and demonstrations took place over the following days, which underlined the rift that the cuts were making in the social fabric of the country.

Up until this point, therefore, the government offered higher taxes and nothing, or very little for recovery, growth, and development, notwithstanding the frequent mentions of the opposite during the election campaign and in the investiture speech.

It is now clear that the economic crisis was not the consequence of the mistaken policies of the previous administration, just as it was not sufficient to change the government to regain the confidence of the markets. In the space of just a few months, the PP's rise to power has disproven the forecasts of those who maintained that Spain would begin to see the light at the end of the tunnel once it voted out the Socialists. It could be added that the worsening economic situation is actually providing further proof that Spain's problems were not caused by the poor political handling of the crisis (even though this has certainly made the situation even worse), but that they are structural, particularly problems related to the economic model for which both of the main Spanish parties that have alternated in government since democracy was reinstated are probably equally responsible, albeit at different times and for different reasons. It does not seem at the moment that the Popular Party and its leaders (just as it was with the Socialists who are now in opposition) have fully grasped this. If it is true that a good diagnosis is a good starting point for the right therapy, one should recognize that it will not only be difficult and painful for Spain to get out of the crisis, but that this outcome is not even in sight.

Notes

1. "'Es un tema opinable si hay crisis o no hay crisis,'" *El País*, June 29, 2008.
2. Seventeen percent declared very strong or quite strong support for Zapatero, 15.6 percent for Rajoy. Centro de Investigaciones Sociológicas (CIS) Study 2847 (October 2010). All CIS studies are available at: www.cis.es.
3. This chapter reexamines and develops some of the points and analyses found in Botti (2012).
4. During these hours, however, Rajoy himself did not hold back from showing his strong moral belief that responsibility for the attacks lay with ETA; see "Mariano Rajoy: 'Tengo la convicción moral de que fue ETA,'" *El Mundo*, March 13, 2004.
5. CIS Study 2802, *Debate sobre el estado de la nación* (May 2009).
6. CIS Study 2842, *Debate sobre el estado de la nación* (July 2010).
7. CIS Study 2907, *Debate sobre el estado de la nación (XXII)* (June 2011).
8. CIS Study 2802, *Debate sobre el estado de la nación* (May 2009).
9. CIS Study 2842, *Debate sobre el estado de la nación* (July 2010).
10. CIS Study 2907, *Debate sobre el estado de la nación (XXII)* (June 2011).
11. See CIS studies 2802, 2842, and 2907, cited earlier.
12. "La espantada de San Gil coloca a Rajoy en su momento más débil del precongreso," *ABC*, May 13, 2008.
13. "Botella irrumpe en la crisis para apoyar a San Gil y pedir a la dirección que 'reflexione,'" *ABC*, May 13, 2008.

14. "San Gil abre una sima entre los dos PP," *El País*, May 13, 2008
15. "Símbolos de PP se vuelven contra Rajoy," *El País*, May 23, 2008.
16. "Juan Costa se piensa su candidatura," *El País*, May 21, 2008.
17. See *Boletín Oficial del Estado* (BOE), January 29, 2011. Available at: http://www.boe.es/boe/dias/2011/01/29/pdfs/BOE-A-2011-1640.pdf.
18. For an analysis of the 2009 Basque election, see Llera et al. (2009).
19. CIS Study 2859 (January 2011).
20. CIS Study 2828 (January 2010).
21. The ministers are as follows: José Manuel García-Margallo (Foreign Affairs), Jorge Fernández Díaz (Internal Affairs), Miguel Arias Cañete (Agriculture, Food and Environment), Ana María Pastor (Infrastructure), José Manuel Soria (Industry, Energy, Tourism), Pedro Morenés (Defense), Fátima Báñez (Employment and Social Security), Cristóbal Montoro (Finance and Public Administration), Luis de Guindos (Economy and Competition), Ana Mato (Health, Social Services and Equality), Alberto Ruiz Gallardón (Justice), and José Antonio Wert (Education, Culture and Sport).
22. "Silencioso Rajoy," *El País*, April 29, 2012.
23. See *Boletín Oficial del Estado* (BOE), February 11, 2012. Available at: http://www.boe.es/diario_boe/txt.php?id=BOE-A-2012-2076.
24. "Rajoy anuncia que espera cerrar el déficit de 2012 en el 5,8% y no en el 4,4%," *El País*, March 2, 2012.
25. A copy of the speech can be found at: www.lamoncloa.gob.es.

WorksC ited

Adagio, C., and A. Botti. 2006. *Storia della Spagna democratica. Da Franco a Zapatero*. Milan: B. Mondandori.

Aguilar, P. 2009. "Le politiche della memoria." In A. Bosco and I. Sánchez-Cuenca, eds., *La Spagna di Zapatero*. Bologna: Il Mulino, pp. 129–48.

Astudillo, J. 2009. "Le sconfitte di Rajoy: la destra dopo Aznar." In Bosco and Sánchez-Cuenca, eds., *La Spagna di Zapatero*, pp. 67–86.

Avilés, J. 2010. "Política antiterrorista y debate público, 1996–2009." *Pasado y memoria* 9: 149–74.

Botti, A. 2004a. "Madrid dopo l'11 marzo." *Il Mulino* 3: 534–43.

———. 2004b. "Le ragioni della ragione. Dall'11 settembre all'11 e poi al 14 marzo 2004." *Giornale di storia contemporanea* 1: 113–19.

———. 2012. "La Spagna dopo il voto." *Il Mulino* 1: 107–14.

Llera F. J., R. Leonisio, and J. García. 2009. "Cambio de ciclo en las elecciones vascas de 2009." *Cuadernos de Alzate* 40: 103–48.

Malet, G., ed. 2008. *Losantos contra Rajoy*. Badalona: Ara Llibres.

Molina, I. 2011. "¿Década perdida? La política europea de España 2002–11." *Política Exterior* 144: 94–101.

Montero, J. R., I. Lago, and M. Torcal, eds. 2008. *Elecciones generales 2004*. Madrid: CIS.

Palomo Cuesta, G. 2011. *El hombre impasible. Historia secreta del PP de Rajoy camino al poder.* Madrid: La Esfera de los libros.

Rajoy, M. 2011. *En confianza. Mi vida y mi proyecto de cambio para España.* Barcelona: Planeta.

Sampedro, V., ed. 2008. *Medios y elecciones, 2004.* Madrid: Editorial Universitaria Ramón Areces.

Zarzalejos, J. A. 2010. *La destitución. Historia de un periodismo imposible.* Barcelona: Ediciones Península.

CHAPTER 4

Governing Spain in Tough Times and in Minority: The Limits of Shifting Alliances

Bonnie N. Field

The contrast between the two Socialist Party (PSOE) governments of Prime Minister José Luis Rodríguez Zapatero is considerable.[1] The first government, which lasted from 2004 until 2008, was notable due to its progressive social legislation, particularly in the area of civil rights and liberties, territorial reforms that expanded political autonomy for several of Spain's regional governments, and for reopening the political discussion of Spain's past of civil war and dictatorship (see Bosco & Sánchez-Cuenca 2009; Field 2011). While the first Zapatero government certainly met with the ire of Spain's conservative political forces, and of the opposition PP, it comparatively received much better reviews from the Spanish public. In polling over the four-year period, an average of 33 percent of Spaniards indicated that the PSOE government was generally governing well or very well. Only 21 percent of Spaniards polled indicated that it was governing poorly or very poorly.[2]

The 2008 parliamentary elections, which brought about Zapatero's second term, came on the heels of a highly polarized period of Spanish politics, particularly manifested in extremely acrimonious interparty relations between the Socialists and the Popular Party (Field 2008; Sánchez-Cuenca 2009). The political atmosphere in Spain during the first Zapatero government was likely the most polarized of contemporary Spanish democracy. The strident environment, however, did not appear to negatively affect the main parties' electoral fortunes. The PSOE's electoral performance improved in 2008 from the general election in

2004. It increased its vote share by 1.3 points and added an additional five seats in parliament. Their 169 seats, however, fell seven seats short of an absolute majority in a chamber of 350 seats. While polarization, which some analysts consider to be a Popular Party (PP) electoral strategy (Sánchez-Cuenca 2009), did not generate a PP victory, the party did improve its electoral performance by an even greater margin than the PSOE: 2.2 points and six seats. In number of votes, the PSOE added approximately 262,000 compared to nearly 515,000 for the PP. This vote concentration in the two largest parties came at the expense of the minor parties.[3]

In contrast with the first, the second Zapatero government that lasted until 2011 failed in the eyes of the Spanish public. Considering the second term in its entirety, polling shows that an average of only 13 percent of Spaniards thought the PSOE government was generally governing well or very well. A near majority (47 percent) indicated that it was governing poorly or very poorly. The latter statistic reached 66 percent in October 2011, before the general elections in November.[4] The second government was inescapably marked by a devastating economic crisis, austerity measures, and structural economic reforms (see chapters 6, 7, and 11 in this volume). Zapatero also saw his personal popularity plummet, even among his prior base of supporters. During his last year in office his approval rating averaged near 3.5 points on a 10-point scale, with 10 being the best evaluation. During his first year in office his approval rating had averaged near 6 points.[5] Zapatero opted not to run as the Socialist candidate for prime minister in the 2011 elections, in which Alfredo Pérez Rubalcaba of the PSOE and Mariano Rajoy of the PP competed. Rajoy and the PP trounced the Socialists with 44.6 percent of the vote compared to 28.8 percent for the Socialists (see table 1.1). Rajoy won an absolute majority of seats in parliament, and, unlike Zapatero, would not need the votes of any other party to pass his legislative agenda.

Both Zapatero governments were single-party minority governments. Minority governments have been extremely common in Spain. In fact, four of the five governments between 1993 and 2011 were minority ones. The first Zapatero government lasted the full constitutional limit of four years, while Zapatero, in this second term, called elections approximately three and a half months early. Early elections are not uncommon in the Spanish parliamentary system, and in fact the duration of the second Zapatero government was longer than all other postconstitutional governments, except for the last three: the two governments of José María Aznar and Zapatero's first (Field 2009). What is interesting about the second Zapatero government is that despite the Spanish public's growing dissatisfaction, the government was not forced to call early elections due to a lack of parliamentary allies. In fact, its habitual allies at the time, the Basque Nationalist Party (PNV) and the Canary Island Coalition (CC), were still ready and willing to negotiate.[6] These parties began to suspect early elections when the government did not begin negotiations regarding the 2012 general budget.[7]

This chapter examines the governing dynamics of the second Zapatero minority government. In particular, it identifies the governing party's alliance partners in parliament, and a change of strategy from one of shifting parliamentary alliances to a more encompassing agreement with PNV and CC. It argues that the worsening economic crisis led to the strategy change; however, to understand the alliance with PNV and CC we must also bring in territorial politics and the government's largely orthodox policy response.

The research is based on interviews with numerous politicians, newspaper reports, and parliamentary voting data. It proceeds as follows: First, it reviews the election of Zapatero as prime minister and the composition of the parliament with which he would need to negotiate. Second, it examines the relationship between the Socialist Party and the main party of the opposition, the PP. Third, it evaluates the voting behavior of the parliamentary parties to identify the government's parliamentary support. The fourth section provides an explanation of the parliamentary dynamics. Finally, the chapter concludes with some observations about the PP absolute majority government of Mariano Rajoy.

Investiture and the Pool of Parliamentary Parties

In the Spanish parliamentary system, the prime ministerial candidate is subject to a formal investiture vote in the Congress of Deputies, the lower and more politically significant chamber of the bicameral parliament. If the candidate receives a favorable absolute majority in the first round, the candidate is elected. However, if an absolute majority is not obtained, the candidate is subject to a second vote two days later in which he or she can be elected with a plurality of more "yes" than "no" votes. Since the approval of Spain's democratic constitution in 1978, five general elections have produced minority situations, in which no single party attained a majority of seats in the Congress. To date, Spain has not formed a national coalition government. Particularly in the post-1993 period, minor regional parties[8] have provided external support for single-party minority governments of the PSOE (1993–96, 2004–2008,

2008–11) and PP (1996–2000). In some instances, the external support has been highly formalized with explicit, public agreements. In the Spanish context these are called *pactos de legislatura* (legislature pacts) (see Heller 2002; Reniu 2002). In academic circles, the governments are what Strøm (1990) calls formal minority governments; if these external support parties were counted the government indeed relies on a majority. The minority governments of Felipe González (1993–96) and José María Aznar (1996–2000) best fit this category. Other minority governments relied on a greater degree of ad hoc support or shifting alliances. This is the case of the minority governments of Zapatero, as well as the Union of the Democratic Center (UCD) minority governments during the initial years of democracy (1977–82) (see Capo 1986).

Setting aside the UCD governments due to the transitional environment, three of the four post-1993 minority governments have sought and attained support from minor parties to assure a win in the first-round investiture vote. González attained the support from the Catalan nationalist party Convergence and Union (CiU) and the Basque Nationalist Party (PNV) in 1993. Aznar in 1996 also got the support of CiU and PNV, as well as of the Canary Island Coalition (CC). Zaptero himself in 2004, though he did not rely on an explicit support agreement or *pacto de legislatura*, received the support of CC, United Left (IU), Initiative for Catalonia Greens (ICV), the Catalan Republican Left (ERC), Galician Nationalist Block (BNG), and the Aragonese Council (CHA).

However, in 2008, Zapatero did not seek the support of additional parties to win an absolute majority in the first-round investiture vote. A common interpretation provided to the author by representatives of the minor parties was that Zapatero thought that a close association with the minority regional-nationalist parties during his first term had been prejudicial. Therefore, Zapatero opted to begin the new parliament without explicit commitments and to seek ad hoc allies on the basis of the content of the legislation. This strategy in the Spanish context is known as *geometría variable* (variable geometry), which was also a parliamentary strategy used during his first term (Field 2009). In effect, the governing PSOE, because of its central policy position[9] in the parliament, could search for the least expensive coalition partner(s) on different issues instead of relying consistently on a single ally or set of allies. Therefore, Zapatero was elected in a second round vote with only a plurality and the support of his own party.

The Spanish parliament is organized on the basis of parliamentary groups. According to the parliamentary rules, there are two standards by which a parliamentary group can be formed: (1) with 15 deputies; or

(2) with 5 deputies if the political formation(s) obtain a minimum of 15 percent of the votes in the districts where they presented candidates or 5 percent of the national total.[10] The chamber has however had an informal practice of flexibility with regard to the formation of parliamentary groups.[11] In 2008 six parliamentary groups formed (see table 4.1): Socialist (PSOE), Popular (PP), Catalan (CiU), Basque (PNV), Left Republican-United Left-Initiative for Catalonia Greens, and the mixed group. In 2004 ERC had for the first time been able to form a parliamentary group on its own; however with only three deputies elected in 2008 they formed a group with IU and ICV.[12] Initially BNG joined the group to facilitate its formation but subsequently joined the mixed group. The mixed group is made up of diverse parties that do not meet the requirements for the formation of their own group (or do not benefit from a side deal). Initially the mixed group contained Navarre Yes (NA-BAI), CC, and Union, Progress and Democracy (UPD). They were almost immediately joined by BNG and later by Union of the Navarre

Table 4.1 Party composition, Congress of Deputies, 2008 and 2004

	Seats		Parliamentary group		Ideology	Statewide or region
	2008	2004	2008	2004		
PSOE	169	164	Socialist	Socialist	Left	Statewide
PP*	154	148	Popular	Popular	Right	Statewide
CiU	10	10	Catalan	Catalan	Right	Catalonia
PNV	6	7	Basque	Basque	Right	Basque Country
ERC	3	8	ERC-IU-ICV	Republican Left	Left	Catalonia
IU[†]	1	3	ERC-IU-ICV	IU-ICV	Left	Statewide
ICV[†]	1	2	ERC-IU-ICV	IU-ICV	Left	Catalonia
CC	2	3	Mixed	Canary Coalition > Mixed	Right	Canary Islands
BNG	2	2	Mixed	Mixed	Left	Galicia
UPD	1	–	Mixed	Mixed	Right	Statewide
NA-BAI	1	1	Mixed	Mixed	Left	Navarre
EA	–	1	–	Mixed	Left	Basque Country
CHA	–	1	–	Mixed	Left	Aragon
Total	350	350				

Notes: PSOE: Partido Socialista Obrero Español; PP: Partido Popular; CiU: Convergència i Unió; PNV: Partido Nacionalista Vasco; ERC: Esquerra Republicana de Catalunya; IU: Izquierda Unida; ICV: Iniciativa per Catalunya Verds; CC: Coalición Canaria; BNG: Bloque Nacionalista Galego; UPD: Unión, Progreso y Democracia; NA-BAI: Nafarroa Bai; EA: Eusko Alkartasuna; CHA: Chunta Aragonesista.

* PP presented candidates jointly with Unión del Pueblo Navarro (UPN), a regional party, in Navarre.

† IU presents candidates jointly with ICV in Catalonia. Here they are disaggregated.

Sources: Congress of Deputies; ideological placement taken from Chapel Hill Expert Survey of Party Positioning (2006), except for UPD and Na-Bai, which were categorized by the author.

People (UPN).[13] Parliamentary groups are significant because resources and debate time are allocated to the parliamentary group; however, voting discipline operates at the party level, and Spain has highly disciplined political parties.

As mentioned earlier, the PSOE occupied the central policy position in both parliaments, which allows the governing party to more easily shift allies (Green-Pedersen 2001; Strøm 1990, 97). During the second term the government needed an additional seven votes for an absolute majority, fewer than it needed during the first term, or it needed to convince some parties to abstain. Typically more "yes" than "no" votes are sufficient to pass legislation; major exceptions are final votes on organic laws and first attempts to lift a veto from the Senate, which require an absolute majority.

Despite gaining more seats, Zapatero faced more difficult parliamentary arithmetic during his second term (see table 4.1). The left held fewer seats overall. In the 2004–2008 parliament the left held 182 seats, and in 2008–11 it held 177, only 1 seat more than an absolute majority. Therefore, if Zapatero wanted to form a leftist alliance, he would need to get the support of four or five additional parties from among IU (1 seat), ICV (1), ERC (3), BNG (2), and Na-Bai (1). On the right, aside from allying with the main opposition PP, Zapatero's pool of potential allies included CiU (10 seats), PNV (6), CC (2), and UPD (1). Subsequently UPN split from the PP parliamentary group and was also a potential ally. Therefore among the minor parties an absolute majority could be formed with CiU alone, or with two of the center-right minor parties. Clearly, a combination of allies that crossed the left-right ideological divide could open up other strategic options. It is important to note that most of the minor parties are regional parties that only present candidates in a limited number of territorial districts and defend regional or substate nationalist interests. Only PSOE, PP, IU, and UPD are statewide parties, which present candidates in all or most all of the districts in Spain and attempt to aggregate the diverse territorial interests of the Spanish population.

Politics as Usual: The Zapatero Government and the PP

Perhaps it is no surprise that the Zapatero government did not find a solid ally in the main party of the opposition. While the period of Zapatero's first term likely marked the height of *crispación* or polarized, acerbic politics, the relationship between the PSOE and PP during the second term can best be characterized as "politics as usual." An examination of parliamentary behavior indicates that interparty politics in parliament between 2008 and 2011 was largely consistent with the prior period.

Table 4.2 presents measures of interparty agreement (or division) using votes in the Spanish Congress of Deputies. It extends two prior studies of all laws passed in the Congress of Deputies between 1977 and 2008 (Field 2005, 2008) to include the 2008–2011 parliament. The dataset includes all organic and ordinary laws with recorded votes.[14] Organic laws regulate the development of fundamental rights and liberties and approve the regional government charters (statutes of autonomy), the electoral laws, and many other laws that regulate the institutions of the state.[15] All other laws are ordinary laws. Ordinary laws in some cases can be passed in committee and do not require a floor vote. The dataset includes laws passed in committee and on the floor.

The first measure averages the support for all laws during the legislative period. Averages are the percentages of votes cast in favor, against, and abstaining. The second measure is the portion of laws that pass during each legislative period with what I call *substantial collaboration*. Since committee voting records do not indicate legislator names, we use an indirect measure. Laws that attain a percentage of votes in favor of the legislation that is equal to or greater than the combined percentage of seats held by the governing party and the principal opposition party are categorized as passed with substantial collaboration.[16] In effect, it is an indirect indicator of the degree of agreement or disagreement across, at a minimum, the two main political parties. Substantial collaboration in some instances indicates wider multiparty consensus.

Many of the data points indicate continuity with post-2000 parliamentary dynamics. Since the 2000 election, the main national parties have agreed on the passage of approximately half of the legislation in parliament, as indicated by the substantial collaboration data. This is the period with the lowest levels of bipartisanship since the transition. There are however two data points that stand out. First, the average number of abstention votes is the highest of the entire democratic period. This indicates that Zapatero had greater difficulty finding allies who were willing to express explicit public support with a "yes" vote. He was better able to negotiate abstention votes, which indeed help the government legislate as abstentions in most cases lower the threshold of votes needed to pass legislation. The second data point that stands out is the percentage of organic laws that were passed with substantial collaboration. While it is not statistically significant, substantial collaboration on organic laws increased 19 points. This percentage is in line with the average of the post-1986 period. However, as I've indicated elsewhere (Field 2008), the

Table 4.2 Interparty collaboration, Congress of Deputies, 1977–2011

Legislature	Governing party-main opposition	Government type	Average support (all laws; in %)			Substantial collaboration (in %)			Cases (N)		
			For	Against	Abstain	All laws	Ordinary laws	Organic laws	All laws	Ordinary	Organic
Legislature C (1977/1979)	UCD-PSOE	Minority	92	4	4	86	86	–	107	107	–
Legislature I (1979/1982)	UCD-PSOE	Minority	90	5	5	79	**76	95	250	212	38
Legislature II (1982/1986)	PSOE-AP/PP	Majority	86	8	6	***57	***62	***36	210	168	42
Legislature III (1986/1989)	PSOE-AP/PP	Majority	88	6	6	***71	72	**71	119	102	17
Legislature IV (1989/1993)	PSOE-PP	Majority	87	7	6	72	73	67	135	111	24
Legislature V (1993/1996)	PSOE-PP	Minority	86	7	7	65	*61	76	147	109	38
Legislature VI (1996/2000)	PP-PSOE	Minority	84	8	8	63	60	78	218	178	40
Legislature VII (2000/2004)	PP-PSOE	Majority	84	11	5	**52	**47	73	191	150	41
Legislature VIII (2004/2008)	PSOE-PP	Minority	82	12	6	50	48	58	167	134	33
Legislature IX (2008/2011)	PSOE-PP	Minority	83	7	11	52	46	77	141	115	26
Entire period			86	8	6	64	63	70	1685	1386	299

Notes: "Substantial collaboration" refers to the percentage of laws that passed with substantial collaboration during the legislative period. Asterisks on the "substantial collaboration" data refer to the statistical significance of the change from the previous legislative period. Statistical significance was determined by the Pearson Chi-Square test. * Statistically significant at the <.10 level; ** Statistically significant at the <.05 level; *** Statistically significant at the <.01 level.

Source: Elaborated by the author based on votes published in the Diario de Sesiones, Congress of Deputies, Spain.

first Zapatero government stood out due to the lack of bipartisanship on issues of state. We should also note, however, that comparatively fewer organic laws were passed.

Unsurprisingly, the PP did not support the government's key legislative responses to the economic crisis, including the first government spending cuts in May 2010 (PP "no" vote), the labor market reform of September 2010 (PP "abstention"), the reform of the financial system in March 2011 (PP "abstention"), the collective bargaining reform of June 2011 (PP "no" vote), and the reform of the pension system (PP "no" vote) also in June 2011.[17] However, remarkably, the two main parties rapidly and surprisingly reached an agreement in late summer 2011 to reform article 135 of the Spanish constitution to introduce the principle of budget stability and to cap public budget deficits. The only other party to vote in favor was UPN, and several parties abandoned the parliamentary chambers in protest while others chose not to vote.[18] Despite numerous debates regarding the need for constitutional reform particularly with regard to the territorial organization of the state and the Spanish Senate, this was the first significant reform since the transition. Opposition from the minor parties came in several forms, including ideological disagreement, concerns about the reform's effect on the autonomy of the regional governments, and the process of deal-making between the two main parties, which some claimed broke the wider spread consensus on which the constitution was written during the transition to democracy.

The Configurations of Parliamentary Alliances

This section sets out to identify the parliamentary alliance patterns prevalent during Zapatero's second term in minority. It highlights four important alliance characteristics: first, the predominance of alliances with PNV and CC; second, the familiar reliance of minority governments on regional compared to statewide parties; relatedly, the comparatively greater reliance on right and right-regional parties compared to Zapatero's first term; and finally, the diminished level of parliamentary support overall.

To identify the government's parliamentary allies, I examine floor votes on legislation in the Spanish Congress of Deputies.[19] The dataset includes votes: (1) on legislation, including government and parliamentary bills and the sanctioning of the executive's decree laws; and either (2) the vote passed—with or without the support of the governing Socialists, or (3) the vote failed despite the favorable vote of the governing Socialist Party. In effect it includes all governing party defeats, if any, and all votes on articles and amendments that passed. Data for both Zapatero terms are presented for comparison. There are 1117 discrete votes from 2004 to 2008, and 657 from the 2008 to 2011 period.

For each vote, I calculate the Rice index of voting likeness (IVL) between each party and the governing PSOE. It is calculated as follows:

IVL = 100 − (A − B),

where A = percentage of party group A voting pro on resolution X, B = percentage of party group B voting pro on resolution X, and (A − B) = absolute value of A − B. The IVL ranges between 0 (maximum disagreement) and 100 (maximum voting similarity) (Raunio 1999, 201).

All IVLs are then averaged. If no one in the party votes, the number of votes on which the analysis is based is correspondingly reduced.

Table 4.3 presents the indexes of voting likeness between the PSOE and each of the parliamentary parties and by various party characteristics (regional or statewide; right or left; right-regional or left-regional). The regional parties are CC, PNV, CiU, BNG, ERC, UPN, Na-Bai, ICV, CHA, and Basque Solidarity (EA). Statewide parties are IU, PP, and UPD along with the governing Socialists. CC, PNV, CiU, UPN, PP, and UPD are considered to fall right of center. BNG, ERC, Na-Bai, ICV, IU, EA, and CHA, along with the PSOE, are considered to be on the left (see table 4.1).

Examining the second term, there are several interesting patterns. At the party level, CC (89.8) and PNV (86.8) were the most frequent parliamentary allies of the Socialist government, followed at a distance by CiU (72.2). As noted earlier the combination of PSOE votes plus those of PNV and CC provided the government with an absolute majority of 177. This reflects the fact that the PSOE negotiated agreements with both the PNV and CC in late 2010 to support the passage of the government's 2011 budget and economic reforms, which will be discussed later. The PSOE's least frequent allies were the new statewide party UPD (38.3) and the main opposition PP (50.2). The three most frequent allies of government during Zapatero's first term were CC, CHA, and BNG, followed closely by IU, ICV, and PNV.

Regarding party types, during the second term regional parties were more likely to vote with the Socialists than the statewide parties, 67.7 compared to 47.4, which is a 20-point gap. This is a well-known trait of the Spanish parliamentary system, where regional parties provide stability for minority governments. This characteristic distinguishes the Spanish case from European trends, where cross-national findings associate

Table 4.3 Average Index of Voting Likeness (IVL) with the governing PSOE, 2004–11

Party	Zapatero II (2008–11) Mean	N	Party	Zapatero I (2004–2008) Mean	N	Zapatero II – I Party	Difference
CC	89.8	635	CC	95.5	1092	IU	−27.7
PNV	86.8	656	CHA	91.4	795	ICV	−26.1
CIU	72.2	656	BNG	84.4	1086	BNG	−20.5
BNG	63.9	656	IU	81.4	1108	ERC	−19.6
ERC	59.0	644	ICV	80.7	1088	NA-BAI	−9.8
UPN	56.0	595	PNV	80.1	1115	CC	−5.8
NA-BAI	55.4	538	ERC	78.6	1116	PP	−4.8
ICV	54.7	615	CIU	76.0	1117	CIU	−3.8
IU	53.7	646	EA	66.7	782	PNV	6.8
PP	50.2	657	NA-BAI	65.2	928		
UPD	38.3	654	PP	55.0	1117		
Total	62.0	6952	*Total*	77.8	11344	*Total*	-15.8

Party type	Zapatero II (2008–11) Gap	Mean	N	Zapatero I (2004–2008) Gap	Mean	N	Zapatero II – I Difference
Regional		67.7	4995		80.2	9119	−12.5
Statewide	20.3	47.4	1957	12.1	68.1	2225	−20.7
Right		65.6	3853		75.1	5223	−9.5
Left	8.1	57.5	3099	−5.0	80.1	6121	−22.6
Right-regional		76.6	2542		80.5	4106	−3.9
Left-regional	18.2	58.4	2453	1.5	79.0	5013	−20.6

Notes: The difference is calculated by subtracting the Zapatero I data from the Zapatero II data. Gap refers to the difference between party types; regional minus statewide, right minus left, right-regional minus left-regional.

regional parties with government instability (Brancati 2005). Regional parties were more likely to support the government than statewide parties during both governing periods. However, the gap (IVL regional parties minus IVL statewide parties) was greater during the second government, 20 points (2008–11) compared to 12 (2004–2008), leaving Zapatero comparatively more reliant on regional parties in his second term.

During the second term right parties were more likely to ally with the Socialists (65.6) than the left parties (57.5). Analyzing only the regional parties, the right-regional parties jointly had an IVL of 76.6 compared to 58.4 for the left-regional parties, a difference of 18 points. Contrasts with the first term are also illuminating here. During the 2004–2008 parliament, left parties were more likely to ally with the Socialists (80.1) than right parties (75.1), and left-regional parties were as likely to support the first Zapatero government as right-regional parties, 79.0 and 80.5, respectively.

Finally, the data reveal that the government enjoyed substantially less parliamentary support overall during the second term, though support from the left and left-regional parties declined more dramatically than for the right and right-regional parties, leaving Zapatero more reliant on parties of the right. The total IVL for all parties was substantially lower during the second term (62.0) than during the first (77.8), nearly a 16-point difference. In fact, except PNV, every party had a lower IVL during the second term, ranging from a 4- to a 28-point difference.

Minority Governing Dynamics: From *geometríav ariable* to the *pacto presupuestario*

This section analyzes the shift from a strategy of *geometría variable* to the government's greater reliance on PNV and CC with the *pacto presupuestario* (budget pact) in the fall of 2010. While the worsening economic crisis is critical to our understanding of this shift, to understand the choice of allies we must also consider territorial politics and the government's largely orthodox policy response.

Contrary to the expectations of minimum-winning coalition theory (Riker 1962), in minority situations at the national level in Spain government coalitions do not form. The common explanation for the lack of coalition governments or, alternatively, for the formation of single-party minority ones in Spain is the differing goals of the regional parties, who do not prioritize executive office at the national level (Reniu 2002, 2011). As mentioned earlier, Zapatero in his second term initially planned to continue a strategy of *geometría variable* or shifting alliances that was used during the his first term (Field 2009). During both periods, the governing PSOE occupied the central position in the parliamentary party system, and therefore would be comparatively better able than a noncentral party (such as the PP minority government under Aznar) to shift allies depending on the content of legislation, with the goal of attaining policy outcomes closer to its preferences or with the fewest concessions.

However, once the economic crisis exploded, and particularly after May 2010, *geometría variable* became an increasingly difficult governing strategy. It was widely perceived that CiU had saved the government with its abstention on the government's deficit reduction decree, which was approved with only PSOE votes and the abstention of CiU (ten votes), CC (two), and UPN (one). Had the government lost this vote, early elections would likely have been called. In the context of heightened economic crisis and external pressure, the Spanish government sought to create confidence in its ability to govern and carry out economic reforms. In the fall of 2010, ultimately the government negotiated a deal with PNV and CC to pass the 2011 state budget and, for their support on economic reforms, it was hoped that CiU would be incorporated following the Catalan regional elections on November 28, 2010.[20] Zapatero closed a deal with Iñigo Urkullu, PNV president, and Paulino Rivero, CC president, on October 15, 2010.

The deal was referred to as a *pacto presupuestario* or budget pact. The exact nature of this agreement is ambiguous. At times, it has been referred to as a *pacto de legislatura*; however, PNV on numerous occasions stated that the pact covered the 2011 budget and that subsequent support was not guaranteed and keeping the government in power was not part of the deal. It also made its support for future economic reforms contingent on their "reasonableness." Nonetheless, it was widely believed to give Zapatero stability to serve out his term, in which elections had to be called before March 2012, even if it meant not passing a new 2012 budget the following year.

The exact content of the deal is also unclear; yet, aspects of it were reported in the press. The PNV attained the almost complete implementation of its regional charter (statute of autonomy), which included the transfer of competencies in 20 areas; yet competencies related to prisons and social security were not part of the pact. Among other provisions, the deal was also reported to include 112 million euros in state investments for the Basque Country, a commitment to change the names of the Basque provinces to Basque names (Bizkaia, Gipuzkoa) or a hyphenated Spanish-Basque name (Álava-Araba), and to include representatives of the Basque Country region within the Economic and Financial Affairs Council (ECOFIN) of the European Union.

Among other provisions, concessions to the CC and the Canary Islands included 25 million euros in state investments; an employment plan that would include temporary tax benefits for companies that create employment in the Canary Islands and 42 million euros for an Integral Employment Plan; subsides for the transport of merchandise and the maintenance of subsidies for the transport of passengers; as well as financing for up to 1 percent of the Canary Islands' GDP from the Official Credit Institute.[21] The agreement led the PP to withdraw from the CC-PP government in the Canary Islands. In response the PSOE assured support from the Canary Island Socialists.[22] A CC minority government was subsequently formed.

For the PNV, there was the additional benefit that the party hoped to overshadow the existing Basque government led by the Socialist Patxi López. A bilateral committee of PNV representatives and Socialists was set up to guarantee the implementation of the agreement. It was later revealed that the PNV had also attained a commitment to gain representation on four state regulatory boards, the Telecommunications Market Committee, the National Energy Committee, the National Postal Sector Committee, and the Public Television (RTVE) Administration Board. The Basque nationalists had not had representation in these institutions since the Aznar government.[23]

Another indication of the government's growing weakness and inability to engage in shifting alliances was that the budget pact also affected the government's social policy priorities. Negotiations with its new allies led to the abandonment of some of its more progressive legislative priorities, particularly the promised bill on religious freedom, which was included in the PSOE's platform and was on the executive's agenda, and antidiscrimination legislation.[24] Of course, in subsequent legislative negotiations, there were also policy concessions. For instance, the collective bargaining reform of June 2011 was adapted to give preference to collective bargaining agreements at the autonomous community level over state-level agreements.[25]

If the economic crisis explains the change from a strategy of shifting alliances to a comparatively more stable agreement, what explains the choice of alliance partners? In addition to the coordination difficulties of negotiating a leftist coalition with multiple small parties, an alliance with the leftist parties was complicated by several factors. First, contextual factors clearly mattered. Several officials from the minor left parties indicated their severe disenchantment with the PSOE government and Prime Minister Zapatero. The Catalan leftist parties, ERC and ICV, who had been closer allies of Zapatero in his first term, felt betrayed by Zapatero when during his first term he did not accept the revision of the Catalan regional charter that emerged out of the Catalan parliament, as promised. This led to an increasingly adversarial relationship, particularly on the part of ERC, which was necessary for any left-wing alliance. Second, the government's increasingly orthodox policy response to the economic crisis met with severe criticism from all of the leftist parties. Furthermore, multilevel governing dynamics also mattered. In a multilevel state, with significant regional governments, and a two-dimensional party system, we must incorporate territorial politics to help explain alliance patterns (Field forthcoming). In addition to the soured relationship with the Catalan governing parties (ERC and ICV), the support

BNG had provided to the Zapatero government declined. The party had governed at the regional level with the Socialists in Galicia from 2005 until 2009. Once the PSOE-BNG coalition lost the government to the PP, BNG's incentives to support the national-level Socialists also diminished.[26]

The substantive policy orientation of the economic reforms also likely facilitated an alliance with the center-right parties. The center-right regional parties claimed that they would also be perceived as more credible allies by the financial markets, the EU, and international financial institutions. But, why wasn't CiU a more prevalent ally? Using the insights of coalition theory, it might appear that CiU would be the party most apt to have entered into an encompassing agreement with the governing PSOE. Aside from the main opposition PP, it was the only party individually capable of forming a minimum winning parliamentary coalition. A PSOE-CiU minimum winning parliamentary alliance would also be the only one that would hold the minimum number of seats, which requires fewer payoffs according to coalition theory (Gamson 1961; Riker 1962), and the smallest number of actors, making bargaining easier (Leiserson 1968).

However, territorial politics are significant here. CiU, which had been the critical support party for the González and Aznar minority governments in the 1990s, lost the Catalan regional government in 2003 to the PSC-PSOE (Socialist Party of Catalonia-PSOE), ERC, and ICV coalition. This placed the party in a more competitive relationship with the governing Socialists and reduced its incentives to support the government because it would not capitalize directly on the side payments attained for their support, as they were not governing.[27]

PNV ironically faced a similar circumstance in 2009, when it lost the Basque government to a minority PSOE government that had the external support of the PP. The PNV's initial reaction was to pledge to oppose the Zapatero government. However, in the face of the government's weakness, the PNV saw an opportunity to accomplish several of its policy priorities and attempt to overshadow the Socialist-led government in the Basque Country.

Conclusions

This chapter examined the parliamentary dynamics during Zapatero's second term at the head of a minority government. It draws our attention to the government's change of parliamentary strategy, particularly from a strategy of shifting parliamentary alliances to a more encompassing and stable agreement with PNV and CC. It argues that while the strategy change can be explained by the economic crisis, the choice of allies has much to do with territorial politics and the largely orthodox policy response.

The Popular Party government of Mariano Rajoy that emerged out of the 2011 elections relies on a very comfortable absolute majority in parliament. Also, due to regional elections held between 2009 and 2011, the Popular Party has control of most of the regional governments in Spain. This, however, is a double-edged sword, particularly in the context of the economic and financial crisis. On the one hand, the PP obviously has the parliamentary majorities to pass its initiatives; on the other, it will also bear responsibility for them, many of which are and will be highly unpopular and painful. During the initial months of the new government, Rajoy sought to attain support from other parties, particularly CiU, to share the burden of the government's policy response to the economic crisis. In some instances, CiU collaboration was forthcoming. This also must be understood in the context of territorial politics, where CiU, which returned to government following the 2010 Catalan elections, was governing in minority, and repeatedly relied on the Catalan branch of the PP to carry out its governing priorities. However, the strains of this relationship began to show in the summer of 2012 and powerfully with the demands of CiU (and other Catalan parties) for a reform of the financial system used to allocate resources to the autonomous communities (referred to as the *pacto fiscal* or fiscal pact), the mass demonstration in Barcelona on September 11, 2012, which is the national day (*diada*) of Catalonia, under the banner "Catalonia: New State in Europe," and the calling of early elections for the Catalan parliament by Artur Mas, leader of the Catalan government and of CiU, with the declared intention of seeking electoral backing to hold a referendum on Catalan sovereignty.

Moreover, the costs of governing are already clear. In the first elections held after the PP's return to the national government, for the regional parliaments of Andalusia and Asturias on March 25, 2012, the PP electoral results were disappointing for the party. The PP anticipated winning enough votes to govern in Andalusia for the first time since Spain's transition to democracy; however, the PP only won 50 of the 109 seats. The PSOE formed a coalition government with IU. In Asturias, the PP maintained their 10 seats in the 45-seat chamber; however, the PSOE, very soon after its tremendous defeat in the general parliamentary elections, was able to increase its seats and govern with the support of IU and UPD.

The Rajoy government also faced significant extrainstitutional opposition, such as the general strike held on March 29, 2012, 15-M *indignados* (indignant) demonstrations in mid-May 2012, the protest march carried out by Asturian miners from the region to Madrid in July 2012, among many other protests against government cutbacks, in addition to the already mentioned mass mobilization in support of Catalan sovereignty in Barcelona in September. Therefore, one of the government's main challenges is to manage extrainstitutional conflict and the demands of substate nationalists yet without having the incentives that minority governments create to accommodate distinct positions.

Notes

1. The author gratefully acknowledges the support of the Ministerio de Ciencia e Innovación, Gobierno de España (CSO2010–16337), the American Political Science Association, and the Program for Cultural Cooperation between Spain's Ministry of Culture and United States Universities. She also thanks Kerstin Hamann for her helpful comments and suggestions on previous versions of this chapter, and Paige Roland, Lourdes Solana, and Teresa Sieiro for research assistance.
2. Centro de Investigaciones Sociológicas (CIS) data. *Valoración de la gestión del Gobierno* (Polling summary). Available at: http://www.cis.es/cis/export /sites/default/-Archivos/Indicadores/documentos_html/sB102030010.html (last accessed on March 31, 2012).
3. All election data are taken from Spain's Ministry of Interior. Available at: www.infoelectoral.mir.es.
4. CIS data. See note 2.
5. CIS Barometers, various dates. Available at: www.cis.es.
6. L. R. Aizpeolea, "Zapatero rechaza un adelanto electoral hasta que se supere esta crisis financiera," *El País*, July 12, 2011.
7. F. Garea, "PNV y CC emplazan al Gobierno a que abra ya la negociación del Presupuesto," *El País*, July 28, 2011.
8. Regional parties are defined as those that present candidates in a limited number of territorial districts.
9. Central policy position refers to the party that contains the median legislator on both the left-right and center-periphery dimensions of political competition. Parties' positions were determined by the Chapel Hill Expert Survey of Party Positioning, 2006 survey. Available at: http://www.unc.edu/-hooghe /data_pp.php.
10. Congressional rules (*Reglamento del Congreso de los Diputados*). Available at: http://www.congreso.es/portal/page/portal/Congreso/Congreso/Hist _Normas/Norm.
11. For example, the PSOE "lent" two Socialist deputies to CC in 2004 to facilitate the formation of a CC parliamentary group. Similarly, as part of the

deal for CC to support the investiture of PP candidate Aznar in 1996, the Union of the Navarre People (UPN) deputies, who were allied with the PP, facilitated the formation of a CC group by temporarily joining it. However, with the new PP majority elected in 2011 this flexibility was not shown to the new Basque leftist-nationalist coalition *Amaiur*, which was not permitted to have a parliamentary group. *Amaiur* won seven seats. It met the 15 percent hurdle in the Basque Country districts, but it only obtained 14.86 percent in the Navarre district.

12. ICV is a party independent of IU, yet they jointly present candidates in Catalonia.

13. UPN is an independent political party that has a special relationship with the PP (see Verge & Barberá 2009). The UPN presents candidates for parliament on PP lists and its deputies until this point had formed part of the PP parliamentary group.

14. It does not include international treaties or royal decree laws. However, royal decree laws are often subsequently processed as ordinary laws, which are included. For a complete explanation of the data and methodology, see Field (2005).

15. Article 81 of the Spanish constitution of 1978. Available at: http://www.congreso.es/portal/page/portal/Congreso/Congreso/Hist_Normas/Norm.

16. For laws passed in committee, the portion of committee seats is used.

17. "Cinco votaciones de reformas clave sin apoyo del PP," *El País*, June 27, 2011.

18. R. Seco and P. R. Blanco, "La reforma constitucional del PP y PSOE sale con el desplante del resto," *El País*, September 2, 2011; N. Junquera, "PP y PSOE fracasan en su intento de lograr apoyos para la reforma," *El País*, September 7, 2011.

19. Since records of committee votes do not indicate how individual legislators vote, we are limited to floor votes taken in the chamber.

20. L. R. Aizpeolea and I. C. Martínez, "Zapatero cierra con el PNV y CC un pacto para el resto de la legislatura," *El País*, October 16, 2010.

21. A. Díez, "El PSOE acoge con alivio el mensaje de que podrá acabar la legislatura," *El País*, October 19, 2010.

22. T. Santana, "El PP dejará el Gobierno canario tras presentar las cuentas," *El País*, October 21, 2010.

23. A. Díez, "El PSOE pacta en secreto con el PNV su entrada en cuatro órganos del Estado," *El País*, November 9, 2010; F. Garea, "El PSOE tiene 110 millones para nuevos pactos en el Presupuesto," *El País*, October 26, 2010.

24. F. Garea and N. Galarraga, "Zapatero achaca a la falta de consenso el frenazo de la ley de libertad religiosa," *El País*, November 11, 2010.

25. F. Garea, "CiU y PNV salvan ahora a Zapatero en la reforma de la negociación colectiva," *El País*, June 23, 2011.

26. Personal interviews with BNG politicians.

27. Personal interviews with CiU politicians.

WorksC ited

Bosco, A., and I. Sánchez-Cuenca, eds. 2009. *La España de Zapatero: Años de cambios, 2004–2008*. Madrid: Editorial Pablo Iglesias.

Brancati, D. 2005. "Pawns Take Queen: The Destabilizing Effects of Regional Parties in Europe." *Constitutional Political Economy* 16(2): 143–59.

Capo, J. 1986. "Party Coalitions in the First Democratic Period in Spain, 1977–1982." In G. Pridham, ed., *Coalition Behavior in Theory and Practice: An Inductive Model for Western Europe*. Cambridge: Cambridge University Press, pp. 232–50.

Field, B. N. 2005. "De-thawing Democracy: The Decline of Political Party Collaboration in Spain (1977–2004)." *Comparative Political Studies* 38(9): 1079–103.

———. 2008. "Interparty Politics in Spain: The Role of Informal Institutions." In B. N. Field and K. Hamann, eds., *Democracy and Institutional Development: Spain in Comparative Theoretical Perspective*. Houndmills and New York: Palgrave Macmillan, pp. 44–67.

———. 2009. "Minority Government and Legislative Politics in a Multilevel State: Spain under Zapatero." *South European Society and Politics* 14(4): 417–34.

———, ed. 2011. *Spain's "Second Transition"? The Socialist Government of José Luis Rodríguez Zapatero*. New York and London: Routledge.

———. Forthcoming. "Decentralization, Regional Parties and Multilevel Governance in Spain." In A. López Basaguren and L. Escajedo San Epifanio, eds., *The Ways of Federalism in Western Countries and the Horizons of Territorial Autonomy in Spain*. New York: Springer.

Gamson, W. A. 1961. "A Theory of Coalition Formation." *American Sociological Review* 26 (3): 373–82.

Green-Pedersen, C. 2001. "Minority Governments and Party Politics: The Political and Institutional Background to the 'Danish Miracle.'" *Journal of Public Policy* 21(1): 53–70.

Heller, W. B. 2002. "Regional Parties and National Politics in Europe: Spain's Estado de las Autonomías, 1993 to 2000." *Comparative Political Studies* 35(6): 657–85.

Leiserson, M. 1968. "Factions and Coalitions in One-Party Japan: An Interpretations Based on the Theory of Games." *American Political Science Review* 62(3): 770–87.

Raunio, T. 1999. "The Challenge of Diversity: Party Cohesion in the European Parliament." In S. Bowler, D. Farrell, and R. S. Katz, eds., *Party Discipline and Parliamentary Government*. Columbus, OH: Ohio State University Press, pp. 189–207.

Reniu, J. M. 2002. *La formación de gobiernos minoritarios en España, 1977–1996*. Madrid: Centro de Investigaciones Sociológicas.

———. 2011. "'Spain is Different': Explaining Minority Governments by Diverging Party Goals." In R. B. Andeweg, L. De Winter, and P. Dumont, eds., *Puzzles of Government Formation: Coalition Theory and Deviant Cases*. London and New York: Routledge, pp. 112–28.

Riker, W. H. 1962. *The Theory of Political Coalitions*. New Haven: Yale University Press.

Sánchez-Cuenca, I. 2009. "Las elecciones de 2008: ideología, crispación y liderazgo." In Bosco and Sánchez-Cuenca, eds., *La España de Zapatero*, pp. 25–48.

Strøm, K. 1990. *Minority Government and Majority Rule*. Cambridge: Cambridge University Press.

Verge, T., and Ó. Barberá. 2009. "Descentralización y estrategias organizativas: las relaciones especiales entre partidos de ámbito estatal (PAE) y partidos de ámbito no estatal (PANE) en España." *Institut de Ciències Polítiques i Socials Working Paper Series* no. #281.

CHAPTER 5

The State of Autonomies between the Economic Crisis and Enduring Nationalist Tensions

César Colino

After a first term (2004–2008) marked by significant controversy surrounding the territorial model of the Spanish state and the reform of six regional statutes of autonomy, the reelection of Zapatero's Socialist Party (PSOE) at the central government level in 2008 ushered in a much calmer environment on territorial issues and partisan confrontation at large.[1] In the context of an international economic crisis that began to affect Spain in a particularly severe fashion, public debate seemed to have turned almost exclusively to the problems of the Spanish economy. However, three main territorial issues remained on the political agenda and garnered media attention for most of Zapatero's second term (2008–11) and have imbued the occasional public discussions and the conduct of intergovernmental relations: the reform of the regional government funding arrangements and the central and regional responses to the economic crisis; the Constitutional Court's ruling on the Catalan statute of autonomy issued in 2010; and the end of violence in the Basque Country.

All three developments posed unprecedented challenges to the efficiency and legitimacy of the Spanish territorial system, referred to as the "state of autonomies." The way they were confronted is bound to have a decisive impact on its viability for years to come (see Colino 2011; Colino & Hombrado 2012). At the end of the term, and since the worsening of the sovereign debt crisis throughout Europe in 2010, the autonomous communities (hereafter ACs) bluntly experienced the consequences of an unprecedented fiscal crisis that forced them to undertake, for the first time, radical cuts in their budgets and public services. Prime Minister Zapatero's second term also witnessed the disappointed reaction of Catalan politicians and citizens to the court ruling on Catalonia's statute of autonomy, seen by many in Catalonia as curtailing the previously agreed-upon powers and recognition for this AC within Spain. The Basque Country, for its part, witnessed for the first time a non-nationalist regional government and what seems to be the end of one of the most infamous anomalies of Spanish democracy so far, nationalist political violence. This occurred through the definitive defeat of the terrorist organization Basque Homeland and Freedom (ETA), forced by government antiterrrorist policies and judicial pressure, and by the interests of its own political allies to definitively give up its violent strategy and to defend its nationalist and secessionist agenda through peaceful and democratic means.

This chapter's general argument is that the evolution of Spain's state of autonomies—after the recent reform of eight regional statutes of autonomy, the 2009 regional funding reform, and the end of political violence—experienced increased devolution of competencies, some additional regional financial autonomy and increased resources for regions, and a certain degree of institutional updating or modernizing, but without a clear blueprint for the future territorial model. At the same time, several ACs, especially Catalonia, attained additional recognition of identity symbols. However, despite these developments, during Zapatero's second term the distributive tensions and the centralizing tendencies reinforced by the economic crisis and the fiscal consolidation imperatives, together with what was deemed a restrictive interpretation of the constitution by the court ruling, meant that the reforms were not perceived in Catalonia as promoting the accommodation of its demands. Renewed fiscal and identity demands, increased secessionist sentiment, and intergovernmental tensions have ensued.

The chapter first sets the historical context and presents some of the features of the Spanish territorial system. It then looks at the relevant issues of territorial governance revolving around the national and regional government responses to the economic crisis and the distributive tensions among the regions and the central government. It proceeds to analyze the issue of the accommodation, or lack thereof, of Catalan nationalism in the system by describing the Constitutional Court's ruling on the Catalan statute of autonomy and the political and citizen reactions to it. The fourth section deals with developments in the Basque Country during the regional legislative term initiated in 2009 and culminating with the announced end of terrorist activity by ETA. The chapter concludes with a reflection on the new and recurring tensions in the system.

The State of Autonomies in Historical Perspective: The Setting before the Crisis

By the mid-2000s, when the recent round of reforms was initiated, the Spanish state of autonomies had evolved through the repeated adaptation of regional statutes of autonomy, which are regional government charters. Reforms occurred by political praxis without formal constitutional change and through Constitutional Court rulings that shaped the evolution of the territorial model from being an asymmetrical one, with different powers across regions, to being a virtually symmetrical and cooperative federal model, with shared competencies and finances as the system's prevailing modus operandi. The distribution of powers, largely accomplished through the intervention of the Constitutional Court, became increasingly coherent and clear for political actors.

To understand recent developments it is useful to refer to several main characteristics of the system at the moment when the recent round of reforms and the crisis began. These include: (1) Strong nationalist movements and parties existed in two of the autonomous communities, and they were demanding increased powers and recognition; (2) the territorial system was relatively decentralized in terms of public spending and authority, with a dominance of shared regional and central state powers and revenues and a growing tendency toward greater decentralization of resources and competencies; (3) in its political dynamics, the Spanish model had produced at the same time a centrifugal and differentiating tendency among some regions and a centripetal and equalizing one among others, articulated by regional governments and parties and manifest in intergovernmental relations; (4) with the main exception of distinct fiscal arrangements in the Basque Country and Navarre, initial asymmetry of regional autonomy had given rise to symmetrical arrangements. To be sure, the evolving model, despite some relative success, was never without opponents. There had always been discontent and criticisms regarding its operation, as well as frustration from regional nationalist parties and governments that had, paradoxically, been the main beneficiaries of the system. Until 2004, this discontent never translated into proposals to reform regional statutes of autonomy or the Constitution. In the last nine years, however, due to a combination of political, ideological, and conjunctural factors, both at the regional and at the central level, and also because of the institutional conditions and rules of the system, initiatives to reform regional statutes of autonomy have been discussed and enacted by regional parliaments in eight ACs. Regional statutes of autonomy have been amended or even drafted anew: Valencia (2006), Catalonia (2006), Balearic Islands (2007), Andalusia (2007), Aragon (2007), Castile and León (2007), Navarre (2010), and Extremadura (2011). Other ACs debated proposals and drafts, but had not yet found the necessary party-political consensus at the regional level, for example, Canary Islands, Castile-La Mancha, and Galicia. In the Basque Country, a reform attempt failed in 2005. Most of these reform processes had been triggered and influenced by the discussion of the reform of the Catalan statute of autonomy (see Colino 2009).

These reforms entailed the devolution of competences, redistribution of resources, the introduction of regional charters of rights, and some other symbolic issues. For the first time, regional parties and parliaments had set the agenda for reform of their statutes, without prior consensus or agreement among the main national political forces regarding the orientation and goals of the reform. In fact, although most reforms were ultimately approved by the two main Spanish statewide parties in the regional and national arenas, these parties have not responded in general to any global plan or scheme concerning the Spanish territorial model ultimately to be achieved. The intervention of the Constitutional Court was triggered by the main national opposition party, the Popular Party, challenging some aspects of the amended Catalan statute of autonomy.

Regarding the Spanish system of fiscal federalism and financial equalization, that is, those arrangements to finance all of the regions and redistribute funds among them, reforms in 2001 increased the resources and fiscal autonomy of ACs, who became mainly dependent on tax-sharing and some unconditional central state transfers. However, reforms did not end demands for more resources from all the regions. Wealthy ACs, such as Catalonia, have long tried to establish a link between their constitutional status as a nationality and more financial powers; the Basque Country and Navarre continued to enjoy a high degree of constitutionally entrenched fiscal power. Politicians in Catalonia also began to complain about the so-called fiscal imbalances: that is, the excessive redistribution produced by the funding system and the negative balance between their region's contribution and what it received from the central government. They began to advocate for putting a limit on the existing solidarity and redistribution mechanisms among autonomous communities, accomplished through the tax system, social security, and the central government's public investments. They repeatedly sought to gain greater control of the taxes raised in their territory.

In this context, the current financial crisis that began in 2008 caused a deteriorating budget situation for the central government and the ACs. The later saw their revenues sharply reduced due to the bursting of the housing bubble and the collapse of the tax yield coming from real estate taxes. At the same time, the new autonomy statute of Catalonia did not seem to satisfy the Catalan parties.

Territorial Governance and the Fiscal Crisis: Responses to Distributive Tensions

The years 2008 and 2009 were dominated by the reform of the funding arrangements for regional governments, which had last been changed in 2001. A requirement for reform by 2008 was established in the new Catalan statute of autonomy passed in 2006, and the Catalan and other regional governments insisted on reaching new funding arrangements that guaranteed additional regional resources to deal with increasing citizen demands. Debate about the regional funding arrangements and the related fiscal equalization scheme, designed to ensure that public services are provided at similar levels in all ACs, was intensified due to the economic crisis. Despite clear signs of an economic downturn at that point, however, the reform of the funding arrangements seemed to respond more to traditional distributive struggles than to the upcoming fiscal crisis. Regional spending and deficits still grew from 2009 to 2010, which implied that the response to the crisis and the externally required fiscal consolidation measures were delayed until they were very difficult to accomplish by the time the sovereign debt crisis hit in 2010 and almost impossible to comply with by the end of the Zapatero government's term.

The Reform of Funding Arrangements in 2009

By 2007, still a time of considerable economic growth in Spain, most ACs complained of receiving insufficient resources to manage their competencies. Experts also pointed to the inequity produced by the equalization system in terms of regional per capita funding. The wealthiest ACs complained about the "overequalizing" effects of the financial equalization arrangements. For some academics and politicians in those wealthier regions, the system was far too redistributive and lacked clear criteria for the central government to allocate redistributive transfers, thus producing no incentives for subsidized regions to improve their performance.

Negotiations to change the funding system by the deadline established in the new Catalan statute of autonomy began in 2008 at a rather unpropitious time for distributive conflicts, due to the already visible effects of the crisis on government revenues. AC governments allied along different fronts, with Catalonia heading a bloc of higher-income ACs versus an "Atlantic Front" of less well-off ACs that argued that population should not become the main criteria for distribution. Also a kind of auction began about the additional resources that the central government was ready or able to inject into the system, with different regions asking for between 4,000 and 12,700 million extra euros.

The funding arrangements finally adopted at the end of 2009 retained the basic features of the previous model, such as population as the main allocating principle, the guarantee of financial equalization in essential public services, and the principle of financial sufficiency linked to the execution of regional competencies. It also provided additional resources injected through two new funds that sought to achieve supplementary goals. The Competitiveness Fund sought to offset the imbalances affecting the most dynamic ACs that were complaining of contributing too much to regional solidarity. The Cooperation Fund tried to support growth and development in the more economically backward ACs that were complaining of having insufficient resources to provide their citizens with basic constitutionally protected services.

According to recent studies on initial results (see Bosch 2012), the new funding arrangements have already had an impact on the equity of the equalization system in terms of per capita funding after redistribution, which had been one of the main criticisms directed at the funding model. The Community of Madrid, for example, has now gone from being ranked the fourth worst off AC in terms of per capita funding after its contribution to regional solidarity to being the third highest ranked. Catalonia, for the first time, was above the AC average in terms of per capita funding after equalization. Andalusia, even though it still receives funds, for the first time ranked below the average. Also, according to this report, the central government provided in the first year of the new funding model a further € 9,198 million. Despite its added complexity, it seems that this funding model has finally ensured that all regions that were above the average in fiscal capacity before equalization remain above the average after horizontal and vertical redistribution.

The Bumpy Road to Fiscal Consolidation

During the first two years of the crisis, 2008 and 2009, coinciding with the first two years of the legislative term, the central government budget figures deteriorated more sharply than did those of the ACs, partly because of the central government's leading role in anticrisis, fiscal policy stimulus measures. The regions, meanwhile, despite seeing their revenues sharply reduced (about 30 percent) due to the bursting of the housing bubble and the collapse of the tax yield from real estate taxes, still saw a growth in spending of over 9 percent in 2008 and 2009, provoking a € 16,992 million deficit in 2008 that reached € 21,164 million in 2009. This increase in spending was due in part to incorrect tax revenue collection forecasts and appropriations contained in the central government's budgets for 2008 and 2009. This led to advance payments or grants from the central government to the regions well above the actual final tax returns. This meant that the deficit from the regions was artificially low during those years and was supported by the central government, and that regional governments would need to pay back the money unduly received from the central government over the following years (FEDEA 2012). More importantly, although they all began to react to the crisis with some microeconomic and social policy measures, the seriousness of the situation for the ACs was not really reflected in an actual reduction of revenues until the central government's budget of 2010.

Furthermore, the crisis did not affect all regional treasuries alike. For example, despite the fact that it did not hit their economies as hard, the Basque Country and Navarre, which due to their special fiscal regime directly manage their revenues, suffered from revenue declines higher than the common regime ACs, where the erroneous forecasts and the central government overadvances cushioned the reduction in revenue in 2008 and 2009. The hardest hit by the crisis were the Balearic Islands, Castile-La Mancha, Catalonia, and the Valencian Community, partly because of their budgetary imbalances prior to the crisis, the greater weight of indirect taxes, the greater exposure to real estate, and above average population growth (Fernández Llera & Morán 2008).

This drastic reduction of revenues and expenditure was combined with the European sovereign debt crisis in 2010 and the ensuing fiscal consolidation agreements and calendar to which Spain committed with the European Union (EU). The regions had to reflect the real situation of austerity for the first time in their accounting, therefore, in the 2010 and 2011 budgets. This implied that the ACs had taken more than two years to start the necessary adjustments and now had to make spending cuts much faster, given the limited autonomy they enjoy in their revenues, to reduce a deficit of 2.8 percent of gross domestic product (GDP) in 2010 to 1.3 percent in 2011. In practice, most regions began to implement austerity and fiscal consolidation measures in major expenditure categories, namely, welfare policies and public investments, from the 2011 budget onward (FEDEA 2012). The electoral calendar also facilitated the delay, with regional elections in most ACs due in May 2011.

Success on the difficult path of fiscal consolidation was uneven and the overall deficit reduction target for the ACs in 2010 was not met (the deficit was 2.8 percent of GDP, when the target was 2.4 percent). Nine ACs had a deficit above the average, with Castile-La Mancha registering the worst figure with a -6.5 percent of GDP. In addition, this region, together with the Balearic Islands, Catalonia, and Valencia, were those with deficits and debts larger than the average. Another group, including Madrid, Extremadura, Basque Country, Castile-Leon, Canary Islands, Cantabria, Galicia, and Asturias, met budgetary targets for 2010. Andalusia deviated slightly from that objective. Aragon, Navarre, La Rioja, and Valencia deviated to a greater extent and were asked for decisive action to meet fiscal targets (FEDEA 2012).

In any case, following the sovereign debt crisis, the central government was forced to use the tools at its disposal to halt AC debt, and at the end of 2010 vetoed new borrowing for those who had overstepped the authorized deficit. This led to tensions with Catalonia that were later resolved when the central government agreed to authorize additional borrowing. The tensions would recur in the following years when the austerity measures and the consolidation targets became even more difficult to achieve.

The Constitutional Court and the (Non)Accommodation of Catalan Nationalism

The amended Catalan statute of autonomy had been challenged in 2006 by the main opposition Popular Party (PP), the national Ombudsman, and other ACs, but the Spanish Constitutional Court was unable to issue a decision on its constitutionality until June 2010. The division among the judges, their politicization by the main political parties, and some political maneuvering—recusals of judges, leaks to the press of draft rulings, media pressure on the judges and the court president, and so forth—led to a protracted process that created increased conflict, public controversy, and a very negative political climate that endangered the court's very legitimacy.[2] Following much of its previous jurisprudence, the court's judgment upheld most of the challenged parts of the Catalan autonomy statute. However, it interpreted many others in such a way that it fundamentally watered down most of the innovations that had been negotiated and agreed upon by the political actors during the long reform process. Many of these innovations had also been incorporated into other amended regional statutes of autonomy. In the end, the court's ruling created some satisfaction and relief throughout Spain, but mainly dissatisfaction and even outrage in Catalonia.

The Court's Ruling on the Catalan Statute of Autonomy

Of the 114 articles that the Popular Party had challenged, judgment 31/2010 declared 14 articles unconstitutional in whole or in part, and proposed a restrictive interpretation of 27 other articles, which were not declared unconstitutional insofar as they are construed in accordance with what is stated in the judgment. The ruling contained five dissenting opinions and mostly followed the court's previous case law and doctrine on most issues (see Castellá 2010).

To understand the court's position on the specific controversial issues and the interpretive approach taken, it is important to note the court's opinion regarding whether regional statutes of autonomy are quasi-constitutional legal instruments with a complementary role to that of the Spanish constitution. Contrary to the advocates of the reformed Catalan autonomy statute, the court explicitly rejected this conception of the statute of autonomy as a quasi-constitutional instrument with the capacity to indirectly define and regulate the distribution of powers and finances across the country. It also refuted that regional statutes of autonomy have a higher legal force vis-à-vis other national organic laws. This allowed the court to reassert its role as the only authority, along with the constitution, able to define the distribution of powers and provide authoritative interpretations of the constitution and its provisions concerning fundamental rights or the allocation of legislative competencies. In this fashion, the court was able to "deactivate" many of the most ambitious provisions of the Catalan autonomy statute without having to declare them unconstitutional. Many of the most innovative provisions of the Catalan autonomy statute concerning the safeguarding of the exclusive competencies from central government encroachment and those concerning the criteria for the funding arrangements, regional participation in central state bodies, and the decentralization of the judiciary in Catalonia were not declared unconstitutional but simply deemed the manifestation of political demands not to be regulated in the regional autonomy statute but rather needed to be established in an organic law by the central parliament.

Regarding the issues related to the recognition of the distinctiveness of Catalonia and its national character and other symbolic issues such as the recognition of historical rights, the ruling accepted the declaration, in the preamble, of Catalonia as a nation and the use of the adjective national related to the "national symbols" of Catalonia in article eight. However, noting that the Spanish legal system is based on the principle of popular sovereignty and that the only holder of sovereignty is the Spanish people at large, those symbolic references were deprived of any legal force in the interpretation of any provision of the regional autonomy statute. According to the court, while a group is entitled to call itself a nation for the purposes of political or cultural debate, when it comes to legal language there is only one nation in the Kingdom of Spain, the Spanish nation. Catalonia is just a "nationality" in the sense of article two of the Spanish constitution and article 1.2 of the Catalan autonomy statute. Regarding historical rights, the court accepted the challenged article five referring to the "historical rights" of Catalonia, provided it is interpreted as to avoid any parallels between the Catalan "historical rights" and the constitutionally enshrined historical rights of the Basque and Navarre territories, which imply a special fiscal regime.

Regarding civil rights, the court also accepted the constitutionality of including a regional charter of rights in the autonomy statute but distinguished those rights from the fundamental rights contained in the Spanish constitution. Regarding language policy and rights, the court largely upheld the existing model of Catalan as the language of normal use in the education system—insofar as this does not involve the exclusion of Castilian as a teaching language—but struck down the term "preferential" as unconstitutional, when applied to the use of Catalan in public administration and media. The court accepted that the Catalan parliament, through ordinary legislation, may approve measures of positive discrimination to correct "historical situations of imbalance." On the other hand, the "right of citizens to address constitutional bodies and the Spanish judiciary in Catalan" and the level of knowledge of the Catalan language needed by judges and notaries was said to lie within the regulatory responsibility of the central Spanish parliament. Finally, the ruling rejected the general obligation to know the Catalan language as being equivalent to the constitutional obligation to know the Spanish language.

With respect to the attempts in the new Catalan autonomy statute to decentralize competencies and to "shield" or safeguard regional exclusive competencies from central government encroachment, by providing a detailed definition and listing of policy subareas and trying to define and limit the scope of central government framework legislation, the judgment rejected them. It declared that a statute of autonomy cannot limit the scope or the substance of central government competencies. At the same time, and for the same reason, the court rejected the attempts to limit the framework powers of the central government to only establishing minimum standards of regulation. In sum, the court embraced a conception of most regional competencies as being shared or concurrent competencies.

At the same time, the judgment accepted some innovations in the Catalan autonomy statute that suggested that autonomous communities may have a say in the exercise of the central government's exclusive competencies. The court interpreted or struck down a few articles that provided regional power to call referendums and some powers related to immigration, taxes, and local government regulation because they were exclusive competencies of the central government. Yet it accepted regional participation in many central decisions, for example, through the bilateral joint commissions established in the autonomy statute, the regional right of initiative to ask the central government to sign international treaties, and the right to be informed of them. The court also accepted the right to make proposals for the composition of different central state bodies and to participate in the execution of several exclusive competencies of the central government, such as economic planning, road communication between ACs, and the determination of the immigration quota (Solozábal 2011).

Finally, with regard to provisions of the Catalan autonomy statute dealing with the funding arrangements, the court's ruling also downgraded most of the provisions to mere normative proposals. But most of them had already been incorporated in Spanish finance regulation after the 2009 reform of regional funding arrangements. The court rejected the notion that the autonomy statute can condition the criteria used to establish the fiscal contribution of the ACs to the common purse, since that would encroach on the central state competence to "regulate the exercise of financial powers of the autonomous communities and set the levels of its contribution to the equalization system and to solidarity." On the other hand, the court accepted the "rank order" principle (meaning that the rank order of regions in terms of fiscal capacity may not be altered after redistribution) as a constitutional limitation on the regional contribution to the equalization scheme. The court also watered down some provisions of the regional autonomy statute that established the obligation of the central government to invest a fixed amount in Catalonia according to GDP share and to devolve certain taxes. Although not necessarily unconstitutional, the court declared that they may not be decided unilaterally by each AC.

Increasing Disaffection toward Spain within Catalonia?

In the political and public sphere the consequences of the court judgment, at least in Catalonia, were bound to be, according to many observers, very negative, causing general disaffection and promoting secessionism and confrontation between political actors from Catalonia and the rest of Spain. One sign of this disaffection was the large public demonstration in Barcelona on July 10, 2010, against the judgment. It was headed by the Catalan regional premier himself and led by a banner with the slogan "We are a nation. We decide" together with thousands of secessionist flags.

In general, opinion poll data from the *Centre d'Estudis d'Opinió* of the Catalan government had consistently suggested a clear division of the citizens of Catalonia between supporters of Catalonia as a state within a federal Spain (30 percent), those who prefer to be an autonomous community (30 percent), and those who want to be an independent state (28 percent).[3] Surveys in the aftermath of the judgment and the demonstration showed a momentary rise in the number of supporters of Catalan secession. A Noxa survey for the newspaper *La Vanguardia* showed that 40 percent of Catalans were in favor of independence and 45 percent against.[4] Additionally, two of every three Catalans claimed that the level of autonomy of Catalonia is insufficient. An increase of secessionism was observed, not just in surveys, but also in repeated public declarations, especially by political and professional elites. For many observers, this seemed to signal the emergence of a new secessionist discourse based less on identity and emotion and more on economic interests.

The Catalan elections in November 2010 were the first test of the real extent of the alleged growing disaffection with Spain among Catalan citizens. However, the situation did not reflect disaffection as much as predicted. The Catalan nationalist Convergence and Union (CiU) won with a comfortable plurality and subsequently shifted to a much more moderate discourse than it had in opposition. Electoral results showed an increase of five points for nationalist parties [CiU, Republican Left of Catalonia (ERC), Catalan Solidarity for Independence (SI), Realignment for Independence (RI)], but explicitly secessionist parties taken together (ERC, SI, RI) lost 10 percent of their votes—ERC alone lost 220,000 votes, a 50 percent decline. At the same time, the more pro-Spanish options (PP, *Ciutadans*) increased their vote by 20 percent. This means that polarization increased, since the more moderate options such as the Catalan Socialist Party (PSC-PSOE) and the leftist Initiative for Catalonia Greens (ICV) lost votes. PSC-PSOE lost almost a third of its votes (Martínez-Herrera & Miley 2011).

Finally, another manifestation of the growing mobilization of secessionism was the informal local consultations, organized by secessionist associations, on Catalan independence in over 550 municipalities in Catalonia from 2009 to 2011. They mobilized a total of about 500,000 Catalans, around 257,000 of them in the capital, Barcelona. These consultations were not supported by the Catalan Socialists, but were symbolically supported by members of the CiU government in Catalonia and its president, who voted to support them in parliamentary motions and voted affirmatively in the consultation held on the streets of Barcelona.[5] Apart from the expected overwhelming victory of the "Yes" option (93 percent), there was a turnout of around 20 percent of Catalans, who for different reasons wanted to show support for independence.[6]

The Beginning of a New Era in the Basque Country? The End of Terrorism

As is well-known, the Basque Country had witnessed persistent political violence and a nationalist terrorist organization supporting independence and the annexation of Basque lands in France and Navarre for many years. Since 1968 ETA has assassinated 829 people and kidnapped 84. From 1995 onward almost 30 percent of the victims were political adversaries—local town councilors (16 people), party leaders or ex-leaders of non-nationalist parties (5), and public officials (5). Most non-nationalist politicians, local councilors and parliamentarians, professors and journalists, and their families had to live with around-the-clock bodyguards. In parts of the Basque Country, in the provinces of Guipúzcoa and Vizcaya, non-nationalists could not campaign freely in elections. Also dozens of journalists and academics were forced into self-exile outside the Basque Country due to fear and intimidation. According to some sources, people who were threatened or extorted by ETA, or its auxiliary legal organizations, and emigrated as a result numbered around 200,000, that is, 10 percent of the population. They include professionals, company executives, and university professors, among others.

Due to this unsustainable situation, the Spanish parliament decided in 2003, through the new law on political parties, to ban those parties clearly linked with the terrorist organization ETA and advocating violence. Despite some political and legal debate and the opposition of the then governing Basque nationalist parties, the law proved somewhat effective at reducing terrorists' resources and limited their room for maneuver. In March 2006, ETA announced an explicit ceasefire that lasted nine months. The ceasefire had raised hopes of a long-term peace and spurred the Zapatero government to conduct direct talks with ETA, which had been prepared in advance by contacts between some Basque Socialists and representatives of ETA (see Eguiguren & Rodríguez Aizpeolea 2011). These talks were deeply controversial and divisive among the main political parties, within the judiciary, and Spanish public opinion.

In December 2006, amid talks with the government, ETA killed two people in a bomb attack at Madrid's airport. The Zapatero government broke off talks with ETA. With the return of violence, the government utilized all means offered by the law on political parties to ban dozens of candidates of Basque National Action (ANV) and Basque Homeland Communist Party (PCTV), the legal successors of the then illegal *Batasuna*, the political branch of ETA, from taking part in the 2007 local elections in the Basque Country. In the March 2008 national elections, candidates of those parties were also banned. At the beginning of Zapatero's second term, there were still 38 terrorist attacks in 2008 alone, of which 8 were car bombs, 4 people were killed, and 64 injured. There were also 227 violent actions by groups supporting ETA. None of the parties close to *Batasuna* or its successors condemned or criticized this violence.[7]

From the Last Ibarretxe Plan to the First Non-nationalist Government

In this context, the March 2008 national elections saw a decrease in votes for nationalist parties, especially for the Basque Nationalist Party (PNV) that was governing at the time in the Basque Country. As he had done in 2004 with his so-called Ibarretxe Plan, which sought to achieve an associated-state status for the Basque Country, the reaction of the PNV leader Ibarretxe to the losses in the 2008 election was, against all odds and against a large part of his own party, to continue on the sovereignty path, defying the central government once more. Despite the evident political and legal failure of the first Ibarretxe Plan, he decided to announce a referendum for October 2008, which the Basque government had no legal power to call, to consult the Basque population about a future process of negotiation with ETA. This was done by passing in the regional parliament in June 2008 a "law on a popular consultation in order to know the citizens' opinion on the opening of a negotiation process to reach peace and political normalization." This law ignored the warnings of illegality that the central government issued and was immediately challenged by the central government before the Constitutional Court. The court rushed to pronounce a ruling (TC 103/2008) in early

September that declared the law to be against the constitution on several legal grounds, not the least of which was the lack of jurisdiction of the Basque parliament to call a referendum and to do it on a subject affecting the Spanish constitution. After the court's rejection, Ibarretxe announced he would appeal to the Court of Human Rights in Strasbourg, which he subsequently did not pursue.

Against this backdrop of political turmoil and the persistence of the terrorist threat, regional elections were held on March 1, 2009, without the participation, for the first time, of the parties supporting ETA. Ibarretxe's PNV won the elections but without enough parliamentary seats to repeat its governing coalition. The Basque branch of the Socialist Party (PSE-PSOE) won 25 seats (an increase of 7), with 30.7 percent of the vote. All nationalist parties lost votes except *Aralar*, a secessionist party that explicitly rejected violence and doubled its votes (to 4 seats and 6 percent of total votes). Radical nationalist voters supporting ETA's goals and means until then apparently decreased by one-third and some of them went to other nationalist parties. Many others remained faithful to ETA's strategies. The Socialist Party, with the second highest vote share, negotiated parliamentary support from the Basque branch of the Popular Party to form a non-nationalist government, and Patxi López became the first non-nationalist premier of the Basque Country in May 2009. The interparty agreement included issues such as language policy, security and antiterrorist policy, media and public television, measures against the economic crisis, further development of self-government, education, health, and housing, among others, as well as the commitment to negotiate the budget each year and not to force a no-confidence motion against the new regional premier.[8]

The Effects of the Party Ban and Antiterrorist Policy on Radical Nationalists' Political Strategy

After the failed negotiations between the central government and ETA, the persistence of the ban on parties tied to violent activity and the effective antiterrorist policy of the government (305 arrested between 2008 and 2010, among them several successive leaders of the group) led the now illegal forces of the Basque radical nationalist left, headed by Arnaldo Otegui, to realize that there would be no legalization as long as ETA was active, and that the Spanish government would never negotiate any demands as long as they maintained their strategy. After some internal discussion, the radical nationalists determined that their political objectives could be achieved without recourse to violence.

The next step was to try to create a new political party that could participate in the forthcoming local and regional elections in 2011 in the Basque Country and Navarre, by meeting or circumventing the requirements of the law on political parties. That meant that out of conviction or pragmatic reasoning they had to pay lip service to nonviolent means and convince the other parties and the judiciary of its democratic credentials. There were several attempts; the first was to create *Sortu*, which presented candidates but was subsequently banned by the Supreme Court. The next attempt to circumvent banning was the formation of the coalition *Bildu*, with other legal left nationalist parties (*Eusko Alkartasuna, Alternatiba*, and *Independientes*). The central government, however, challenged 254 candidate lists before the Supreme Court again, arguing that they were inspired by the terrorist group. The Supreme Court judges upheld the ban but were highly divided (nine to six) in their votes. *Bildu* appealed to the Constitutional Court, which only minutes before the start of the election campaign upheld the coalition's right to participate in the elections. This allowed them to become the second strongest political force in the local elections, attaining 25 percent of the votes and many local councilors.

ETA's Final Ceasefire in 2011

As part of this strategy of legalization, the terrorist group announced on September 5, 2010, through a video sent to BBC1, a cessation of "offensive armed actions." In January 2011, ETA announced a "permanent, general and verifiable" ceasefire. These declarations were met with skepticism by the government and other political parties in the Basque Country and the rest of Spain. But several months after that, and three days after a so-called Peace Conference held in San Sebastian that had asked ETA for a declaration of ceasefire, ETA announced "the definitive cessation of its armed activity" on October 20, 2011. The declaration underlined that ETA remained committed to the goal of Basque independence, but said it was ready to "agree to the minimum democratic conditions" to achieve it without violence. A long history of terrorist violence on Spanish soil seemed to have reached an end.

Conclusions: The Prospects for the State of Autonomies

During Zapatero's second term, the growing fiscal restrictions generated by the financial crisis turned debt crisis hit regional governments hard and put an unprecedented strain on the governance and coordination capacities of the Spanish territorial system. That system had to respond, at the same time, to the international requirements of fiscal consolidation and to the demands of their citizens in times of sky-rocketing unemployment, growing social and economic divergence across regions, and pervasive democratic disaffection and protest. The system seemed to muddle through these various challenges without implementing a clear overall institutional reform strategy. The financial tensions and the media attention to certain perceived inefficiencies of the system, together with scandals about regional corruption and the squandering of public money led to an intense public discussion in 2010 and 2011 about the inefficiency and deficiencies of the Spanish decentralization model.

The Spanish territorial model had usually been criticized by regional nationalist parties for its lack of accommodation of nationalists' demands and the insufficient power and resources of ACs. At the same time, it had been criticized by the more centralist-oriented media outlets for what was deemed to be excessive decentralization and diversity-promoting policies. During Zapatero's second term, additional criticisms about its efficiency were raised by various political and economic sectors. Influenced by the media debate, these critics saw the Spanish territorial model and some of its regions as a scapegoat for the current crisis (De la Quadra-Salcedo 2012). In this climate, several conservative and right-populist media outlets took the opportunity to organize an authentic media attack campaign against the state of autonomies and some of the regions. Without a clear alternative in mind, and without daring to explicitly defend a centralized model, and occasionally joined by the opposition Popular Party and its main think tank (FAES), they blamed ACs for the crisis. This has already had some visible effects on the public's attitudes (Grau 2011).

During the Socialists' second term, even though a couple of regional statutes of autonomy were amended, most attempts at institutional reform were abandoned. An exception was the so-called express reform of the constitution in the summer of 2011 to entrench the EU requirements of fiscal stability and budgetary consolidation. There seemed to be no clear diagnosis, feasible alternative, or blueprint for reform able to reach the necessary consensus among the two main Spanish state-wide parties and with the nationalists. Despite the change in the PP's oppositional style and the presence in office of the Socialist Party at the national and in most regional governments (including Catalonia and the Basque Country), the, for many, indispensable constitutional reform of the territorial model was put to rest for the moment (Tudela 2011).

In practical terms, the key question is the extent to which the Spanish state of autonomies, which had mostly evolved under good economic conditions, will still be viable and adaptable to new conditions of austerity and increasing secessionist tensions. A look at this period raises the question of whether the Constitutional Court with its 2010 ruling derailed a painfully negotiated solution that would have guaranteed the accommodation of reasonable demands under the current constitution for years to come, or, on the contrary, whether it prevented, by safeguarding the traditional interpretation of the constitutional pact, the potentially perverse consequences of the peculiar institutional openness of the Spanish territorial model and its vulnerability to centrifugal and dysfunctional tendencies in terms of cohesion and equity.

After the summer of 2012, history seemed to be accelerating and the state of affairs to have worsened in terms of nationalist tensions, risk for the unity of the country, and an impending constitutional crisis. A large demonstration was held on the Catalan national day on September 11 in Barcelona; civil society secessionist organizations, with the support of the Catalan official public media and the Catalan government itself, were able to mobilize the general discontent of thousands of Catalans due to the crisis and other alleged grievances around the banner of sovereignty. The Catalan government and its premier in particular had been articulating these grievances since the 2010 ruling of the Constitutional Court and before through a very effective populist rhetoric against "Spain" and focused on the "plundering" or "pillaging" of Catalonia by Spain and the alleged disregard for Catalonia within Spain. This rhetoric, which thus far had been used as a justification for the demand for a new "fiscal pact" (full fiscal powers for Catalonia), included in the 2010 Catalan ruling party's manifesto, transformed into an outright striving for sovereignty, justified by the central government's refusal to accept the new fiscal pact and the lack of recognition of its national character through asymmetry and special treatment. Given the success of the Barcelona demonstration and a growing outlook among elites and part of the population that the solution to Catalan problems is independence, Artur Mas, the Catalan premier, after the Spanish prime minister's expected refusal to negotiate a new fiscal agreement along the lines of the Basque one, boldly embraced the idea of secession, which was not contained in the party's manifesto, and announced early elections for November 2012, only two years into the parliament's legislative term. His party, CiU, also approved a proposal in the Catalan parliament to hold a referendum on sovereignty, even if it is not authorized by the Spanish parliament, which has the sole jurisdiction in Spain to do so.

The Catalan nationalists' challenge to the constitutional settlement of 1978, the Catalan prime minister's sudden and far-reaching tactical and strategic change, and the soaring secessionism sentiment among the Catalan population detected in polls, even if some time in the making, have generated bewilderment in the rest of Spain and within the Rajoy government, which has reacted with warnings about the pernicious effects of this constitutional crisis on the fight against the economic crisis and the country's debt problems and with some clumsy threats to enforce the constitutional order if challenged. Many have attributed this unexpected move by Mas simply to electoral reasons and the need to achieve a majority in the Catalan parliament and to avoid blame for harsh cutbacks of public services in Catalonia, moving the discussion away from the economy and the dismal public finances of the Catalan government to issues of identities and economic grievances that put the blame on the government in Madrid. It seems evident that in some sense Mas has achieved these two objectives. At the same time, others, led by the Socialist Party now in opposition, have begun to argue for the need to reform the constitution to reinforce federalism and better accommodate some of the Catalan demands, for example, by again reforming the funding arrangements. In any case, the decentralization model is at a crossroads and the way in which the different actors react in the coming months will be critical to its future survival and development.

Notes

1. Portions of this chapter were previously published in Colino and Hombrado (2012).
2. This section draws heavily on Colino and Hombrado (2012), Colino (2011), Castellà (2010), Solozábal (2011), and Tornos (2010).
3. J. Matas, "Tres modelos de Estado," *El País de Cataluña*, November 10, 2011.
4. "El apoyo a la independencia remite y cae al 40%," *La Vanguardia*, September 7, 2010.
5. "Más de 257.000 personas participan en la consulta independentista de Barcelona," *La Vanguardia*, April 10, 2011.
6. The question asked in the consultations was: "Do you support Catalonia becoming an independent, democratic welfare state based on the rule of law and integrated in the European Union?"
7. The last fatal terrorist attack in Spain occurred on July 30, 2009, in Mallorca, where two civil guards were assassinated. However, the last attack was the killing of a French policeman in France on March 16, 2010.
8. F. Llera, "Aritmética y política," *El Correo Digital*, March 12, 2009.

WorksC ited

Bosch, N. 2012. "Horizontal Equity in the 2009 Regional Financing Model." In Institut d' Economía de Barcelona, ed., *Report on Fiscal Federalism 2011*. Barcelona: Institut d' Economía de Barcelona, pp. 54–59.

Castellà, J. M. 2010. *La sentencia del Tribunal Constitucional 31/2010, sobre el estatuto de autonomía de Cataluña y su significado para el futuro del estado autonómico*. Working Paper. Madrid: Fundación Ciudadanía y Valores. Available at: http://www.funciva.org.

Colino, C. 2009. "Constitutional Change without Constitutional Reform: Spanish Federalism and the Revision of Catalonia's Statute of Autonomy." *Publius* 39(2): 262–88.

———. 2011. "What Now for the Autonomic State? Muddling through Growing Tensions amidst the Aftermath of the Court's Ruling and the Painful Fiscal Crisis." In EZFF Tübingen, ed., *Jahrbuch des Föderalismus 2011*. Baden-Baden: Nomos Verlag, pp. 309–22.

Colino, C., and A. Hombrado. 2012. "El Estado autonómico: superando la resaca estatutaria y capeando la crisis." In C. Colino and R. Cotarelo, eds., *España en crisis. Balance de la segunda legislatura de Rodríguez Zapatero*. Valencia: Tirant Humanidades, pp. 191–218.

De la Quadra-Salcedo, T. 2012. "El federalismo español ante la crisis económica y el debate estatutario." *Sistema* 224: 3–19.

Eguiguren, J., and L. Rodríguez Aizpeolea. 2011. *ETA: las claves de la paz*. Madrid: Editorial Aguilar.

FEDEA, ed. 2012. *Observatorio fiscal y financiero de las comunidades autónomas*. Madrid: FEDEA.

Fernández Llera, R., and E. Morán. 2008. "Reacciones fiscales de las comunidades autónomas ante una crisis global." *Revista Asturiana de Economía* 42: 57–80.

Grau, M. 2011. "Self-government Reforms and Public Support for Spain's Territorial Model: Changes and Stability (1992–2010)." *Revista d'Estudis Autonòmics i Federals* 13: 186–214.

Martínez-Herrera, E., and T. J. Miley. 2011. "Cría cuervos. España en manos de CiU." *El Viejo Topo* 278(March): 27–35.

Solozábal, J. J. 2011. "La sentencia sobre el estatuto de Cataluña: una visión de conjunto." *Revista de Estudios Políticos* 151: 203–29.

Tornos, J. 2010. "El estatuto de autonomía de Cataluña, y el estado autonómico, tras la Sentencia del Tribunal Constitucional 31/2010." *El Cronista del Estado Social y Democrático de Derecho* 15: 18–25.

Tudela, J. 2011. "¿Reforma constitucional en clave federal? (sistematización de problemas generados por las reformas y posibles soluciones)." *Revista de Estudios Políticos* 151: 231–79.

CHAPTER 6

Economic Reforms and the Labor Market: Zapatero's Endless Period inthe Wilderness

Óscar Molina and Alejandro Godino

S pain is no longer a success story and has instead become the sick man of Europe. Recent reports seem to suggest that far from being left behind the crisis is likely to produce a new and deeper recession (European Commission 2011; OECD 2010). Unemployment is increasing and it reached more than five million people, amounting to 24.5 percent of the active population, in the first semester of 2012. Most analyses conclude that 2012 and 2013 will also register negative growth and worsening labor market conditions due to the depressing effect of austerity packages and fiscal consolidation. Per capita gross domestic product (GDP) has decreased to 2002 levels, while inequalities have grown remarkably, hence challenging social cohesion in a context of declining unemployment benefits and social spending cuts. Spain missed the opportunity to overcome some of the historical problems that made the country lag behind in Europe during the 1996–2007 growth years and will face enormous difficulties in recovering a growth path and catching up with the continental and northern European countries.

The worrying economic situation in Spain by the end of 2011 was the main factor behind the Socialists' worst ever performance in general parliamentary elections. When Prime Minister Zapatero announced early elections, most surveys already foretold a defeat of the Socialists. However, it was not clear how large the defeat would be. To the inevitable loss of votes caused by the growing deterioration in economic and labor-market performance, in the case of Spain we must add the feeling among the citizenry that the executive lacked the skills and ability to manage the economic crisis due to erratic and very often contradictory policy responses.[1] The overreliance on the construction sector, together with a late and bad diagnosis of the challenges facing the Spanish economy in the early months of the crisis, resulted in costly and ineffective policies, which not only hampered recovery but also aggravated the conditions Spain would have to confront with the sovereign debt crisis from 2010 on.

The aforementioned considerations about the economy have to be placed in the context of a deep and multifaceted political crisis. The lack of confidence in the Socialist executive is probably the most remarkable aspect of the political crisis, which was aggravated by the abrupt end of the honeymoon between the government and social partners that characterized Zapatero's first term (see chapter 7 in this volume). However, the crisis has political implications that go far beyond discontent with the executive. On the one hand, there is an increasing perception among the citizenry about the need to reform a political system that is seen as undemocratic, both with regard to the institutions as well as the functioning and representativeness of the political parties. These demands have been aggravated by the perception that technocratic European Union (EU) economic governance institutions imposed fiscal adjustment in order to resolve the debt crisis (Erne 2008). Moreover, the negative impact of adjustment on social cohesion threatens the stability and characteristics of the democratic system. The *indignados* (indignant) movement must be interpreted accordingly as an expression of political and economic discontent as will be shown later (Armingeon & Baccaro 2011).

In light of the aforementioned considerations, we analyze the economic developments and economic reforms during Zapatero's second term (2008–11), as well as their implications. We start by highlighting the need to refocus on the structural problems facing the Spanish economy, paying particular attention to low productivity and the reasons for it. In order to interpret and analyze recent developments, the chapter provides a longer-term perspective that highlights the persistence of structural weaknesses in the Spanish economy. The chapter then analyses the strategies and policies implemented by the government and their potential impact on the future development of the economy. We argue that the internal devaluation strategy imposed as a consequence of euro membership will have a long-lasting impact on the institutional pillars and dominant forms of coordination in the economy, not to mention the consequences for democratic governance at domestic and EU levels.

The chapter is organized as follows. The first section provides an overview of the state of the Spanish economy and the structural problems facing it at the time Zapatero was reelected in 2008. Section two analyses the main policies of the 2008–11 period and the reforms enacted to overcome the crisis. Section three turns to the implications of the policies and the adjustment for the labor market, the welfare state, and more generally the role of the state in the economy. Section four provides an overview of the economic policies under the newly elected Popular Party (PP) government and section five offers a conclusion.

The Economic Crisis in Spain: Short-Term Imbalances and Structural Determinants

When Zapatero was reelected in May 2008, it was difficult to imagine that his second term would end with the calling of early elections and the worst-ever results in that election for the Socialist Party (PSOE) since Spain's transition to democracy. Even though the first symptoms of deceleration were already noticeable, the general feeling was that the Spanish economy was in a strong position to be able to manage the international economic deterioration. The impressive growth registered in the previous decade, together with record-low unemployment and healthy public finances, made it difficult to think that Spain would suffer from the crisis to a greater extent than other EU countries.

This legacy certainly influenced the early decisions of the Socialist government. The executive led by Mr. Zapatero argued first that there was no crisis and then blamed external factors both for its inception and intensity. However, an overemphasis on the temporary and international character of the crisis led the executive to underestimate the structural and endogenous problems facing the Spanish economy. Notwithstanding several reports by the Organization for Economic Cooperation and Development (OECD) and the European Commission (EC) that had issued warnings about the weaknesses of a brick-and-mortar-based growth model, little was done by previous executives to correct the economic path. Economic policies under Zapatero represented continuity with the previous PP executives. The economic policy paralysis that characterized the early months of the second Zapatero term is accordingly explained by the belief that the economy was well prepared for a temporary shock and little action was needed.

In the early months of the crisis, unemployment was to a large extent driven by the severe adjustment of the construction sector, hence explaining the comparatively stronger impact of the crisis on the Spanish labor market. However, as job destruction continued and spread to most sectors of the economy, other causal factors had to be considered. Some of these factors are related to the growth path followed in the precrisis years, such as the housing bubble and the increase in private indebtedness, while others—including the characteristics and role of the banking sector, the labor market, and collective bargaining institutions as well as the statist character of the Spanish variety of capitalism (Molina & Rhodes 2007)—have a structural character. It is accordingly necessary to adopt a longer-term perspective when interpreting recent developments as the imbalances that characterized the precrisis years are partly a legacy of historical processes.

It is precisely the interaction between short-term and structural processes that explains the deeper and longer-lasting impact of the 2010 sovereign debt crisis in Spain. First of all, Spain shares with the other Southern European economies low and stagnant productivity that is related to the production structure and the pattern of economic specialization. Second, Spain also shared with Ireland a housing bubble leading to unprecedented development of the construction sector and a rapid increase in private indebtedness (López & Rodríguez 2011). This unique problem load differentiates Spain from the rest of the countries most affected by the debt crisis, and must be considered when interpreting economic and labor market developments.

The first aspect to be considered is the difficulties companies had accessing credit due to banks' increasing restrictions on lending. This had an immediate effect on the construction sector, which spread to the rest of the economy. In spite of the essentially financial character of the economic crisis, the banking system in Spain appeared not to be as badly hit as banks in other countries in the early months of the crisis. The general feeling was that the largest private banks in Spain were well buffered and provisioned. However, as the economic crisis evolved, banks became more vulnerable and a target of citizens' discontent. In this vein, the executive and the public blamed banks for fueling the housing boom and for providing excessive credit in good times, and then significantly limiting access to credit during the recession and the euro sovereign debt crisis.[2] Moreover, the problems facing the banking sector, partly as a consequence of speculation with poisoned assets, forced governments to devote significant resources to avoiding bankruptcy. The rescue of the banking sector fueled discontent as very few conditions were imposed on banks in exchange for receiving massive public resources.

On top of this, some research highlighted the structurally negative impact of the financial sector on the Spanish economy due to a historical pattern of financial interventionism that guaranteed the selective alloca-tion of credit to strategic industries and large companies and favored political stability. In the reforms of the financial sector since the 1960s, the government and public officials accommodated the demands of banks, which contributed to the maintenance of an oligopolistic struc-ture. The transition to democracy was characterized by continuity due to the privileged political position of banks as sovereign debt holders in a moment of rapidly increasing public spending. Imperfect liberalization perpetuated the oligopolistic position of the major banks in Spain and contributed to the maintenance of high interest rates and limited access to credit for small- and medium-sized enterprises (SMEs) (Cabrera & Del Rey 2007; Pérez 1997). As a consequence, companies' capacity to invest in productivity-enhancing technologies was curtailed because many could not access credit. This favored the gradual specialization of the Spanish economy in labor-intensive sectors. The soft approach adopted in the rescue of the banking sector confirms the maintenance of its privileged position vis-à-vis the government.

In order to fully understand the role of the banking sector in the crisis, it is necessary to explain individuals' excessive borrowing to finance private consumption. Colin Crouch's (2008) notion of privatized Keynesianism becomes particularly useful in this context. The growth of the Spanish economy between 1998 and 2007 was strongly dependent on the addi-tional resources provided to families by easy access to credit. The housing bubble had the effect of reducing disposable income for a large number of families due to rapidly increasing residential housing prices, which almost doubled from 2000 to 2008. As López and Rodríguez (2011, 11) note, "[D]eficit spending in the years 1997–2007 was decisively trans-ferred from the Spanish state to private households, which, in the final years of the cycle, became net demanders of financing." In other words, banks contributed to expanding private demand in a context of restrictive fiscal policies that were reflected in government budget surpluses. Private indebtedness increased while public indebtedness decreased. However, the reduction in private savings was significantly higher than the surplus in public accounts between 2005 and 2007.

An additional reason for the excessive reliance upon credit is related to labor market conditions. Moderate inflation yet with skyrocketing housing prices, and a high rate of temporary, often low-pay, employ-ment encouraged individuals to increase borrowing to make up for the shortfall. The financially vulnerable position of many workers coincided with increasing private indebtedness thanks to lax lending practices by banks.

Other authors have stressed the role of collective bargaining and wage increases as an additional structural factor that helps explain the crisis in Spain and other Southern European countries (Carballo-Cruz 2011; Wölfl & Mora-Sanguinetti 2011). According to this argument, industrial relations in Southern European countries, characterized by politicized trade unions, weakly articulated social partners, low coordination, and high levels of conflict, have historically delivered high wage increases that resulted in rising unit labor costs and reduced the competitiveness of these economies. In the context of the European Monetary Union (EMU), wage discipline becomes even more important due to the impossibility of relying on the competitive devaluation of the currency. Social partners have accordingly been asked since the mid-1990s to further restrain wage increases. When one looks at the outcomes of the bargaining processes in terms of negotiated wage increases, the picture is indeed one of considerable wage moderation. Figure 6.1 shows that since the late 1990s average negotiated wage increases (i.e., those agreed in the context of collective bargaining between unions and employers) moved along with inflation and in some years triggered losses in the purchasing power of earnings. This evidence is reinforced when we take into account the evolution of labor's share of national income, defined as the percentage of wages and salaries in GDP, which has declined since the early 1980s (Arpaia et al. 2009). It could accordingly be argued that the long-running current account

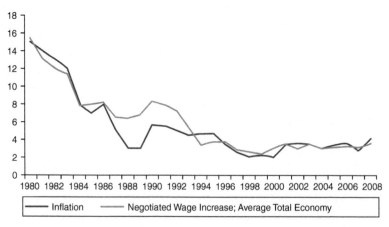

Figure 6.1 Inflation and negotiated wages in Spain, 1980–2008 (percent increase over previousy ear).

Source: National Statistics Institute (INE).

deficit is not only caused by cost-competitiveness problems (i.e., high wage increases), but also by a pattern of specialization in sectors with weak and declining demand that are more exposed to the competition from emerging economies.

It is only when we take into account productivity that we start getting a clear picture of the real structural limitations of the Spanish economy and the implications for understanding the extent and duration of the current crisis. As a matter of fact, if we jointly consider the evolution of wages and productivity through real unit labor costs (average cost of labor per unit of output) the picture changes significantly, particularly so when we compare Spain with other EU economies. As can be observed in figure 6.2, real unit labor costs evolved along with those of Germany and the EU average in the precrisis period. This confirms that the problems of the economy are not so much related to cost-competitiveness, but rather to low output per person employed.

In light of the evidence given earlier, the question we need to answer is why productivity is so low in Spain. The productivity problems of the Spanish economy and, in particular, its evolution in the growth years are related to three main factors. The first factor is the sectoral composition of GDP and the unbalanced growth path with the remarkable

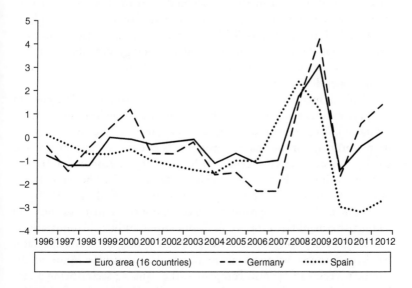

Figure 6.2   Real unit labor costs, 1996–2012 (percent increase over previous year).
Source: Eurostat.

contributions of the construction sector and tourism. These two sectors are highly labor intensive and as a consequence have very low productivity levels. But when we compare sectors with higher productivity, we still see that Spain in general has lower productivity levels due to less advanced production technologies (OECD 2007). The predominance of SMEs also contributes, as these companies have more difficulty accessing capital markets in order to finance innovations or to invest in research and development.

Another factor that helps explain the low productivity levels of Spanish firms is the high rate of temporary employment. As the expectation of employee permanence in the company decreases, so do the incentives of both employers and employees to invest in specific skills, as they do not expect to benefit from the returns of the investment. Provided the positive relationship between investment in firm-specific skills, innovation, and hence productivity, a high percentage of employees on fixed-term contracts translates into lower aggregate levels of productivity.

Related to the aforementioned points, the massive inflow of immigrant workers during the past decade needs to be considered. Mass immigration had three major implications. First, it contributed to expanding demand, which was a key contributor to the growth of the Spanish economy after the late 1990s. Second, the incorporation of mostly medium- to low-skilled workers in the service and construction sectors helped keep wages low at a moment when labor market shortages were pushing wages up. Moreover, the availability of immigrant labor led some companies to opt for maintaining the same technology and labor-intensive techniques, as the cost of hiring one person relative to investing in new technologies decreased.

Finally, as mentioned before, it is also necessary to adopt a longer-term perspective to explain the structural weaknesses of the Spanish model of capitalism. More specifically, it has been argued that the low productivity performance of the Spanish economy is due to a pattern of late and partial industrialization together with the legacy of economic interventionism during the Franco dictatorship (Sapelli 1995). The implications of these two elements for economic development since the late 1970s are multifarious. On the one hand, Spain could not consolidate a strong and competitive manufacturing sector. More importantly, the comparatively more significant role of the state as an economic actor and regulator has been a source of noncompetitive practices that have hindered the competitiveness of Spanish companies, the banking sector being a case in point. On the other hand, the organizational weakness of collective social actors (trade unions and employer organizations) has hindered the development of strong forms of autonomous nonmarket coordination, which is a defining trait of so-called coordinated market economies (CMEs) such as Germany's (Molina & Rhodes 2007). According to the varieties of capitalism literature, it is precisely the hybrid or statist character of the Spanish economy that constitutes a hindrance to achieving higher economic performance (Hall & Soskice 2001).

To sum up, even though the crisis had an external trigger common to other EU countries, its greater impact in Spain is due to a series of historical legacies and structural imbalances that characterized the growth years. The housing bubble and structurally low productivity constitute the context in which the effect of economic policies of Zapatero's second term must be analyzed.

The ReformPr ocess

From Denial to Accelerated Deceleration

The adjustment of the Spanish economy to the financial crisis has gone through several phases. The crisis began at the global level during the second semester of 2007, shortly after the subprime mortgage scandal was revealed. The most immediate impact of the crisis in Spain was the barriers banks placed on lending. This automatically depressed consumption and caused troubles for many SMEs due to a sudden fall in demand. As a result, purchasing power was severely cut, affecting the most important sector for driving growth during the previous years, that is, construction, which accounted for 17.9 percent of GDP in 2007. However, this figure would be substantially higher if we added manufacturing and service activities linked to the construction sector. Consequently, the collapse of the housing bubble was reflected in the rapid increase in the unemployment rate, going from 7.95 percent in the second quarter of 2007 to 10.44 percent one year later.

Evidence indicating a significant deceleration and a likely recession—based on increasing inflation and unemployment, decreasing car purchases and mortgages, a downward-trending industrial production index, and so forth—was already available to the Spanish government by early 2008. However, Spain was in its preelection season and the Socialist government opted to deny the existence of the crisis, hence refusing to take any action. Once they won the elections in March 2008, data on job losses and a significant deterioration of the labor market was evident as the unemployment rate reached 11.3 percent. Only then did Zapatero accept the existence of an "accelerated deceleration."

It was only in the fall of 2008 that the Socialist executive publicly acknowledged the difficult economic situation and started to act. Table 6.1 presents a list of the most important reforms enacted by the

Table 6.1   Summary of economic reforms implemented by the Socialist executive, 2008–11

Reform	Date	Description
Rescue package for the banking sector	October 2008	Granting of €100,000 million
Plan E	November 2008	Stimulus plan for the construction sector (€55,000 million)
Temporary unemployment protection and labor integration program	October 2009	€426 noncontributory monthly unemployment allowance with six-month duration
Sustainable economy law	April 2010	Policy package aimed at reorienting the economy toward more sustainable activities.
Deficit reduction measures	May 2010	A cut of 5 percent in civil servant salaries. Freeze on pensions. Abolition of the *cheque-bebé* (baby check)
Labor market reform	June 2010	Reduction of severance compensation. Further limits placed on the use of temporary contracts
Social and economic agreement	February 2011	Tripartite social pact on pensions, active labor market policies, collective bargaining, energy and R&D policy
Pension reform	2011—Agreed in February and passed into law in June	Increase of the retirement age and of the minimum number of working years to have access to a pension
Limit on regional government deficits	April 2011	A limit of 1 percent
Collective bargaining reform	June 2011	Measures aimed at increasing internal flexibility and collective bargaining at company level
Constitutional reform	August 2011	Modifies article 135 and establishes a ceiling for the public administration deficit
Labor market reform	September 2011	Increase of the maximum age for fixed-term training contracts and employment-promotion contracts
VAT reduction for new home purchases	September 2011	Reduction from 8 to 4 percent
Tax on capital gains	September 2011	Reactivation of the tax on holdings over €700,000

Socialist executive. The first measure increased the provision of guarantees to the banking sector with a value of 100,000 million euros. However, this massive injection of money was not accompanied by a requirement that the banks grant loans to companies and individuals and was accordingly heavily criticized by a large sector of the citizenry.

At the same time, the government approved the controversial *Plan E*, with a budget of 55,000 million euros, aimed at financing public works and hence facilitating the reemployment of construction workers. This measure was also heavily contested because of its exorbitant budget and short sightedness. Overall, the initial reforms implemented by Socialist government were late and more importantly did not address the structural problems facing the economy.

The increase of government spending due to growing unemployment and public investment programs in addition to the decrease in social security contributions led to the rapid growth of the deficit, from a 1.9 percent surplus in 2007 to a 4.2 percent deficit in just one year. The deterioration of labor market conditions produced an 18 percent unemployment rate in 2009 and an increase of the long-term unemployment rate to 4.3 percent. Given the high rate of temporary employment in Spain, many of those who lost jobs were only entitled to low unemployment benefits or none at all. At the same time, as the economic crisis deepened, many of those whose last jobs were based on indefinite contracts also started to exhaust their unemployment protection with the consequent threat to social cohesion. Confronted by this social emergency, the executive approved the Temporary Unemployment Protection and Integration Program (PRODI) with the support of trade unions. It consisted of a 426 euro noncontributory unemployment allowance for six months, extendable for another three, for the unemployed who had exhausted their unemployment benefit rights.

The Debt Crisis and the Implications of Austerity Measures

It was only at this stage that the Socialist executive acknowledged the structural character of the crisis and hence the need to introduce substantial reforms. Until that moment, the executive was convinced that little could be done against a crisis with an essentially financial and exogenous character. This explains the mostly reactive nature of the policies implemented until 2010. The first structural reform was the sustainable economy law of April 2010. The objective of this law was to transform the Spanish production model with a focus on developing the sustainable energy sector and innovation. However this law had very little impact as it was vague and lacked the financial support necessary to ensure adequate implementation.

As a consequence of the worsening fiscal position of most EU countries, but particularly of the Southern European countries and Ireland, fears of default led to the euro sovereign debt crisis. The average deficit of the European Union had increased from −0.9 percent in 2007 to −6.8 percent in 2009. In the Spanish case, it was even worse, rising from 1.9 percent (2007) to an unprecedented −11.1 percent (2009). Up to this point, the strategies to overcome the crisis had mostly been regarded as domestic affairs where each country should develop its own policy. However, as the debt crisis deepened, the EU took on a more active role and put pressure on the Spanish government to implement significant cost-cutting measures.

The meeting of the Eurogroup in early May 2010 concluded with strong demands that the Spanish government implement austerity policies aimed at calming the financial markets that were attacking Spanish and Italian debt. As a result, on May 12, the government presented a set of "measures to accelerate the reduction of the public deficit." These included a 5 percent reduction of the salaries of civil servants and a freeze on wage increases in the forthcoming years; nonapplication of the cost-of-living indexation of pensions; the ending of the *cheque bebé* (an allowance of 2,500 euros to families with newborn children); and a significant reduction of public works and investment. These measures were vehemently rejected by the trade unions and opposition parties as they considered the sudden change to be the result of external imposition and economic mismanagement. A large part of the Socialist electorate perceived the executive's shift in social and economic policy as a betrayal while a majority of the population perceived it as a loss of sovereignty. Partly as a response to the critical economic situation and to the executive's policies, on May 15, the *indignados* (indignant) movement arose. Certainly, the critical attitude toward political parties and their alleged detachment from social problems was considered to be one of the main factors contributing to the appearance and growth of this movement.[3] Moreover, politicians and the political system were perceived as the third most important problem affecting Spain, after unemployment and the economy.[4]

The new austerity measures were accompanied in June by a labor market reform that introduced two main changes: a reduction of severance pay and the opening of spaces for company-level agreements to opt out of higher-level agreements. The reform was unilaterally passed and was strongly criticized by trade unions that called for a general strike in

September 2010. Social dialogue was nonetheless restored some weeks later as the executive looked for the support of social partners on a vast number of issues, including pensions and collective bargaining reform. As a result, the Economic and Social Agreement was signed in February 2011. This pact contained an increase of the pensionable age to 67 as well as a commitment by the social partners to initiate social dialogue on a number of issues, such as active labor market policies, vocational training, collective bargaining reform, industrial policy, energy policy, and research and development and innovation (R&D + i). Negotiations on some of these issues continued but had varying degrees of success. For instance, negotiations around the reform of collective bargaining broke down and the government intervened unilaterally again.

After several months of austerity policies and no sign of recovery, social discontent had grown significantly as shown by the momentum of the *indignados* movement. Even though there are many factors that may help explain this important social mobilization (such as high unemployment and political corruption in the two main parties), the discontent it expressed was also a response to the undemocratic imposition of economic policies by the EU and other international organizations. The contrast between what had been the political program of the Zapatero government for its second term and the policies implemented generated frustration among their voters and the citizenry more generally. In this vein, 81 percent of the population declared in June 2011 that they were sympathetic to the *indignados* movement and approximately 20 percent indicated they had participated in some demonstrations, assemblies, or other activities.[5]

As a result of the adjustment program, the budget deficit decreased from −11.1 percent in 2010 to −9.2 percent just one year later. In addition to the aforementioned policies, other initiatives were implemented. For instance, the ceiling on regional government deficits was set to 1 percent. Moreover, in only the second reform of the Spanish constitution in 33 years, guarantees for the stability of public finances were introduced and passed without any public consultation or referendum. These budgetary constraints may be detrimental to the quality of welfare services as regional governments are responsible for providing important public services. Similar far-reaching cost-cutting packages were adopted simultaneously in regions such as Catalonia, Valencia, Madrid, and Castile-La Mancha. These reforms have augmented the perception of decreasing accountability of executives to citizens. The imposition of more stringent budgetary rules and in some cases the monitoring of public finances by supranational institutions strengthened the perception of decreasing sovereignty at the national level. German authorities' recommendations to the Spanish executive to reduce labor costs and holidays and to enhance labor productivity have created a tail wagging the dog effect. Even though citizens generally acknowledge the executive's inability to prevent and overcome the crisis and its consequences, there is nonetheless strong reluctance to be monitored by supranational institutions. This contrasts with Spaniard's strongly favorable attitudes toward European integration. However, as pointed out by Szmolka (2008), this positive attitude is grounded in purely instrumental motivations regarding economic and political issues. If citizens perceive reduced benefits accruing from the European Union, indifference or even opposition to European integration processes may grow. The last important measure approved by the Socialist executive before its electoral defeat consisted of the reactivation of taxes applied to capital gains over 700,000 euros. In the context of predominantly expenditure-based adjustment, tax increases like this have been the exception.

Notwithstanding the political and economic costs, the Socialist government's commitment to further austerity policies remained strong. As a result, the Spanish economy witnessed a further deterioration of growth and employment figures during the summer of 2011. Placing public deficit reduction as the focal point of economic policies in the second half of Zapatero's second term de facto meant a postponement sine die of economic stimulus measures for economic growth. GDP contracted -0.3 during the last quarter of 2011 due to a drop in public investment together with further reductions in private consumption. Moreover, OECD and International Monetary Fund (IMF 2011) projections predicted a new recession period in Spain during 2012. This would confirm the insight of some economists, such as Joseph Stiglitz, that "austerity is a suicide path" as budget cuts imply shifting risks to the private sector and raise the economic stakes in the short and long term.[6] The implementation of further austerity packages consisting mostly of cost-cutting measures, with little emphasis on revenue-based adjustment or policies to stimulate demand, certainly constitute a threat to growth and the maintenance of public services.

The Consequences of the Adjustment

Generally speaking, the reforms enacted have not managed to address the structural problems affecting the Spanish economy. In spite of some measures aimed precisely at facilitating a gradual transition toward a more sustainable and high-productivity economic structure, little seems to have been achieved in this regard. Rather, the lack of credit for companies together with public spending reductions will very likely have a negative impact on investment and firms' innovation decisions.

The most distinctive feature of Spain's adjustment to the crisis has been the volatility exhibited by the labor market. Whereas in the period preceding the crisis employment grew more than in any other EU country, during the crisis the Spanish economy has been the EU champion in job destruction. The decrease in employment relative to the fall of GDP was remarkably higher in Spain, leading to skyrocketing unemployment that reached 24 percent by early 2012. Even though this is not a new feature of the Spanish labor market, where an abuse of temporary contracts allows companies to lay off workers to adjust to economic downturns, what is particularly worrying is the deepening dualization, characterized by increasing polarization between stable and precarious workers. Some groups have been particularly harmed by the adjustment. This is the case of young workers, most of them with short, fixed-term contracts. There was only a cyclical reduction of temporary employment due to the fact that temporary workers were the ones laid off first. However, the structural level of temporary employment remains very high. Moreover, individuals who left school early to enter the workforce increased significantly during the growth years, hence making this a particularly vulnerable group. Immigrants have also been more exposed to the risk of unemployment, informal work, and temporary employment due to their comparatively lower qualification levels and reduced capacity to rely on family networks.

The 2010 labor market reform had very little impact on existing labor market dynamics. The objective of the reform was to halt employment destruction and set the foundations for employment growth. In order to achieve these goals, the reform modified the conditions for firing employees, facilitated working time adjustments, and improved some aspects of public employment services. However, this reform had very little impact: first, because the changes introduced were marginal and incomplete; and second, because the fiscal adjustment required by the worsening sovereign debt crisis neutralized any possibility of employment creation irrespective of the contents of reform. The repeated failed attempts to overturn existing labor market dynamics highlight the need to adopt a broader perspective that articulates labor market reforms within broader policy packages aimed at setting the foundations for systemic change. This would mean, among other things, carrying out a reform of the education and training systems, and developing a clear strategy regarding industrial policy that provides clear guidelines for an inclusive and sustainable growth model.

Regarding social protection, the most significant impact of the adjustment has come through spending cuts affecting public services, most notably education and health (see also chapter 11 in this volume). The adjustment undertaken in May and June 2010 meant the abolition of a 2,500 euro allowance for a newborn child and a freeze on old age and other pensions. By contrast, unemployment assistance was extended initially, though some months later the executive was obliged to retreat from this. The 2011 old age pension reform contained an increase of the pensionable age and was aimed at making the system sustainable in the context of an aging demographic structure.

Overall, the policies implemented during the second half of the 2008–11 term reduced social protection due to a combination of lower expenditures and mounting social risks. High unemployment together with lower social spending helps explain the increase in poverty rates and inequality, which are well above the EU average. Expenditure on unemployment protection constitutes a case in point. Social spending increased from 20.7 percent by 2007 to 25 percent in 2011. This increase is explained by a contraction of total GDP combined with mounting unemployment and hence unemployment benefits. In fact, by 2011 unemployment protection in Spain amounted to 15 percent of total social spending, more than twice the EU average of 6.8 percent. And yet, the number of unemployed who do not receive contributory or noncontributory benefits is increasing and reached 32.3 percent of the unemployed by the end of 2011.

As the debt crisis persists, many voices have proposed a co-payment model for health and education that is becoming a new roadmap for the reform of the public sector in Spain—a cost-cutting roadmap shared by the new conservative PP government elected in November 2011. State retrenchment is even more worrisome in the present context as the family can no longer provide sufficient protection due to the large number of households with all their members unemployed. The risk of dualization in social protection is accordingly high, with the most vulnerable groups in society increasingly needing to resort to social assistance and those with more resources being reliant on the market.

To sum up, the most important outcome of the crisis and the adjustment has been a reconfiguration of state's role in the economy. Austerity policies implemented in 2010 and 2011 meant cuts in public services such as transport, education, and health, which are very likely to have a long-lasting impact. The financial crisis and the risk of default by some of the Eurozone countries is forcing the governments of Greece, Italy, Ireland, Portugal, and Spain (the so-called GIIPSs) to implement additional cost-cutting packages with devastating effects on consumption, employment, and growth prospects. Particularly worrying in this context are expenditure cuts in social policies and more importantly public services such as education and health as they are reducing the capacity of states to maintain social cohesion in a context of unprecedentedly high unemployment. Moreover, the scaling down of the public sector and institutional changes associated with it will also have effects on the role of the state and the dominant forms of socioeconomic coordination that open the door to the further liberalization of markets. The expenditure-based character of fiscal adjustment is having very negative effects on demand and hence limiting consumption and economic activity and reducing the prospects for employment creation.

Economic Policy of the Rajoy Government

After eight years of Socialist government, the general elections held in November 2011 sanctioned a shift toward the PP headed by Mariano Rajoy. Even though the polls pointed to a clear victory of the right-wing party, PP leaders were very careful not to fully explain their plans for economic reforms so as not to lose votes. In this regard, there was a strong contrast between the PP's guarantees to EU partners that it would carry out an aggressive reform program in order to bring down the deficit and restore trust in the Spanish economy, and the significantly more moderate tone used in the campaign, where no details were provided about the form and extent of the adjustment to be undertaken.

Right after the election, the executive announced an ambitious reform plan including the banking sector, labor market and industrial relations, education, and more. The first reform was aimed at consolidating the banking system and was followed by announcements of a labor market reform. Contrary to what had been the practice since the restoration of democracy, the right-wing executive did not consult trade unions or employer organizations about its reform plans and the labor market reform law was unilaterally passed with the PP's comfortable absolute majority in parliament.

Generally speaking, economic policies under the Rajoy government have been characterized by some continuity with respect to the previous government, but the legitimacy obtained in the elections together with the support of EU partners have translated into more aggressive plans for fiscal adjustment. The labor market reform however implies a remarkable shift with respect to the previous orientation of labor market reforms in 2010 and 2011. On the one hand, a focus on enhancing firms' ability to move employees into different positions and reduce working time remains, but this was done by increasing the bargaining power of employers at the company level and their ability to make unilateral decisions. There has also been a clear shift toward facilitating individual firing, by means of increasing the circumstances for lawful firing and reducing firing costs.

Following the approval of the aforementioned reforms, attention shifted to the general budget law for 2012. This process was extremely controversial for several reasons. First, the executive never revealed any details about the characteristics of the budget and how cuts would be distributed. Moreover, and notwithstanding the critical economic situation, its approval was delayed in order not to jeopardize the PP's prospects of supplanting Socialist dominance in Andalusia in the March 2012 regional election. Finally, the whole process was also marked by negotiations between the Spanish government and the European Commission (EC) over the deficit objective that concluded with a 5.3 percent objective, higher than initially announced by the EC, but lower than sought by the Spanish executive. This amounted to a deficit reduction of 3.2 percent of GDP in just nine months, hence accounting for the largest spending-cut package in the history of democratic Spain. These cutbacks are nonetheless distributed differently across departments. Continued spending-based austerity measures will not only delay the recovery of the economy, which faces an acute demand problem, but will also impact very asymmetrically upon different groups as a good amount of the adjustment will come through cuts in universal public services such as health, education, public works, and transport.

ConcludingRemar ks

Since the beginning of the crisis in the early months of 2008 until the Socialists' defeat in the November 2011 elections, the Spanish economy experienced increasing performance deterioration, which is particularly worrying when one looks at the labor market. According to data released at the end of October 2011, the unemployment rate had reached a historical maximum of 24.5 percent. After four years of uninterrupted recovery plans and reforms, the data call for a reassessment of the characteristics of the adjustment and the extent to which it has contributed to addressing some of the structural failures of the Spanish economy.

The analysis in this chapter shows that, far from having solved these problems, the adjustment has delivered very poor results with regard to restoring growth and tackling the deterioration of labor market conditions. Structural reforms were initially delayed and then subordinated to the rescue of the banking sector, and in a second stage to the requirements of fiscal adjustment arising from the euro sovereign debt crisis. Adjustment based on expenditure reductions has had two main effects on the economy. In the short term, it has further depressed demand hence limiting the prospects for a prompt recovery. In the long term, public sector adjustment and in particular cuts in public services, together with moves toward privatization and liberalization, have opened the door to a reconfiguration of the state's role in the economy.

But the most important conclusion emerging from the analysis of Spain's adjustment is the fact that the structural weaknesses of the economy, those that help explain not the crisis, as this was common to all EU countries, but its depth and intensity, remain. In other words, the aforementioned factors underlying the low productivity of the Spanish economy remain untouched. Labor market reforms have contributed very little to changing labor market dualization that affects a large part of the working population, particularly younger people. Furthermore, the economy still relies upon labor-intensive sectors, and laws aimed at reorienting economic activity toward alternative sectors that have higher value added and are more sustainable have had very limited impact.

One additional aspect we have highlighted throughout the chapter is the fact that the economic crisis is accompanied by a political crisis, which goes beyond the traditional left-right debate and takes the form of a crisis of representation and legitimacy. The single European currency is now demonstrating that it is more than just an economic instrument as its stability forced the resignation of prime ministers in Greece and Italy. Moreover, the imposition of severe adjustment packages by technocratic EU economic governance institutions, in order to safeguard the euro, is having perverse effects on member states' democratic legitimacy. Even though this constitutes in itself a cause for concern, it also has negative implications for the economy; the weakness of the Spanish executive reduced the effectiveness of its reform attempts. In order to circumvent this problem, the executive has always sought the support of social partners, but the limited effectiveness of the negotiated reforms reinforce the idea that social pacts have been conceived more as legitimating devices to accompany policies rather than mechanisms to enhance the effectiveness of the policy at stake.

Notes

1. "El 61% desaprueba la gestión de Zapatero," *El País*, October 4, 2009.
2. "Corbacho culpa a los bancos de la crisis inmobiliaria," *El País*, August 25, 2009.
3. J. J. Toharia, "Las raíces del desencanto," *Metroscopia—Blogs El País*, June 21, 2011.
4. Centro de Investigaciones Sociológicas (CIS), Barometers, November 2009–June 2012. CIS data are available at: www.cis.es.
5. F. Garea, "Apoyo a la indignación del 15-M," *El País*, June 5, 2011.
6. A. Yalnizyan, "Austerity Kills: Conservative Cure Worst Thing for What Ails the Economy Says Stiglitz," *Rabble*, October 31, 2011.

WorksC ited

Armingeon, K., and L. Baccaro. 2011. *The Sorrows of Young Euro: Policy Responses to the Sovereign Debt Crisis*. Paper presented at the Council for European Studies conference, Barcelona, June.

Arpaia, A., E. Pérez, and K. Pichelman. 2009. *Understanding Labour Income Share Dynamics in Europe*. European Commission, European Economy, Economic Papers 379. Brussels: European Commission.

Cabrera, M., and F. Del Rey. 2007. *The Power of Entrepreneurs. Politics and Economy in Contemporary Spain*. New York: Berghan Books.

Carballo-Cruz, F. 2011. "Causes and Consequences of the Spanish Economic Crisis: Why the Recovery Is Taken So Long?" *Panoeconomicus* 58(3): 309–28.

Crouch, C. 2008. "What Will Follow the Demise of Privatised Keynesianism?" *Political Quarterly* 79(4): 476–87.

Erne, R. 2008. *European Unions. Labor's Quest for a Transnational Democracy*. Ithaca: Cornell University Press.

European Commission. 2011. *European Economic Forecast*. Brussels: European Commission.

Hall, P., and D. Soskice, eds. 2001. *Varieties of Capitalism: The Institutional Foundations of Comparative Advantage*. New York: Oxford University Press.

International Monetary Fund. 2011. *World Economic Outlook 2011*. Washington DC: IMF.

López, I., and E. Rodríguez. 2011. "The Spanish Model." *New Left Review* 69 (May–June): 6–29.

Molina, O., and M. Rhodes. 2007. "Conflict, Complementarities and Institutional Change in Mixed Market Economies." In B. Hancké, M. Rhodes, and M. Thatcher, eds., *Beyond Varieties of Capitalism: Contradictions, Complementarities and Change*. Oxford: Oxford University Press, pp. 223–53.

OECD. 2007. *Economic Surveys: Spain*. Paris: OECD.
———. 2010. *Economic Surveys: Spain*. Paris: OECD.
Pérez, S. 1997. *Banking on Privilege: The Politics of Spanish Financial Reform*. Ithaca: Cornell University Press.
Sapelli, G. 1995. *Southern Europe since 1945. Tradition and Modernity in Portugal, Spain, Italy, Greece and Turkey*. London and New York: Longman.
Wölfl, W., and J. S. Mora-Sanguinetti. 2011. *Reforming the Labour Market in Spain*. OECD Economics Department Working Papers, n. 845.

CHAPTER 7

The Relationship between Unions and Zapatero's Government: From Social Pacts to General Strike

Kerstin Hamann

W hen Zapatero was reelected to head a second Socialist Party (PSOE) government in 2008, there was no reason to doubt that the cooperative atmosphere that had dominated the relationship between unions and the government during his first term would continue. In fact, the economic crisis that manifested itself about the same time appeared to strengthen rather than undermine social dialog between the government and unions. However, Zapatero's commitment to overcoming the crisis through concertation was questioned when negotiations on labor market reforms failed and the government announced unilateral reforms against vehement union opposition, leading to a general strike on September 29, 2010. Zapatero's second government thus illustrates that union inclusion in policymaking remained contingent rather than institutionalized and that the patterns developed during the earlier years of Spanish democracy were thus continued rather than reformed. Furthermore, it is not just economic factors that shape the relationship between unions and the government, but also electoral factors and the strength of the government. Underlying issues and problems in the area of labor market policies remained unaddressed during Zapatero's administration, and the current conservative Popular Party (PP) government faces similar issues.

This chapter traces the changing relationship between unions and the second Zapatero government (2008–11) while providing comparisons with Zapatero's first government (2004–2008). It also briefly discusses the implications of the November 2011 election, which propelled the PP under Prime Minister Rajoy to executive office, for organized labor and its relationship to the government. The chapter concludes by arguing that despite eight years of Socialist government, unions have remained in a structurally vulnerable position as the imbalances in the labor market have not been resolved and unions' access to policymaking has remained contingent.

Social Pacts, General Strikes, and the Industrial Relations System in Spain

The dynamic relationship between the major union confederations in Spain and the second Zapatero government is better understood against the background of the peculiarities of the industrial relations system in democratic Spain. The history of the relationship between the unions and the Socialist Party has been marked by periods of cooperation, often expressed in national-level social pacts, but also by more confrontational periods, perhaps most clearly evidenced by general strikes staged by the unions against the government.

Since the transition to democracy, Spanish industrial relations have been dominated by the two main union confederations, the General Workers Union (UGT) and the Workers Commissions (CC.OO.). The UGT was founded in 1888 and had a historically close relationship with the PSOE. In contrast, CC.OO. only emerged in the 1960s during the Franco regime and was closely tied to the Communist Party (PCE). The two unions played a crucial role during the democratic transition and consolidation periods, where they supported the onset of democracy, despite occasional strike waves, and cooperated with employers and the Union of the Democratic Center (UCD) government in encompassing social pacts addressing wages, the industrial relations system, and employment relations. During the PSOE governments under Felipe González (1982–96), unions increasingly opposed the government's economic program that was focused on modernizing the economy and joining the European Community in 1986. These policies, emphasizing industrial restructuring and widespread privatization of state-owned companies, resulted not just in rising unemployment but also in weakening links between the party and the union. For instance, social pacts between the government and unions all but disappeared by the late 1980s, while both unions jointly called three general strikes against government policies (1988, 1992, and 1994). At the same time, CC.OO. and the UGT, previously engaged in competition over members, influence, and resources, began to align their goals and coordinate their strategies in a collabora-tive relationship known as "unity of action." By the mid-1990s, as the PSOE ruled with a minority in Congress and the general strikes had demonstrated little effect on modifying government policy, negotiations between unions and the government occurred more frequently and sev-eral agreements, smaller in scope, were signed. During Prime Minister Aznar's conservative PP administration, social pacts with the government resurfaced again, especially during his first term (1996–2000), while his second term (2004–2008) witnessed a decline in national-level agree-ments. The unions also staged a general strike against the government's proposed unemployment policy reforms, resulting in substantial modi-fications of the reforms.

Union involvement in national-level agreements with the government presents an important indicator of the role and political influence of unions in Spanish politics, especially in light of the peculiarities of the country's industrial relations system. Conventionally, union density (the proportion of the workforce that is unionized) serves as an important indicator of union strength. In Spain, union density fluctuated between 8.3 percent in 1981 and 14.3 percent in 2008, one of the lowest levels of union density in Western Europe (Hamann 2012, 5).[1] At the same time, however, density in Spain has remained remarkably stable overall and has, in fact, grown since the early 1980s, in contrast to many other Western European unions, which have experienced marked declines. As organi-zational strength has been low in Spain, other indicators have gained in significance in signaling union strength and influence. The proportion of the workforce covered by collective bargaining agreements (bargain-ing coverage) has remained relatively high despite a decline in recent years from 84.3 percent in 1996 to 70 percent in 2008.[2] Furthermore, relative union strength in the workplace is better indicated by the sup-port workers express for each union in the elections to the works com-mittees. These competitive elections allow affiliated workers as well as those not belonging to a union to vote for their preferred union. The two major confederations, UGT and CC.OO., have dominated these elections in the past 25 years, although regional unions have also gained considerable vote shares, especially in Galicia and the Basque Country. Furthermore, the "most representative unions" as determined by these election outcomes are also legitimized to participate in bargaining above the workplace level. This "electoral unionism" (Martínez Lucio 1992, 501) has, since the transition to democracy, positioned the UGT and CC.OO. as the only unions that are legitimized to participate in bar-gaining at the national level with the employers' organization CEOE

(Spanish Confederation of Employers' Organizations) and CEPYME (Spanish Confederation of Small and Medium Enterprises). Similarly, Spanish unions have been among the most strike-prone in Western Europe (Monger 2003; Rigby & Marco Aledo 2001). In addition to workplace strikes, unions have also organized a relatively high number of general strikes against policy reforms planned or adopted by governments both of the left and the right (Hamann et al. 2013). Thus, unions have exerted considerable influence on Spanish politics not just as workplace organizations but also through their involvement in national politics.

The presence or absence of social pacts between governments and unions in the past was not clearly related to the party of the chief executive—social pacts were signed with some frequency with the UCD governments during the early years of Spanish democracy, under the González Socialist governments, and also under Aznar's PP administration. Yet, the González and Aznar governments also experienced periods where social pacts failed or were absent and the government passed legislation without union support, especially during the second and third González administrations (1986–93) and the second Aznar term (2004–2008). Thus, variations in patterns of policy inclusion have not been clearly linked to the party of the incumbent. Similarly, social pacts did not neatly match patterns of economic growth and decline (see Hamann & Kelly 2011, ch. 7).

It is against this context of the industrial relations system in Spain and the noninstitutionalized nature of union inclusion in policymaking through social pacts that the relationship between the unions and the government during Zapetero's second term has to be understood. These factors informed the strategies of both the government and the unions during Zapatero's rule, which witnessed a period of cooperation and dialog as well as a period marked more clearly by conflict and confrontation.

The Preponderance of Social Dialog under Zapatero I

While Zapatero continued many of the economic policies of his conservative predecessor, José María Aznar, he set a distinct policy course in other areas, especially social policy and the "historic memory" of the Franco dictatorship (see Field 2009). With respect to labor issues and unions, Zapatero's commitment to include unions in economic and social policymaking through national tripartite negotiations was particularly remarkable and put his administration into sharp relief to Aznar's second government (2004–2008), when many policy reforms in areas relevant to labor had been decided without agreement with unions (see Hamann 2012).

During much of Spain's democracy, social pacts between the government and unions primarily reflected political contingencies rather than economic necessities. Zapatero's governments proved to be no exception as the presence or absence of social pacts during his rule was closely related to political factors, especially the PSOE's electoral position. The party's victory at the polls in 2004 did not, in fact, reflect a widespread and profound ideological turn of the electorate to the left. Instead, it was a result of several factors, including the PP's response to the terrorist attacks on Madrid commuter trains just days before the election, which, in turn, led to an elevated voter turnout that benefitted primarily the PSOE by mobilizing abstainers and young people; and former IU (United Left) voters switching votes to the PSOE. Furthermore, voters overall judged the PP government as competent on economic policies but were more critical of Aznar concerning other issues, including the sinking of the oil tanker *Prestige* and the ensuing environmental disaster; the country's entry into the Iraq War despite widespread popular opposition; and questions related to regional autonomy (Fishman 2007; Lago & Montero 2006; Torcal & Rico 2004). Nonetheless, the PSOE failed to secure a legislative majority, leaving Zapatero to head a minority government supported by leftist and regionalist parties.

The economic upswing observed during the Aznar government continued during the first part of Zapatero's administration (see table 7.1, and chapter 6 in this volume). Growth was primarily fueled by private consumption and construction,[3] and surpassed the European Union (EU-15) average. Notably, unemployment fell to less than 10 percent in 2005 for the first time in over 25 years, and to 8.3 percent in 2007 (European Commission 2009, 155–56). Yet, the proportion of temporary contracts remained high with over 30 percent of all contracts. It is noteworthy that unemployment and temporary employment were not evenly distributed across the Spanish workforce as young people were particularly affected. For example, unemployment for young people (15–24 years old) stood at 37.8 percent in 2009, more than twice the overall unemployment rate of 18 percent (European Commission 2010, 175). Similarly, the mean share of temporary contracts out of all contracts between 2005 and 2008 for people 20 years of age was 71 percent in Spain (compared to an EU average of 47 percent) and 49 percent for those of age 25 (EU average for this age group was 25 percent), while the mean for all age groups (15–64 years of age) stood at 32 percent in Spain

Table 7.1 Macroeconomicd ata,S pain,2004–11

	Unemployment (% of labor force)	Inflation (% rate of change of CPI)	Real GDP (% change)	Public deficit (as % of nominal GDP)
2004	10.5	3.1	3.3	−0.4
2005	9.2	3.4	3.6	1.0
2006	8.5	3.6	4.0	2.0
2007	8.3	2.8	3.6	1.9
2008	11.3	4.1	0.9	−4.1
2009	18.0	−0.3	−3.6	−11.2
2010	20.1	1.4	−0.2	−9.3
2011	21.5	0.6	0.7	−6.2

Notes: CPI: consumer price index; GDP: gross domestic product.

Source: *OECD Economic Outlook* No. 87 (June 2010); OECD Spain-Economic Forecast Summary (November 2011). Available at: http://www.oecd.org/document/6/0,3746,en_2649_34109_45270278_1_1_1_1,00.html.

(European Commission 2010, 128). This is of significance also because it has implications for future employment prospects and the access to the social safety net that comes with steady employment. Young people who leave school early and have a low level of qualifications are particularly prone to be trapped in the temporary employment situation, illustrated by the fact that five years after finishing their initial education, 40 percent of young people with low qualifications still find themselves dependent on temporary contracts (European Commission 2010, 129), which tend to be poorly paid and do not grant the same social welfare rights as do permanent contracts.

Many of Zapatero's policies were aimed at improving the situation of the workforce. The government raised the minimum wage and increased minimum pensions in real terms; other policies included basic care for dependent persons, a law that entitled fathers to paid paternity leave, and financial support for families with children (Bernardi & Sarasa 2009); and the share of the unemployed who receive benefits increased from 61 percent in 2004 to 75 percent in 2009.[4]

In addition, during Zapatero's first government important policy areas were reformed in close cooperation with the social partners through bi- or tripartite negotiations. The prime minister met with the unions and employers shortly after his election to set an agenda for future negotiations. In July 2004 the government, both major union confederations, and the employers' organization signed the *Declaración para el Diálogo Social 2004* (Declaration for Social Dialog), designed to increase economic competitiveness, productivity, stable employment, and social cohesion through social dialogue on issues such as immigration, training, active labor market policies, minimum wage, collective bargaining structure, and social security (Sala Franco 2007, 144–45). Negotiated reforms also comprised a new procedure to extend collective bargaining agreements, which was signed by the government and the social partners and issued as a royal decree in 2005 (Albarracín 2005). Of particular significance was the agreement on the tripartite May 2006 labor market reform (*Acuerdo para la mejora del crecimiento y del empleo*), which was subsequently passed in Congress and effectively revised the workers' statute. The agreement provided incentives for employers to convert temporary to permanent contracts and improved unemployment protection. Other agreements included a pension reform, integration of immigrants, and minimum wage increases, among others (see Mulas-Granados 2009, 18; Pitxer i Campos & Sánchez Velasco 2008, 112–13; Sala Franco 2007, 145–7).

Union confederations and employers' organizations also engaged in bilateral agreements. One example is the bipartite Third Agreement to Resolve Labor Disputes out of Court (Martín Artiles 2005). In 2006, the fourth National Agreement for Continuous Training (*Acuerdo nacional de la formación continua*, ANFC IV) was negotiated between the social partners, and was subsequently supplemented by a tripartite agreement with the government. Most important, perhaps, were the annual accords (with the exception of 2009) on collective bargaining (*Acuerdo Interconfederal para la Negociación Colectiva*, ANC) between employers and unions, which contained wage guidelines in line with projected inflation rates and additional adjustment clauses.

In sum, the first Zapatero government witnessed an overall strong economy that extended to improved employment indicators, and social and welfare reforms, many of which were negotiated with the unions and on occasion with the employers. Zapatero's policies raised discussions of a new "left" agenda, which included his emphasis on formulating policy reforms through social dialog. At the same time, however, important issues concerning employment had been left unchanged, perpetuating some of the existing imbalances in the structure of the Spanish economy and labor market. Among those was the continuing fragmentation of the labor market with a high proportion of temporary contracts and a relatively high level of job security among those with permanent contracts, which, it has been argued, limits the flexibilization of the labor market and discourages employers from hiring workers on permanent contracts; the heavy reliance on consumption and especially the expanding construction sector as an engine of economic growth; and the continuing fragmentation of the collective bargaining process. Thus, when the economic and financial crisis hit Spain almost simultaneously with Zapatero's reelection to executive office, the labor market was poorly equipped to weather the challenge.

Zapatero'sSecond Term

Conflict and Cooperation

The March 9, 2008, elections returned the Socialist Party, again led by Zapatero, to office as a minority government with 43.9 percent of the vote and 169 seats in Congress. While the economy began to exhibit signs of decline in 2007, macroeconomic indicators deteriorated rapidly and dramatically in 2008 (see table 7.1, and chapter 6 in this volume). This downturn was prompted by the global financial crisis, which exacerbated existing imbalances in the Spanish economy, in turn driven by a rapid expansion of the construction sector.

The effects on the labor market were particularly detrimental. Unemployment rose from 17 percent, over twice the EU average, in February 2009, to 18.5 percent in July, the highest in the OECD[5]; by 2011, unemployment stood at 22.8 percent.[6] The contraction of the labor market was notable especially in the construction sector, where employment was reduced by 40.4 percent between 2008 and 2010 (European Commission 2011, 26). Rapid job shedding resulted in a decline of the proportion of temporary contracts to about 25 percent in early 2009 (CES 2009, 288–89).

At the onset of the economic and financial crisis, Zapatero first attempted to continue reform through concertation, resulting in the July 2008 *Declaración para el Impulso de la Economía, el Empleo, la Competitividad y el Progreso Social* (Declaration to Stimulate the Economy, Employment, Competitiveness, and Social Progress) between the government and the unions. The declaration proclaimed that in "the current economic context, the contribution of Social Dialog is even more crucial than in previous periods" (cited in CES 2009, 349). Furthermore, the declaration established the *Comisión de Seguimiento y Evaluación del Diálogo Social*, a commission charged with prioritizing and providing oversight to negotiation topics, processes, and outcomes (CES 2009, 30–31). This led to the formation of new bargaining arenas to assess a multitude of issues, including the modernization of employment services, possible reforms of the office for Employment and Social Security Inspection (*Inspección de Trabajo y Seguridad Social*, ITSS), immigration (in relation to employment), the *Ley de Estatuto de Trabajo Autónomo* (Workers' Statute for the Self-Employed), employment equality, social protection, public sector employment, and industrial and energy policies, among others (CES 2009, 31). A 2009 proposal elaborated jointly by the unions, the government, and leftist parties to extend unemployment coverage was subsequently approved in Congress (Sainz de Miguel 2009).

The 2004 Declaration for Social Dialog and its 2008 successor appeared to indicate that regular social concertation had become an institutionalized part of the policymaking process that stood in marked contrast to the more sporadic and cyclical concertation processes of the past. However, when the crisis deteriorated rapidly and concertation was unable to produce a quick fix to the downturn, Zapatero committed to several "shock therapy" economic reforms, including a 5-percent wage cut for public servants and a freezing of pensions in May 2010. The government's severe budget cuts were passed in Congress with a one-vote majority.[7] It was not just the change in the type of policies that met with union opposition, however, but also Zapatero's strategy of formulating these policies. Zapatero's new reforms indicated a shift in the government's policy course, but they also questioned the policy process as they were elaborated without seeking prior agreement with the unions, thus breaking the pattern established by the earlier years of the PSOE government. Social dialog had first been challenged in 2009, when the government as well as the unions opposed the employment policy reforms suggested by the employers (Sanz de Miguel 2010). With the government's turn in policies, concertation now came under additional attack. Unions, for their part, criticized the government's plans to increase the retirement age from 65 to 67 years, announced in February 2010, and organized demonstrations in Spain's major urban centers to protest these pension reform plans. In response, the government declared that the announced reform was not a policy, but merely a proposal open to negotiation.[8] Soon after, Zapatero made public plans for cuts in civil servants' pay and a pension freeze in order to reduce the budget deficit; union leaders again vociferously criticized these reforms as they worried that they would result in even higher unemployment. A meeting between the government and union leaders failed to produce an agreement. The public service federations responded to the government plans by staging a general strike for the public sector in June 2010. But the consequences of Zapatero's reforms went beyond the specific policy plans and instead affected the policymaking process. As UGT secretary general Méndez pointed out with respect to the pay cut for civil servants, "The decree law has found its first victim: the social dialog between public sector unions and the administration."[9]

Another contentious issue surrounded the labor market reform, which had been negotiated between the unions and the employers without, however, reaching consensus. This reform, like several other labor market reforms implemented previously, aimed at making employment conditions more flexible in an attempt to stimulate new employment even though past experience illustrated powerfully that the flexibilization of the labor market was unlikely to redress the underlying problems of the Spanish economy, including high unemployment (see Fishman 2012). When negotiations broke down in July 2010, Zapatero announced that if the negotiations failed to produce an agreement on the labor market reform, he would impose a reform since adjustments in the labor market formed an integral part of the reform package that was deemed necessary to reduce the budget deficit. The reform addressed two main issues— the reduction of rigidities in the labor market by easing restrictions on dismissal of workers on permanent contracts, and changes in the collective bargaining process. Employers generally assert that the rigidities in employment limit their flexibility to fire, and therefore to hire, workers on permanent contracts; employers, according to this line of reasoning, need more flexibility in dismissing workers to adjust more quickly, and more cheaply, to the changing exigencies of the labor market. Unions, on the other hand, criticize these demands to decrease workers' job security as they fear they would add to the problem already posed by the large contingent of temporary workers. Instead, unions have pushed for incentives to transform temporary employment into permanent employment and have blamed the productive model for the unevenness of employment. Zapatero's labor market reform aimed at making dismissals easier and also cheaper for employers by widening the use of a specific type of contract, the "permanent employment promotion contract," to all workers. Unions opposed the facilitation and reduction of costs of dismissals as they predicted that workers laid off in the process would be replaced with cheaper temporary workers lacking employment security. The reform also addressed the collective bargaining process by allowing firms "under certain conditions, to opt out of sectoral agreements and negotiate separate agreements" at the company level instead (Sanz 2010), thus further decentralizing the bargaining process. Unions opposed these measures. The reform also included measures to stimulate the conversion of fixed-term contracts into permanent ones and incentives for employers to hire young people since it is this population group that is disproportionately more affected by unemployment than are older workers (Sanz de Miguel 2010).

Pointing out that the government did not depend on the unions for pushing through the reform package, labor and immigration minister Corbacho commented that "[w]hat does or does not get approved by decree will depend on the unions."[10] When the negotiations were unsuccessful, the unions announced a general strike for September 29, 2010. In the meantime, the government passed the reform as a decree law on June 16, shortly after the EU published a report on Spain's financial situation, in an attempt to establish Spain's credibility within the EU to avoid a financial bailout. The highly contentious reform was then introduced in Congress as a regular piece of legislation subject to parliamentary approval and was narrowly approved, even breaking party discipline within the PSOE, thus illustrating the weakness of Zapatero's minority government in Congress.[11] The general strike in September 2010 had an overall moderate and uneven turnout and left the labor market reform unchanged.

At the same time as the collaborative relationship between the unions and the government was challenged, unions engaged in bilateral agreements with employers. In 2009, the social partners failed to consent on a new Interconfederal Agreement on Collective Bargaining (ANC), an accord between unions and employers that had been signed on an annual basis since 2002 (CES 2009, 355–58).[12] Yet, in 2010, the social partners agreed on a new ANC, this time spanning a three-year period, which outlined modest wage increases in an attempt to stimulate employment.[13]

Explaining the Turn toward Confrontation

The early years of Zapatero's second term in office continued the pattern of concertation with the unions established during his first administration as the prime minister attempted to address the economic and financial crisis through reforms with the consent of organized labor. Yet, this pattern came under strain as the recession deepened. This changing relationship raises the question of the motivation for the turn from negotiated agreements to failed negotiations and conflict. Research on social pacts proposes that governments resort to pacts with unions when the economy is in a slump and social pacts offer an efficient and effective way of addressing the crisis. In the Spanish case, however, the dynamic appears to be reversed: After the democratic transition period, governments and unions agreed on social pacts quite frequently when economic indicators were positive, whereas negotiations tended to fail—or governments preferred to reform policies through legislation—during economic downturns. Consequently, we need to consider not just the economic and financial crisis, but also the political context to explain why social pacts came under pressure during the second Zapatero administration.

Existing research finds that the preponderance of governments to opt for policy reforms through concertation is linked to electoral factors (Hamann & Kelly 2011). From this perspective, Zapatero's announcement of unilateral measures is perhaps not surprising as his leadership had come under severe criticism when the economic crisis deepened. Both the PSOE and Zapatero suffered the erosion of popular opinion: While several opposition parties called for the prime minister's resignation, the PSOE's electoral support among the center-left had been reduced by over 10 percentage points in the 2008 election compared to 2004 (Urquizu 2008, 50). Opinion polls further illustrate the decline of Zapatero's popularity with voters. In April 2010, just 3.3 percent of respondents evaluated the prime minister as "very good," while 26.7 percent judged him as "very bad"; less than one-quarter (24.5 percent) stated they would support him if there was an election the next day. Over half of the respondents thought that the PSOE government's performance had been "bad" or "very bad" and three-quarters proclaimed that they had "no" or "little" confidence in Zapatero.[14] Union popularity had similarly been eroded in the public's view: While on a scale of 0 (lowest) to 10 (highest), survey respondents evaluated unions on average as 4.93 in March 2006, and 4.95 in September 2007, by March 2010 this figure had fallen to 4.11.[15] Given the public's poor evaluation of the governing party, the chief executive, and the unions, a turn away from concertation with the unions and toward unilateral action might appear as a reasonable strategy for Zapatero to regain voters' confidence as it would indicate decisive action and a distancing from the unpopular unions. In addition, the failure of previous concertation and wage agreements to prevent massive job shedding questioned their effectiveness and pointed to the potential usefulness of an alternative approach.

Given this reasoning, it is perhaps surprising that in early 2011 the government returned to pursue pension reform through social dialog, and an agreement was reached between the government and the two major union confederations in late January. Again, it is useful to look at public opinion data for a possible explanation. According to surveys, Zapatero's turn against the unions had been of little assistance in boosting his popularity with voters. In an October national survey, right after the general strike, 81.4 percent of respondents stated that Zapatero inspired "little" or "no" confidence; 58.5 percent rated the PSOE government as "bad" or "very bad," almost 10 percentage points more than half a year earlier; and on a scale of 0 (very bad) to 10 (very good), Zapatero scored a mean of 3.46, barely putting him ahead of the PP leader Rajoy with 3.42.[16] Thus, passing the labor market reform against union opposition had failed to help Zapatero recover the public's confidence. Unions were likewise motivated to return to dialog, even at the cost of making concessions: In the same survey, 70.5 percent of respondents evaluated the general strike as a failure, and a mere 7.5 percent judged it as successful.[17] Thus, confrontation had failed to boost either the government's or the unions' popularity. And public opinion mattered for the government, especially given electoral considerations: As the regional and local elections of May 2011 approached, PSOE leaders commented that the disagreement with the unions "delegitimizes our policies," also reasoning that "[i]t is not the same whether we begin the election campaign with a strike or the threat of a strike, or with a pact with the unions."[18]

The reestablishment of social dialog led to a successful tripartite agreement in February 2011. The Social and Economic Agreement on Growth, Employment, and Guaranteed Pensions, in addition to the pension reform, also included an agreement on industrial policy and one on active labor market policies. Moreover, it included a bipartite accord between the government and the unions on a public administration reform and a bilateral agreement between the unions and employers on a reform of the collective bargaining system. The unions made considerable concessions as they accepted a rise in retirement age in return for active labor market policies and measures to improve the social protection of the unemployed. The agreement on active labor market policies was subsequently adopted as a royal decree, the *Acuerdo Social y Económico para el Crecimiento, el Empleo y la Garantía de las Pensiones* 2011 (Sanz de Miguel 2011).

Unions and the Popular Party Government

The victory of the Popular Party under the leadership of Mariano Rajoy during the November 20, 2011, general election was unsurprising given the government's poor ratings in public opinion surveys and the depth of the recession. With 44.6 percent of the vote, the PP won an absolute majority of the seats (186 out of 350). The PSOE, in turn, suffered a crushing defeat, gaining just 28.8 percent of the votes and 110 seats, a loss of 15 percentage points of votes and 59 seats. Notably, the leftist IU almost doubled its vote share from 3.8 percent to 6.9 percent, winning 11 seats.

Rajoy was confronted with the continuing economic recession, necessitating cutting the budget, resolving the soaring unemployment rates that exceeded 20 percent, and restoring international confidence in the

Spanish economy. Prior to his inauguration as prime minister, Rajoy met with the leaders of the UGT, CC.OO., and CEOE separately to announce that he was willing to negotiate an agreement on the labor market reform.[19] Negotiations between unions and employers early on in Rajoy's administration produced agreements on several issues, such as moving several holidays to a Monday to limit the number of extended "bridge holidays" between weekends and midweek holidays, training, and early retirement. Since then, however, it has become obvious that in case of failed negotiations or when the government lacks interest in involving the social partners, Rajoy can easily pass a reform in Congress given the PP's ample majority as an alternative way of reforming policies. While the unions preferred issues such as wage policy, a reform of the collective bargaining system, and dismissals to be subject to negotiations, the government pushed a profound labor market reform through in Congress. The new law makes dismissals considerably cheaper for the employers, gives employers more leeway in determining employment conditions, such as work schedules and times when economic reasons can be claimed, and changes the collective bargaining structures in several ways, including prioritizing firm-level agreements over higher-level agreements.[20] The unions, in return, reacted by staging a general strike on March 29, 2012, on the 100-day anniversary of the Rajoy government and on the eve of his announcements of far-reaching budget cuts. While the turnout for the general strike was stronger than for the one against Zapatero, it nonetheless failed to change the government's policy reform.

Given the continuing financial and economic crisis in Spain, the strong majority of the PP in Congress, the EU pressures on Spain in light of the crisis of the euro, the weak labor market, and the PP's unilateral labor market reform, it is difficult to interpret the earlier agreements between the social partners as an indicator of union strength, thus perpetuating the debate on whether the social pacts are an expression of union strength or weakness (see Martínez Lucio 2011, 334). By July 2012, Rajoy's administration had not met once with the unions since the government's inauguration. When the government announced the most far-reaching economic adjustments since Spain's return to democracy on July 13, 2012, public opposition to these measures became visible immediately as widespread demonstrations and protests were held in Madrid following the announcement of the adjustment policies. These measures include cutting the Christmas bonus for public workers (a pay cut of about 7 percent), fewer holidays for public workers, an increase in sales taxes (VAT, value added tax), additional environmental taxes, an acceleration of pension cuts, and cuts in unemployment benefits, among others.[21]

Unions had not been consulted on these or other measures designed to meet the pressures of the EU to reform the economy and the financial system. At the same time, miners demonstrated in Madrid against cuts in subsidies for coal mines, leading to mine closures; the demonstration turned violent, leading to over 70 protesters and police officers being injured.[22] Thus, the government's actions face profound public resistance, and unions fear that the measures announced by the government will lead to yet higher unemployment rates, which in turn would weaken the economy even more. It is unlikely that the government will resort to bipartite or tripartite concertation in the near future, given its strong position in Congress. At the same time, demonstrations, strikes, and social unrest against the government's austerity measures are likely to continue, especially if the economy continues to perform sluggishly and unemployment remains high. It is unclear how the government will respond to social unrest and expressions of popular discontent with its policies. Unions will certainly continue to play a role in organizing and channeling this public discontent and will thus retain an important role in Spanish politics, even if they are not in a position of direct negotiations with the government.

Conclusion: Implications for Unions and Spanish Democracy

The second government of José Luis Zapatero in many ways continued existing patterns of union-government relationships. While the specifics of this relationship have been variable in the past, the general pattern highlighted contingency and lack of institutionalization. In other words, unions and the government were close during some periods and found themselves in opposition during others. These patterns did not neatly fit economic patterns, nor did they easily correspond to the party of the chief executive. Rather, the strength of the government and electoral considerations appeared to be more closely linked to the relationship between the government and the two major union confederations, especially as it was expressed through union inclusion in policy formation through national-level social pacts.

Union involvement in policymaking through concertation has been an important strategy for unions to exert influence. The Spanish industrial relations system provides few incentives for workers to join unions, given the existence of extension clauses for collective bargaining agreements; similarly, the system provides little incentive for unions to privilege membership and organizational strength over political action as union strength is better measured by results in union elections at the workplace. In addition, the structure of the Spanish economy with its emphasis on small enterprises presents another obstacle for strengthening membership and organization. The major union confederations' reliance on political influence through agreements with governments and also employers thus appears as a logical choice. At the same time, however, the second Zapatero government demonstrated that despite periods of union inclusion and influence in policymaking, this approach leaves unions vulnerable when agreements fail or when governments are not inclined to seek consent with the unions, be it out of choice or necessity. Having formerly participated in the policymaking process concerning labor market and employment issues, unions can be seen as partially responsible for the structural problems that still exist in these areas and that became evident when the economic crisis propelled the unemployment rates to new heights. This includes the duality of the labor market, as the massive job shedding of workers with fixed-term contracts during the second Zapatero government vividly demonstrated. The ability of the unions to defend workers' interests thus remains to a large extent contingent on the willingness of the government to include unions in the policymaking process.

The measures taken by Prime Minister Rajoy in 2012 in response to EU bailout measures and pressures to propel the economy and financial system out of the profound crisis will likely further deteriorate labor market conditions, which are characterized by high unemployment, particularly of people under 30 years of age, and a large proportion of employed people on temporary contracts rather than in stable employment situations. These patterns in employment conditions are not new, but rather have been a characteristic of Spanish democracy since its inception in the mid-to-late 1970s, which coincided with the global economic crisis caused by the global oil crisis. In Spain, these economic pressures had to be met before a new system of employment relations and welfare system were institutionalized. As the economic pressures were immediate and urgent, the reform of labor market policies was postponed, and remnants of the labor market regulations and collective bargaining institutions and procedures established under the dictatorship were only repealed in the 1990s. Thus, the problems currently observed in the labor market have their roots in the institutions of the Franco regime, and the nature of the transition to democracy, which privileged the transition of some parts of the political system (such as the party system) over others (such as labor market regulations, or the system of the autonomous regions). The implications of this gradual and prolonged reform of the labor market have far-reaching implications, since employment is closely tied to access to the welfare system as well as social unrest, as the demonstrations and general strikes during the last years of Zapatero's government as well as Rajoy's administration to date powerfully illustrate.

Notes

The author would like to thank Bonnie Field and Manfred Bienefeld for helpful comments and suggestions on previous drafts of this chapter.

1. Online OECD employment database. Trade union density in OECD countries, 1960–2008. Available at: http://www.oecd.org/document/34/0,3343, en_2649_33927_40917154_1_1_1_1,00.html#union.
2. Instituto Nacional de Estadística (INE), *Notas de prensa: encuesta de población activa (EPA)*. *Cuarto trimestre de 2009*, January 29, 2010. Available at: http://www.ine.es/daco/daco42/daco4211/epa0409.pdf.
3. The percentage of the workforce employed in construction increased from 8.7 to 14.3 between 1997 and 2007 (Ruesga 2007, 195).
4. Ministerio de Trabajo e Inmigración, "Beneficiarios de prestaciones según tipo de prestación," in *Boletín de Estadísticas Laborales*, January 2011. Available at: http://www.mtin.es/estadisticas/bel/PRD/prd1_top_HTML.htm.
5. INE, *Notas de prensa: encuesta de población activa (EPA)*. *Cuarto trimestre de 2009*, January 29, 2010, p. 1; V. Burnett, "Unemployment in Spain Hits 17.4%," *New York Times*, April 25, 2009; OECD, *Employment Outlook 2009—How Does SPAIN Compare?* Available at: http://www.oecd.org /dataoecd/62/35/43707074.pdf.
6. European Commission, *Key Figures on the Employment and Social Situation in EU Member States*, December 2011. Available at: http://ec.europa.eu /social/BlobServlet?docId=7267&langId=en.
7. F. Garea, "Zapatero salva el plan de ajuste por un voto gracias a la abstención de CiU, CC y UPN," *El País*, May 27, 2010.
8. L. Abellán, "Protesta de guante blanco por las pensiones," *El País*, February 24, 2010; M. González, "Zapatero: 'A los que discrepan les digo: mi Gobierno es de diálogo, no de decretazo,'" *El País*, February 24, 2010.
9. M. V. Gómez and L. R. Aizpeolea, "La respuesta de los sindicatos al recorte arranca con una huelga de funcionarios," *El País*, May 14, 2010.
10. "CCOO y UGT ven cada vez más cerca la huelga general," *El País*, May 21, 2010.
11. F. Garea, "El PP no obstaculizará la tramitación urgente de la reforma laboral," *El País*, June 18, 2010; F. Garea and A. Díez, "El PP se abstendrá en la convalidación de la reforma laboral," *El País*, June 22, 2010; F. Garea, "El PSOE convalida en solitario una reforma laboral provisional," *El País*, June 23, 2010; A. Díez, "El PSOE pone en marcha la sanción a Antonio Gutiérrez," *El País*, June 24, 2010.
12. UGT, *UGT y CCOO presentan los criterios para la negociación colectiva ante la no renovación del ANC*, 2009. Available at: http://www.ugt.es/actualidad/2009

/marzo/a09032009.html. In 2008, no new agreement was negotiated; instead, the 2007 ANC was extended in an amended form for another year.
13. L. Abellán, "El pacto de convenios insta a atajar la temporalidad en las empresas," *El País*, February 10, 2010. For the text of the agreement, see http://www.boe.es/boe/dias/2010/02/22/pdfs/BOE-A-2010-2844.pdf.
14. Centro de Investigaciones Sociológicas (CIS) study 2834. Available at: www.cis.es.
15. CIS studies 2636, 2732, 2831.
16. CIS study 2847.
17. CIS study 2847.
18. Cited in A. Díez, "El PSOE llama a rebato a 300 cargos para la defensa del gran pacto social," *El País*, January 17, 2011.
19. C. E. Cué, "Rajoy da un mes para un acuerdo muy difícil sobre la reforma laboral," *El País*, November 30, 2011.
20. See M. V. Gómez, "La reforma laboral definitiva se publica en el BOE y entra en vigor," *El País*, July 7, 2012.
21. F. Garea, "Rajoy trata de evitar el derrumbe con el mayor recorte en democracia," *El País*, July 12, 2012.
22. F. J. Barroso, "La 'marcha negra' minera termina con ocho detenidos y 76 heridos leves," *El País*, July 12, 2012.

WorksC ited

Albarracín, D. 2005. *New Procedure Introduced for Extending Collective Agreements.* EIROnline. Available at: http://www.eurofound.europa.eu/.
Bernardi, F., and S. Sarasa. 2009. "Las nuevas políticas sociales del Gobierno de Zapatero." In A. Bosco and I. Sánchez-Cuenca, eds., *La España de Zapatero: Años de cambios.* Madrid, Editorial Pablo Iglesias, pp. 227–48.
CES (Consejo Económico y Social). 2009. *Memoria sobre la situación socioeconómica y laboral de España en 2008.* Madrid: CES.
European Commission. 2009. *Employment in Europe.* Luxembourg: Office for Official Publications of the European Communities.
———. 2010. *Employment in Europe.* Luxembourg: Office for Official Publications of the European Communities.
———. 2011. *Labour Market Developments in Europe, 2011.* Available at: http://ec.europa.eu/economy_finance/publications/european_economy/2011/pdf/ee-2011-2_en.pdf.
Field, B. N. 2009. "A 'Second Transition' in Spain? Policy, Institutions and Interparty Politics under Zapatero (2004–8)." *South European Society and Politics* 14(4): 379–97.
Fishman, R. M. 2007. "On Being a Weberian (after Spain's 11–14 March): Notes on the Continuing Relevance of the Methodological Perspective Proposed by Weber." In L. McFalls, ed., *Max Weber's "Objectivity" Reconsidered.* Toronto: University of Toronto Press, pp. 261–89.

————. 2012. "Anomalies of Spain's Economy and Economic Policy-Making." *Contributions to Political Economy* 31(1): 67–76.

Hamann, K. 2012. *The Politics of Industrial Relations: Labor Unions in Spain.* London & New York: Routledge.

Hamann, K., and J. Kelly. 2011. *Parties, Elections, and Policy Reforms in Western Europe: Voting for Social Pacts.* London & New York: Routledge.

Hamann, K., A. Johnston, and J. Kelly. 2013. "Unions against Governments: Explaining General Strikes in Western Europe, 1980–2006." *Comparative Political Studies.* First published on October 29, 2012 as doi:10.1177/0010414012463894.

Lago, I., and J. R. Montero. 2006. "The 2004 Election in Spain: Terrorism, Accountability, and Voting." *Taiwan Journal of Democracy* 2(1):13–36.

Martín Artiles, A. 2005. *Third Agreement Signed on Resolving Labour Disputes Out of Court.* EIROnline. Available at: http://www.eurofound.europa.eu/.

Martínez Lucio, M. 1992. "Spain: Constructing Institutions and Actors in a Context of Change." In A. Ferner and R. Hyman, eds., *Industrial Relations in the New Europe.* Oxford: Basil Blackwell, pp. 482–523.

————. 2011. "El contexto de las relaciones laborales." In M. González Menéndez, R. Gutiérrez Palacios, and M. Martinez Lucio, eds., *Gestión de recursos humanos: Contexto y políticas.* Cizur Menor: Editorial Aranzadi, pp. 327–42.

Monger, J. 2003. "International Comparisons of Labour Disputes in 2001." *Labour Market Trends* 111(4): 181–89.

Mulas-Granados, C. 2009. "La economía española: del 'boom' a la crisis." In Bosco and Sánchez-Cuenca, eds., *La España de Zapatero,* pp. 179–204.

Pitxer i Campos, J. V., and A. Sánchez Velasco. 2008. "Estrategias sindicales y modelo económico español." *Cuadernos de Relaciones Laborales* 26(1): 89–122.

Rigby, M., and M. L. Marco Aledo. 2001. "The Worst Record in Europe? A Comparative Analysis of Industrial Conflict in Spain." *European Journal of Industrial Relations* 7(3): 287–305.

Ruesga, S. 2007. "Treinta años de movimiento continuo en el mercado laboral español." In F. Valdés Dal-Ré, ed., *30 años de libertad sindical.* Madrid: Fundación Francisco Caballero, pp. 186–215.

Sala Franco, T. 2007. "La concertación y el diálogo social durante el período 1990–2007." In Valdés Dal-Ré, ed., *30 años de libertad sindical,* pp. 134–49.

Sainz de Miguel, P. 2009. *Green Light for New Unemployment Protection Measure.* EIROnline. Available at: http://www.eurofound.europa.eu/.

Sanz, P. 2010. *Cause and Effect of General Strike.* EIROnline. Available at: http://www.eurofound.europa.eu/.

Sanz de Miguel, P. 2010. *Government Approves Law Proposing Urgent Labour Market Reform.* EIROnline. Available at: http://www.eurofound.europa.eu/.

————. 2011. *Agreement Signed on Growth, Employment and Guaranteed Pensions.* EIROnline. Available at: http://www.eurofound.europa.eu/.

Torcal, M., and G. Rico. 2004. "The 2004 Spanish General Election: In the Shadow of Al-Qaeda?" *South European Society & Politics* 9(3): 107–21.

Urquizu, I. 2008. "9-M: Elecciones tras la crispación." *Claves de Razón Práctica* 181: 48–54.

CHAPTER 8

Youth Protests and the End of the ZapateroGo vernment

Carmelo Adagio

The year 2011 marks the end of José Luis Rodríguez Zapatero's political trajectory. In 2004 he became a symbol of renewal for the European left, taking power at a time of crisis for social democracy. He had presented himself as an innovator, setting out a plan for a "citizens' socialism," which made Spain a leading country as far as the recognition of important citizen rights are concerned (Calvo 2009; Maravall 2009). An assessment at the end of his first mandate as prime minister already revealed some negative signs, particularly in immigration and economic policy, as well as positive ones (Field 2011). In his second mandate, however, his destiny was linked to the economic crisis, which hit Spain harder than the rest of Europe. Indeed, in Spain the European crisis was preceded by the implosion of the construction boom, which in the space of just a few years destroyed millions of jobs.[1] From the beginning of 2010 Zapatero was dragged into a sad decline made up of errors, a fall in both internal and international credibility, and a loss of decision-making autonomy vis-à-vis European bodies. Within this context, Zapatero witnessed the growth of a significant youth opposition movement that reached its peak in 2011, bringing Spain back under the international spotlight.

The extent and breadth of the mobilizations against the political and economic system throughout the entire country were without doubt among the most important events in 2011, which was an election year (first the local and regional elections in May, then the early general elections in November). Young people took a leading role in the early days of *Zapaterismo*; they made up the majority of those taking part in the preelection day events in March 2004, when the Spaniards who were "indignant" about Prime Minister José María Aznar's lies about the terrorist attacks at the Atocha train station took to the streets; and much of the support for Zapatero's policies on civil rights, the withdrawal of troops from Iraq, and the recovery of historical memory came from the young. Yet an even more widespread youth movement took center stage in 2011, when Spain's city squares were occupied in protests against Zapatero, who was by then seen as no less of an adversary than the European Union (EU) bureaucrats or the opposition Popular Party (PP). The movement came to be known as 15M (due to its launching on May 15) or *los indignados* (the indignant).

The spectacular size of the protest raises a number of questions. First of all, how did the movement that took to the Spanish streets and squares form and spread between May 15 and October 15, 2011? Who did it consist of? What were its core issues? How did it rise up? Finally, when considering the elections, it is fair to ask whether it had any effect on the results. We will attempt to address these questions in the sections that follow.

May 15–October 15: A Crescendo of Mobilizations

On Sunday, May 15, 2011, at 6 p.m., a popular demonstration took place in 60 Spanish town squares by a newly formed group of associations called *Democracia real ya* (Real Democracy Now). Those taking part were asked not to carry any symbols of a political or trade union nature. This demonstration was hugely successful: tens of thousands of people marched through Madrid.[2] When the demonstration in Puerta del Sol, the central square in Madrid, came to an end, a spontaneous sit-in was staged in Plaza de Callao; when the police intervened and made a few arrests, a group of protestors decided to stay and occupy the square. Around 40 people, according to some reports, slept there on Sunday night (other sources refer to 150 or 200 people). The next morning, the police cleared the occupation, which led to clashes on several streets in the city center and traffic was blocked along one of Madrid's main thoroughfares, Gran Vía. A number of protestors were detained and 18 were arrested, which led to more crowds gathering and calling for their release.[3] In Barcelona, too, they created #acampadabcn and the city's central square, Plaza de Cataluña, was occupied for the night by 150 people, following the example of Madrid. These came to be known as *acampadas* or campouts. Similar events took place in Malaga, Granada, Seville, Bilbao, and Zaragoza.

A spontaneous popular assembly took place on the Monday evening in Madrid, and other protestors decided to remain for the night. At dawn on Tuesday the police once again moved in to clear the streets. When several dozen protestors put up passive resistance there were scuffles with the police dressed in antiriot gear, who attempted to break up the protestors by carrying out a number of detentions and one arrest. The protestors appeared to surrender, but in reality they were using their cell phones and the Internet to send out a call for another demonstration that same evening at 8 P.M. in Puerta del Sol. The demonstration was a huge success, and another *acampada* was set up. These camps were beginning to emerge in all Spanish cities, and they were all reporting to each other. There was no longer one single organizing body: communications were moving horizontally through the social networks. The hashtag #acampadasol became a "trendy topic" on Twitter. The Puerta del Sol assembly began to organize into work committees, with the support of shopkeepers and residents of the area, who took charge of supplies. In the evening there were an estimated 12,000 people.

There were *acampadas* in 30 Spanish cities on the night of May 17,[4] including Barcelona, Seville, Bilbao, Burgos, Segovia, la Coruña, Toledo, Cáceres, and Salamanca. In spite of the police ban, tents were set up and preparations made to stay all night.

On the morning of May 18, the Madrid square became the symbol of the movement that now took the form of a camp ground; the movement activists formed a number of committees to take care of logistical matters (cleaning, communications, food, coordination, legal support, and so forth), while the assembly continued to act as the decision-making body. A webcam began to provide minute-by-minute coverage of events in Puerta del Sol. In various locations across Spain, squares were cleared (Valencia, Tenerife, Las Palmas, and Granada), as the entire international press began to report on the "Spanish revolution."[5]

The movement of assemblies and campouts had by now spread all over the peninsula. According to a survey carried out by the Ikimap website,[6] it had already spread to 52 localities by May 18. During the day of May 18, there was a possible turning point when the election board in Madrid declared a ban on demonstrations due to the disruption they could cause during the preelection period (the local and regional elections in Madrid were due to be held on May 22).[7] Similar bans were announced in Seville and Granada. But the reaction to the bans merely served to bolster the number of people in the square. The police in Madrid held off from intervening, while thousands of young people stayed until dawn.

By Thursday the entire square was occupied. A number of meetings were held at the same time, while in the evening there was a large concentration of protestors in open defiance of the ban. A petition declaring the ban null and void was signed by 100,000 people in just a few hours. A website for the movement published a very long list of cities in Spain and outside Spain in which demonstrations were taking place, either in city squares or outside Spanish embassies.[8] At midnight on Thursday the election council prohibited all gatherings on Saturday, May 21, and Sunday, May 22, the former being the day before an election on which no campaigning is allowed and the latter election day, but no ban could halt the demonstrations in the squares, which on the contrary were growing. It was no longer just in Puerta del Sol; it was all of Spain that was seeing an unprecedented wave of participation, whose shape and spread was without no precedent.

On May 21, despite the bans, tens of thousands of people demonstrated all over Spain. According to police figures, there were 28,000 in Madrid, 10,000 in Valencia, 7,000 in Malaga, 4,000 in Seville, 5,000 in Barcelona, 3,000 in Bilbao, and 3,000 in Palma de Mallorca.[9] The movement ignored the May 22 elections, and continued for the next few days. The most significant event of the week following the elections took place on May 27 in Barcelona when the police used brute force to clear the square, with injuries (several dozen) and arrests.[10] The force used by the police (which was repeated in Lérida and Sabadell) provoked more protests, and squares all over Spain were filled.

When faced with the danger of a silent withdrawal, the Madrid *acampada* made a decision on Sunday, May 29, to dismantle the camp and to move their protest to the different town halls of the Madrid region and to districts within the city. A smaller camp was to remain in Puerta del Sol until Sunday, June 12. The fact that the decision to decentralize the protest was not a sign of backing down was made clear by a new day of protests on June 19. The movement took to the squares in 60 cities to protest against the euro agreement,[11] with over 15 million people taking part. The largest demonstrations were in Madrid, Valencia, Seville, Malaga, and Murcia.

This mobilization was large, despite taking place in the summer. In July a "popular indignant march" took place, bringing the entire nation together. Groups of protestors on foot or on bicycles set out from various locations in Spain to reach Puerta del Sol square, where between July 23 and 26 various rallies and national meetings were held to work out plans and to build mobilization campaigns for the fall (the first 15M Social Forum).[12] A date was chosen for the fall (October 15), which would correspond with demonstrations in other cities around the world. Hundreds of thousands of people throughout Spain were joined in protest against the crisis. This time, with the usual variations in the numbers reported, there were an estimated 600,000 people in Madrid and 400,000 in Barcelona.[13]

What Type of Movement Was This?

It is obviously impossible to provide an exhaustive list of those who took part in the camps and assemblies. However, the movement has left its very clear mark on websites, blogs, social network pages, leaflets, posters, and books.[14] A number of TV websites (e.g., http://www.soltv.tv/) provided live broadcasts of many of the demonstrations and assemblies. There were various amusing photographs that attempted to build a montage showing those who took part (e.g., on the website http://acampadabcn. wordpress.com/), underlining the cross-section of generations within the movement, and the variety and levels of cultural and class components. There were also a number of newspaper features emphasizing the different generations represented. However, all the evidence points to the huge preponderance of young people. Other reports highlighted the presence of "two souls." On the one hand, activists from alternative social movements, activists from squatter social centers, and *okupas*. These activists had been involved in countless protests over a number of years, were continuously active and in the public eye during the 15M days and at other times, driving trucks, playing music, carrying out the actual organization of demonstrations, and preparing slogans and rallying cries. But, on the other hand, a second soul was soon emerging. A large number of young people without a clear leftist activist identity were soon to represent what was really new about the Spanish movement. These young people were mainly in the postschool and postadolescence stage, that is, an age group for which the economic figures in Spain revealed alarming trends: dizzyingly high levels of unemployment for 18- to 29-year-olds, the highest in Europe; and a very high percentage of young people still living at home with their parents. A generation of young Spaniards, the so-called Neither-nor (*Ni-ni*) generation because they do not work or go to school, who are unemployed and unable to live independently, and whose only realistic prospects are poor work contracts, low salaries, and precarious jobs, often in spite of having excellent educational backgrounds.[15]

The picture that emerges from newspaper accounts, anecdotal evidence, and films is confirmed by the first sociological analysis of the *acampadas* participants and those attending the assemblies; the bulk of the movement was made up of people between the ages of 19 and 30 (Calvo et al. 2011). It is more difficult to analyze the broader social make-up of the *indignados*. In the absence of statistics, this has to be based on subjective impressions, anecdotal evidence, descriptions, and self-portrayals. The impression is that, socially, they were a section of the middle class, albeit one that was largely impoverished and forced into unstable jobs. They were either jobless or in temporary employment, but there were also salaried employees and professionals. Above all, however, they were from the highly educated middle class. There was not a high degree of working-class participation, at least not via its organizations, although some individuals did become involved.

Research carried out a few weeks after 15M also outlines the appeal of the movement. According to a study by Metroscopia on behalf of the *El País* daily newspaper, 64 percent of the population supported the movement, 71 percent considered it a peaceful movement whose aim was to rebuild democracy (it is interesting to note that the percentage rises to 83 percent among PSOE voters and drops to 54 percent among PP voters), and only 17 percent considered it a radical, antisystem movement. In a word, as far as 79 percent of Spaniards were concerned, the *indignados* were right.[16] However, the number sympathizing with the 15M movement drops to 44.8 percent in the survey carried out by NC Report for the newspaper *La Razón*.[17] The disparity between these figures means that it is not possible to speak of strong support. However, evidence that support was indeed widespread is also provided by the poll conducted by IPSOS, which showed that not only did 78 percent of Spaniards know of the 15M movement, but even more significantly somewhere between six and eight million people took part in one way or another in an *acampada*, the demonstrations or assemblies, at least on one occasion. Among these, two-thirds consider themselves to be on the left, while the others are center-left or not affiliated with any party; only 3 percent described themselves as on the right.[18]

To grasp one of the most interesting aspects of the movement, it is worth examining the forms of participation that it preferred. These forms clearly show the importance of a large, educated, middle-class presence among the ranks of the movement. First of all, the use of social networks played a key role. The 15M movement would have been impossible without the use of cellphones connected to the Internet. The countless connections that amplified and multiplied rallying cries and slogans but also invitations to take part in demonstrations and assemblies made it possible to rapidly spread the word about meetings and to share information, enabling the horizontal multiplication of participants. The concept of network in the birth of the movement and in the structure it developed is crucial: every single point in the network acted as an exponential multiplier.[19] Far from creating isolation, connecting to the Internet increased the opportunities to create communities on the social networks. Thus a new N-1 network[20] was created as an alternative to the Facebook and Twitter services to promote internal communications and the organization of events.

The horizontal nature of the movement was underlined by the lack of recognized leaders and by the crucial role played by the assemblies. There were different ways and opportunities to be present and active: the assembly, which held sovereign decision-making powers, ran alongside the activities of logistical committees (legal, communications, food supplies, cleaning, childcare, and so forth) and various working groups (culture, ecology, work, economy, gender, politics, housing, among others). Thus the ability to take part was determined by the availability of free time, with a circular decision-making process from the assembly to the committees, on to the working groups, and then back to the assembly. The study carried out on the Salamanca *acampada* made it clear that participation levels fluctuated between one-third of activists being involved in committees, working groups, and the running of the camp and two-thirds who only attended assemblies because they had less free time (Calvo et al. 2011). The creativity displayed by the movement was accompanied by a respect for the different individuals involved and the participation of a wide range of professions in the assemblies, which was useful both for logistics and communications. The running of the assemblies and in particular the decision-making brought the presence of mediators and facilitators into play, making it possible to allow more informed types of participation.[21]

This great ability to manage meetings and communications, to organize the squares and assemblies, also derives from the dense network of mobilizations that had taken place in Spain over the prior recent months, opening the way for the 15M explosion. In fact, this movement came about as a result of a combination of hard work by a number of young individuals and others who became antagonized as the crisis went out of control and youth unemployment figures soared.

Preliminary assessments by journalists identified a variety of origins from which the movement grew. Some have spoken of a wave that brought together *Nunca más*, the group of associations created in Galicia after the Prestige oil tanker disaster, and the anti–Iraq War demonstrations held by pacifists in 2003, and also demonstrations called (once again largely organized via the Internet and text messages) following the

Atocha atrocity of March 13, 2004. However, in my opinion, that wave of protests was directed mainly against Aznar's Popular Party, and played a significant role in bringing about a change of government, allowing the Socialist Party (PSOE) to regain power and return to the Moncloa government palace. It is more interesting, in my view, to examine the emergence of the various youth groups characterized by a growing hostility and/or disaffection toward Zapatero's policies, as a result of the onset and the persistence of the economic crisis. Zapatero's reelection in 2008 coincided with the outbreak of the economic crisis caused by the bursting of the construction bubble. Zapatero's entire second mandate was therefore marked by continuous protest movements, which, although modest in size to start, challenged the social and economic policies of the PSOE and also of the European Union, whose commanding influence on Spanish national policies was seen to be growing.

Connected to the later 15M movement, as testified by some of the iconographic materials, was the *V de vivienda* movement, inspired by the name of the graphic novel *V for vendetta* by Alan Moore, which became a successful film thanks to James McTeigue. In May 2006, two separate demonstrations were held on May 14 and 21, the first of which moved along the streets of Madrid, from Puerta del Sol to the seat of the Congress, and the second met with severe repression on the part of the police in antiriot gear. In spite of that, on July 2 several thousand people marched in Madrid shouting slogans about the right to a home and the struggle against unstable work. The protest was organized through various websites and covered a number of cities. Activism against evictions and in favor of a new policy on housing grew until the housing crisis struck, after which it was an issue that bubbled below the surface in other mobilizations up to the 15M. Mortgages, bank debts, and evictions have been at the center of discussions, blogs, and planning discussions at numerous sit-ins, *acampadas*, and demonstrations for many years.[22]

During the following months a university movement composed of a number of groups arose with the common aim of fighting against the so-called Bologna process. Set into motion as early as 1999 to create a European space for higher education, the agreement between the European nations was not formally ratified until March 2010, and it provoked the rise of a university movement aimed at opposing what was seen as the "marketization" or privatization of universities. In a more concrete sense, it was the increasingly precarious job situation and the impression of the growing pointlessness of educational qualifications that created a sense of unease among the student population. This unease, as expressed in various slogans, was directed at the implementation of the "Bologna plan," and it took root in all of the leading Spanish universities.

The protest continued on the web, against the *Sinde* law (drafted by the minister of culture Ángeles González-Sinde) the Zapatero government introduced in 2010 to fight computer piracy, which was criticized for gagging certain websites and accused of reintroducing censorship. The fight against the law actually directly affected the minister, who had been a scriptwriter and film director, and it was led by a number of activist media groups, such as *anonymus* and *nolevotes*.[23]

The issues connected to unstable work, housing, employment, and university education, in a climate of a worsening economic crisis, provided a common platform for a new group known as *Juventud sin futuro (JSF—Youth without a future)*, whose initials first appeared at the beginning of 2011 when various university groups that had been fighting for some years against the "Bologna plan" came together to oppose the labor reforms introduced by the Zapatero government during 2010 and the reform of pensions early in 2011. The movement staged a demonstration on April 7, 2011, and its success surpassed all expectations, with around 10,000 young people taking part. At that point JSF responded to the call for the May 15 (15M) demonstration, thereby positioning itself as one of the "basic ingredients" of the future movement. The first few months of 2011 also saw the appearance of *Democracia real ya*, a group of associations that was the first to put forward the idea of the 15M demonstration, and whose manifesto covered similar issues to those of *Juventud sin futuro*, but couched in language that was drawn less from the militant left than JSF's manifesto.[24]

It is not the task of this chapter to extract a coherent programmatic platform from the multiplicity of interest groups represented. However it seems clear that those who organized the demonstrations and those who took part were demanding a change in Spanish politics and society, and that above all they did not feel represented in the political system, at least not in the current two-party dominant one. The protest is definitely linked to the prolonged economic crisis, which took unemployment levels to 22.8 percent in 2011, the highest in the European Union, and youth unemployment (people below the age of 25) reached 48.5 percent.[25] These levels had not been seen in Spain since the early 1990s. The unstable work situation, the pressure on families caused by debt, the tightening of credit, and the government's welfare cuts all created a situation that favored 15M's success. The Zapatero government's economic policy had already sparked a general strike on September 20, 2010. The strike had been called by the Workers Commissions (CC.OO.)

and General Workers Union (UGT) opposing the labor reform proposed by Zapatero and approved by Congress earlier in September and the announced new pension reform (Rubio Lara 2012). An important role was also undoubtedly played by the publication of Stéphane Hessel's book *Indignez-vous!*, as well as the example of protests and revolutions that took place in the Arab world in the spring of 2011.[26]

The issues that were common to those who took part in the movement were therefore a protest against the existing political class, the need to end the two-party dominant system and the electoral law that favored it, as well as a protest against the many cases of corruption in the political system. Finally, an equally significant factor in its success was the decision to call the 15M demonstration in the middle of the election campaign before the local and regional elections of May 22. The context of the election campaign created a background that permitted the 15M's truly new and discordant messages to emerge and gain sympathizers.[27]

But Did 15M Have Any Influence on Zapatero's Downfall?

As soon as the local and regional elections were over, people began to ask whether and in what way the 15M movement had affected the results. A *Centro de Investigaciones Sociológicas* (CIS) study regarding the elections in the Madrid area shows that the influence on the vote was not significant, and that its effect was mainly on the minor parties. Only 25 percent of voters stated that they had been influenced by the demonstrations, while the *indignado* vote mainly benefited the United Left (IU) and Union, Progress and Democracy (UPD).[28] The analysis carried out by the *Fundación Alternativas* (Jiménez Sánchez 2011) was more ambitious. It took as a basic point the fact that the municipal elections of 2011 had seen the biggest increase in the number of blank and null votes since 1987, and that the increase of these votes was connected to the decrease in votes for the majority parties, which led them to conclude that the 15M demonstrations had had a direct effect on the election results, especially on the increased number of protest votes (blank ballots, null and void ballots, and an increase in the votes for the minor parties).[29]

The concerns about the possibility of evaluating the electoral influence of 15M also stems from the fact that it is impossible to identify a single position emanating from the movement as far as elections were concerned. Many and varied demands emerged from the heterogeneous world of 15M, swinging between campaigns for abstention, encouraging null votes, or strategic votes (*voto útil*), or voting for minor parties, in order to punish PSOE and PP as much as possible. At a national meeting held in Madrid on October 8 and 9, it proved impossible to come to any consensus on calls to promote null votes or appeals to refuse to vote for the PSOE or PP. The only agreement that was reached was on the motions that stated: "(a) the only voice of 15M is its assemblies, and (b) no political party represents us."[30] As far as the elections of November 20 are concerned, and any influence 15M may have had on them, the postelection survey results published by CAPDEA (*Centro de Análisis y Documentación Política y Electoral de Andalucía*) are available. Although about 25 percent of those interviewed state that they had been influenced by the movement when expressing their vote, this only led to very few null votes or abstentions. As far as the majority of interviewees were concerned, they had been influenced either by becoming more convinced about which party they should vote for or by shifting their vote to another party, but the survey does not investigate in which direction these shifts occurred.[31]

The impression is that if we wish to quantify the influence of 15M on the election results, it appears to be negligible[32] or not immediately perceptible. A brief examination of the results, compared with those of 2008, confirms this: there is a barely noticeable growth of blank votes and greater growth in the number of null votes, which double in number but remain quite low in absolute terms, moving from 165,000 to 317,000.[33] The drop in the turnout of 1,400,000 is without doubt more significant (over 6 percent). But the most important data lie elsewhere: the PSOE lost four million votes (one-third of the PSOE's electorate!), while the PP won only about 600,000 more votes than in 2008. In absolute terms IU (around 700,000 votes more than in 2008, with an increase of over 70 percent) and especially Rosa Díez's UPD party, which went from 300,000 to over 1,100,000 votes, gained the most.

Rather than simply analyzing the possible electoral impact of 15M, it is probably more interesting to take a broader perspective, looking at the drop in support for Zapatero's government between its first and second mandates. There is no doubt that the arrival of the crisis in 2008 caught both the governing party and the opposition party unprepared. In the preelection debates of 2008 Zapatero was hopeful in predicting that full employment would be reached during the 2008–12 term.[34] Until 2010, the PSOE government did not appear to have a clear understanding of the crisis situation. Only in May 2010, when there was evidence of a public deficit and negative growth forecasts, along with strong international pressure, did the government begin to take action (reform of the labor market, spending cuts, reduction in salaries for civil servants); it was questionable whether these actions would be effective and in any case their effects would be spread out over a period of time.[35] When faced with a crisis that was bringing unemployment levels back to those of the early 1990s, the Spanish people's awareness of the seriousness of the crisis grew, while at the same time their confidence that the government would be able to tackle it fell in equal measure. The study carried out by Pérez-Díaz and Rodríguez (2011) on the perception of the economic crisis is very significant; when responding to questions asked between the end of 2009 and early 2010 about whether they agreed with the government's approach to tackling the crisis, 78 percent of respondents stated openly that they disagreed. It is particularly interesting to note the separate data about voting intentions: 61 percent of PSOE voters disagree with Zapatero's economic policy, while 53 percent think that Zapatero, when speaking of the economic crisis, does not know what he is talking about (Pérez-Díaz & Rodríguez 2011, 200). The unemployment figures, which get worse from one month to the next (settling around the 20 percent mark in 2010 in overall terms, while youth unemployment reaches over 40 percent), point to an increasingly precarious situation, a return to the family as a social buffer, and work prospects for the young consisting of unemployment, illegal labor, temporary jobs, unemployment assistance, and the impossibility of living independently of the family. The generation that was expecting to move into the labor market between 2008 and 2012, far from experiencing full employment, is destined to face a series of work obstacles, whose medium- and long-term effects on their career paths and on their own sense of satisfaction are not easily predicted.

Therefore, from the end of 2010 growing youth mobilization was the expression of an ever-increasing dissatisfaction with the political class in general and above all with the PSOE government. This youth mobilization took an antiparty stance, although the values expressed by the protestors, along with their individual perceptions, were clearly leaning toward a left-wing political and cultural viewpoint. Consequently, this new youth movement showed indifference toward the 2011 elections. The various studies alluded to earlier also show that the PSOE voters were more sensitive than their PP counterparts to the issues raised by the 15M protests. The picture that emerges suggests that if 15M had any impact on the elections, it was mainly to highlight the predictable downfall of the PSOE, which was caused mainly by a huge drop in confidence among its traditional voters. In sum, it seems fairly clear that it was not so much a case of the PP winning the elections as of the PSOE losing them. The 15M movement, as the same studies show, had no effect whatsoever on the center-right vote, but it did contribute to the collapse in support for Zapatero, thereby punishing the party in government against which four years of youth protests and struggle had been aimed. Future analyses will need to clarify whether the votes lost by the PSOE went to IU, UPD, or PP, or whether they turned into abstentions. Nevertheless, the rejection of the PSOE is clear.

The Movement and the Escalating Financial Crisis in 2012

In the months after the Socialist defeat, the worsening economic situation and the Rajoy-led Popular Party government's choice to implement fiscal policies based on spending cuts and tax increases generated numerous reasons for protest. From the beginning of 2012 there were successive protests against the cuts, which took on mass proportions on several occasions, including the general strike on March 29, the so-called *primavera valenciana* (Valencian spring), and the Asturian miners' demonstrations beginning in May. The government's announcement in July 2012 of a plan for major cuts (65 million euros in two years), requested by the European Union in exchange for the rescue of Spain's faltering banking system, coincided with the arrival in Madrid of the miners' march (July 11), which was a prelude to a rekindling of social conflict in the fall. The *indignados* were present in all of these demonstration, and continued to call an international demonstration one year from the original May 15 demonstration, the so-called 12M 15M.[36] Their sites are active, and the reasons for the protests grow with the worsening of the financial situation in the eurozone.

It is not this chapter's task to speculate about how the new actors immersed in these events will confront the resumption of trade union and workers' mobilization, nor even whether and how the Spanish political system will be modified by the escalation of the crisis. However, it is clear that, as always in the history of democratic Spain, the outcome of the current crisis will be determined more by the influence of the vicissitudes of the eurozone than by local choices.

Notes

1. On the origins of the building crisis, see, among others, Naredo and Montiel Márquez (2011).
2. "Indignados en la calle," *El País*, May 17, 2011. The police announced the figure, probably an erroneous one, of 20,000 demonstrators in Madrid

alone. In all of Spain, adding together the scores of demonstrations, figures are estimated at several hundreds of thousands of protestors.

3. "La manifestación de 'Indignados' termina con 24 detenidos y cinco policías heridos," *Informativos Telecinco*, May 16, 2011.

4. "Acampadas en cadena hasta el próximo 22-M," *El Mundo*, May 17, 2011.

5. The hashtag #spanishrevolution proved to be very popular not only in Spain; media all over the world were talking about the *indignados*.

6. Available at: http://www.ikimap.com/map/2CYF.

7. "La Junta Electoral de Madrid prohíbe la concentración en la Puerta del Sol," *El País*, May 18, 2011.

8. See: http://tomalaplaza.net/lista-de-ciudades-que-ya-han-tomado-la-plaza/. Also see: "El espíritu de la acampada de Sol se reproduce por las ciudades españolas," *El País*, May 20, 2011, which refers to mobilizations in 67 Spanish cities and 15 cities outside Spain.

9. "Las concentraciones en toda España marcan la jornada de reflexión," *El País*, May 21, 2011.

10. "Los 'indignados' recuperan la plaza de Catalunya tras la retirada de la policía," *El País*, May 27, 2011; "La dureza policial multiplica la indignación en Barcelona," *El Mundo*, May 28, 2011.

11. Signed in March by the heads of state and government to tackle the crisis and to increase the competitiveness in the eurozone, the pact highlights the need for strong measures for countries hit by the crisis (particularly Spain, Greece, and Italy), and it came under fire as it could cause further deterioration of welfare levels and living standards in the countries caught in the crisis.

12. One surprising participant was the Nobel Prize winner Joseph Stiglitz.

13. "Sol ilumina medio mundo," *El País*, October 16, 2011.

14. Giving website references is often risky for a volume that is due to appear many months after it has been written. Some sites visited in previous months have in fact already disappeared. Here is a list of the sites that could be consulted on June 15, 2012: www.democraciarealya.es; www.tomalaplaza. net; http://acampadabcn.wordpress.com/; www.spanishrevolution.es; www .takethesquare.net/es; www.tomalosbarrios.net; www.movimiento15M. org; http://www.juventudsinfuturo.net/; http://bookcamping.cc/; http:// acampadas15m.blogspot.it/, http://acampadas.posterous.com/. Other publications that include primary materials and documents are: *Juventud sin futuro* (Barcelona: Icaria, 2011); *Las voces del 15-M* (Barcelona: Los Libros del Lince, 2011); *Hablan los indignados* (Madrid: Editorial Popular, 2011); Botey et al. (2011); Velasco (2012). There are different voices and testimonies in the comic book titled *Indignados! Suggerimenti per una Ri(E)voluzione* (Torino: 001 Edizioni, 2011), Spanish edition: *Yes, we camp! Trazos para una (R)evolución* (Madrid: Dibbuks, 2011) while, again in comic form, there is a reconstruction of the movement in Fuentes and Clarey (2011).

15. Pastor Verdú (2012) talks of the key role, as a driving force behind the movement, of young graduates, who have a strong educational background and face the rising threat of unstable work, bearing in mind that unemployment

rates among young Spanish graduates is around 12 percent, i.e., twice as high as the European average.

16. "El 15-M mantiene su apoyo ciudadano," *El País*, June 26, 2011.

17. "Más de la mitad de los españoles tacha de antidemocrático el 15-M," *La Razón*, June 20, 2011. The daily newspaper draws attention in its headline to the fact that half of those interviewed in the survey it commissioned were against the movement.

18. "Hasta ocho millones de personas aseguran haber participado en el 15-M," *El Mundo*, August 4, 2011. The CIS also refers to an enormous level of support for 15M, which was closely watched by 77 percent of the population, while only 0.9 percent stated that they had not heard of it. See Centro de Investigaciones Sociológicas (CIS) study 2.905 (June 2011), p. 12. Available at: www.cis.es.

19. For more on the Internet as an organizational structure, please see http://madrid.tomalosbarrios.net/reflexion-colectiva-de-la-c-de-barrios-sobre-la-asamblea-popular-de-madrid/.

20. See http://n-1.cc.

21. There are a number of very interesting and detailed pieces of work such as the *Guía rápida para la dinamización de Asambleas Populares* (written by the Comisión de Dinamización de Asambleas of the Acampada de Sol) and the *Propuesta de acuerdo del grupo de barrios para unas asambleas saludables*, collected in *Hablan los indignados*, pp. 69–95 (see Note 14).

22. See www.viviendadigna.org; madrid.vdevivienda.net; www.sindominio.net; www.encapuchadonaranja.com/v-de-vivienda; radiovdevivienda.blogspot.it; www.hipotecados.es. On the history of the Madrid movement for housing from 2006 to 2010, see Blanco Tomás (2011).

23. Alex de la Iglesia, Spanish film director, resigned as president of the Spanish Film Academy (*Academia de cine de España*) in protest against the Sinde law. The controversy lasted a long time, and, while it was not the main cause, it led to the announcement in September 2011, just a few weeks before the elections, of the minister's decision to leave politics in order to dedicate herself to cinema: "González-Sinde dejará la política tras el 20-N," *El País*, September 17, 2011. Regarding *Anonymous*, see *El País*, January 16, 2011, where there is reference to a group of 2,000 media activists who use the name *Anonymous*, inspired by the cartoon by Alan Moore and the film that was based on it. The hashtag #nolesvotes, however, first appeared in February 2011, following the approval of the Sinde law, and it becomes one of the most visited and retweeted "trendy topics" on Twitter in Spain. The movement of media activists aimed to punish the parties that supported the Sinde law, i.e., PSOE, PP and CIU, but it did not call for people to abstain. After a cyber-attack on the PSOE website in April 2011, the #nolesvotes activists joined in the call for the May 15 (15M) demonstration.

24. It is interesting to compare the founding manifestos and the websites. See http//www.democraciarealya.es and http://www.juventudsinfuturo.net/.

25. Instituto Nacional de Estadística (INE), *Encuesta de población activa*, third trimester, 2011. Available at: http://www.ine.es/daco/daco42/daco4211 /epa0311.pdf. Also see García (2011).

26. On the influence of the new forms of mobilization attempted during the Arab spring, see Cotarelo (2012).

27. The bibliography on 15M is beginning to grow. Leaving aside the endless list of articles in newspapers and news magazines, we refer here only to a few attempts at a reconstruction of events, which, notwithstanding their openly "activist" nature, are nevertheless quite useful. A first "instant" analysis is contained in the volumes published a few weeks apart by Carlos Taibo (2011a, b). There is a study that is part analysis and part political proposal in Charnock et al. (2011, 3–11). While the present study was being written, new studies were already beginning to emerge whose aim was to put the events into a historical and economic context, which I have been able to consult in draft form: I refer to the previously cited Pastor Verdú (2012), but also to Fishman (2012), who instead attempts a retrospective positioning within the history of Spanish democracy.

28. See http://www.electometro.es/2011/09/el-15m-beneficio-a-los-partidos -minoritarios/.

29. According to Jiménez Sánchez (2011): "In this paper we have conducted a preliminary analysis of the influence of the 15M movement on the results on the May 22, 2011 municipal elections. To do so, we selected a sample of 89 municipalities with more than 75,000 inhabitants and studied if the variations in blank votes, null votes and votes for major party candidates compared to the 2007 municipal elections are associated with the presence of the 15 M movement. The analysis shows that in those municipalites where protest votes are most intense the holding of demonstrations (and campouts) during the week prior to the election was more frequent. In this sense, we can tentatively conclude that the 15 M movement influenced the voting behavior of citizens in the local elections of 2011." Translated from the original Spanish.

30. See http://encuentro15m.tomalaplaza.net/consensos-8-y-9-de-octubre-2011/.

31. See http://cadpea.ugr.es/Egopa_ArchivoDocu.aspx.

32. According to Pastor Verdú (2012): "The election results seem to show a limited influence of the movement, expressed above all in the increase in votes for minor parties (especially United Left, Equo and, also, Union, Progress and Democracy), as well as in null votes and blank votes, particularly in the Senate election, widely considered an inefficient institution given its nature and functions under the current political system."

33. According to Hernández Castro (2012): "If we assume, and it is a big assumption, that the sum increase of these two quantities is the result of the influence of the appeals made on social networks, we would have a total of 0.9%, which would mean that appeals to cast a blank or null vote had an absolutely marginal electoral influence."

34. As early as July 2007, in the Congress of Deputies, Zapatero stated: "In the next legislature, we will achieve full employment," and again in April 2008 he promised two million new jobs (*El País*, March 5, 2008). Both quotations appear in Pérez-Díaz and Rodríguez (2011, 20).
35. A fairly harsh assessment of Zapatero's economic policy appears in Velarde Fuertes (2010).
36. A map of the cities involved can be found at: http://mapa.12m-15m.org/.

WorksC ited

Blanco Tomás, R. 2011. *¿Qué pasa? Que aún no tenemos casa*. Madrid: Fundación Aurora Intermitente.

Botey, J., R. Díaz-Salazar, O. Mateos, and J. Sanz. 2011. *Indignados*. Rome: Editori Riuniti.

Calvo, K. 2009. "Qualità della democrazia, diritti civili e riforma della política." In A. Bosco and I. Sánchez-Cuenca, eds., *La Spagna di Zapatero*. Bologna: Il Mulino, pp. 169–85.

Calvo, K., T. Gómez-Pastrana, and L. Mena. 2011. "Movimiento 15M: ¿quiénes son y qué reivindican?" *Zoom político* 4: 4–17.

Charnock, G., T. Purcell, and R. Ribera-Fumaz. 2011. "¡Indígnate! The 2011 Popular Protests and the Limits to Democracy in Spain." *Capital & Class* 36(1): 3–11.

Cotarelo, R. 2012. "La expansión de la ciberpolítica." In C. Colino and R. Cotarelo, eds., *España en crisis (Balance de la segunda legislatura de Rodríguez Zapatero)*. Valencia: Tirant Humanidades, pp. 331–55.

Field, B. N., ed. 2011. *Spain's "Second Transition"? The Socialist Government of José Luis Rodríguez Zapatero*. London & New York: Routledge.

Fishman, R. 2012. "On the Significance of Public Protest in Spanish Democracy." In J. Jordana, V. Navarro, F. Pallarés, and F. Requejo, eds., *Democràcia, Política i Societat: Homenatge a Rosa Virós*. Barcelona: Universitat Pompeu Fabra and L'Avenç, pp. 351–66.

Fuentes, L., and P. Clarey. 2011. *15M. Voces de una revolución*. Torroella de Montgrí: Panini.

García, J. R. 2011. *Desempleo juvenil en España: causas y soluciones*. BBVA Research, Working Paper 11/30. Available at: http://www.bbvaresearch.com.

Hernández Castro, D. 2012. "El 15-M tras el 20-N." *El viejo topo* 288: 38–45.

Jiménez Sánchez, M. 2011. "¿Influyó el 15M en las elecciones municipales?" *Zoom político* 4: 18–28.

Maravall, J. M. 2009. "La socialdemocrazia di Zapatero." In Bosco and Sánchez-Cuenca, eds., *La Spagna di Zapatero*, pp. 203–23.

Naredo, J. M., and A. Montiel Márquez. 2011. *El modelo inmobiliario español y su culminación en el caso valenciano*. Barcelona: Icaria.

Pastor Verdú, J. 2012. "El movimiento 15M y la política extraparlamentaria." In Colino and Cotarelo, eds., *España en crisis*, pp. 357–81.

Pérez-Díaz, V., and J. C. Rodríguez. 2011. *Alerta y desconfiada: La sociedad española ante la crisis*. Madrid: Fundación de las Cajas de Ahorros.

Rubio Lara, M. J. 2012. "Los avatares del estado del bienestar: mercados, política y reformas de pensiones de jubilación en España." In Colino and Cotarelo, eds., *España en crisis*, pp. 383–410.

Taibo, C. 2011a. *Nada será como antes*. Madrid: Los Libros de la Catarata.

———. 2011b. *El 15-M en sesenta preguntas*. Madrid: Los Libros de la Catarata.

Velarde Fuertes, J. 2010. *Preparación y estallido de una crisis. De 2004 a 2010: seis años de peregrinación de Casandra*. Madrid: Instituto de Estudios Económicos.

Velasco, P. 2012. *Non ci rappresentano*. Milan: Tropea.

CHAPTER 9

The Spanish Catholic Church from the Zapatero Era to the Rajoy Government

Mireno Berrettini

Since 1983, the year of John Paul II's visit to Spain, the church in Spain has organized collectively through the pastoral plans. In this regard, Prime Minister José Luis Rodríguez Zapatero's years in government are located within the coordinates laid down by a document drawn up during the José María Aznar government in 2002, *Una Iglesia esperanzada. "¡Mar adentro!" (Lc 5:4)*, and above all by the plan *Yo soy el pan de vida (Jn 6:35)*, written in the midst of a controversy with the Socialists in 2006. There is strong continuity between the two documents, but it is certainly the second one that had a greater influence on the decisions made by the church during the years the Socialist Party (PSOE) was in government. The 2006 plan moves between warnings about the danger of an "immanent humanism" and of "internal secularization," referring, respectively, to the idea that man can live independently from God and the confusion and doubts that are increasingly affecting priests. According to the bishops, on the one hand, Spain was under attack from "laical tendencies as far as the organization of society is concerned, a disregard for the reality of marriage and family, attacks on the life of unborn conceived, restrictions on freedom of education, the drifting of young people, now subjected to new forms of slavery." On the other hand, they state that "the main issue that the church in Spain must face today is not to be found in society or in the cultural environment, but within itself; it is an internal problem and not an external one."[1] While the second set of issues could lead to stricter doctrinal control, the others all stem from the PSOE's initiatives. In fact, when faced with a series of legislative initiatives whose aim was generally to promote the recognition of new civil rights, part of the Catholic Church (hierarchical Catholicism) was constantly present in the Spanish public arena, organizing various demonstrations or through the media outlets that were closest to it. As for the relations between Socialists and the Catholic Church, the first Zapatero legislature has often been considered among the most problematic since the years of the transition to democracy (Botti 2005).

There were a number of issues that provoked controversy: same-sex marriage, laws on assisted reproduction and education, as well as the so-called express divorce and the historical memory law. The last of these seemed, as far as the church hierarchy was concerned, to sum up the revanchist mentality of Socialist laicism, and represented the first move in an attack on religion and on traditional Catholic morality. Laicism is, for the Spanish bishops, a radical, antireligious version of secularism. Members of the episcopacy spoke out openly against the Socialists, talking on a number of occasions of "national-laicism" (Agustín García-Gasco); "anti-religious [...] totalitarianism" (Julián Herranz Casado); "laicist-fundamentalism" (José Gea Escolano); "secularist fundamentalism" (Manuel Ureña); and going so far as to declare the existence of a "new religion: laicism" (Antonio Cañizares). But the bishops did not stop there. Their documents, which resonated in the media, provided a prompt response to the government's initiatives, while at the same time the Popular Party (PP) appealed to the Constitutional Court in order to stop some of the Socialist policies in their tracks. The bishops' opposition to the Zapatero government focused on three main areas: the family, with the 2004 document *En favor del verdadero matrimonio* (For true marriage); education, with the 2005 document *Ante el Proyecto de Ley Orgánica de Educación* (Regarding the organic bill on education); and finally, bioethics in 2007, with *Algunas orientaciones sobre la ilicitud de la reproducción humana artificial y sobre las prácticas injustas autorizadas por la Ley que la regulará en España* (Some guidance on the wrongfulness of artificial human reproduction and on unjust practices authorized by the law that will regulate it in Spain). At the same time, some prelates began to organize demonstrations: 19 bishops took part in the demonstration *La familia sí importa* (The family matters) against same-sex marriage on June 18, 2005; 6 in the *Por la libertad y la calidad de la enseñanza* (For educational freedom and quality) demonstration on November 12, 2005.

The second Socialist legislature began with the biggest crisis between government and the church since the times of Aznar. There was tension between the PSOE and part of the Spanish hierarchy following the demonstration in Madrid's Plaza Colón on December 30, 2007 (where the then archbishop of Valencia, Cardinal Agustín García-Gasco, had spoken of the "disintegration of democracy"), and after the *Nota de la Comisión Permanente de la Conferencia Episcopal Española ante las elecciones generales de 2008* (Note from the Permanent Commission of the Spanish Episcopal Conference regarding the 2008 general elections) that condemned the government for having held a dialogue with ETA (Basque Homeland and Freedom) and urged citizens to vote for the PP. The tension that followed was eased thanks to Zapatero and Manuel Monteiro de Castro, who was the papal nuncio at the time. Their broth-based (*caldito*) dinner and the statements of reciprocal respect were an attempt to demonstrate that there were excellent relations between Madrid and the Holy See, and seemed to repudiate the harsh positions taken by the bishops, indicating that the Vatican preferred to tone down the controversies. In fact, the years between 2008 and 2011 were markedly different from the previous four years: more timid Socialist policies on one hand, and the bishops' lower profile on the streets on the other.[2] Despite that, there was still some friction. The long wave of previously mentioned issues was joined by other issues: the possible reform of the special status enjoyed by the Catholic Church in a then anticipated new law on religious freedom; the reappearance of the abortion issue (with a proposed law introducing new rules for the termination of pregnancies); and the issue of the *Valle de los Caídos* (particularly, the plan to transform the Francoist monumental complex into a learning center on the atrocities of the dictatorship, with the associated question regarding the fate of the Benedictine basilica that is part of it).

Catholic bishops again used harsh words, such as "laicist totalitarianism" (Antonio María Rouco Varela) and references to a "damaged" Spain (Antonio Cañizares), on several occasions. In a similar vein the episcopacy directly organized large religious events in the capital that were also laden with political significance: the *Fiesta de la Sagrada Familia* (Festival of the holy family; December 28, 2008), *El futuro de Europa pasa por la familia* (The future of Europe passes through the family; December 27, 2009), and *La familia cristiana, esperanza para Europa* (The Christian family, hope for Europe; January 4, 2011). The church also financed awareness-raising campaigns with powerful emotional impact: the year of life in 2009, *Mi vida está en tus manos* (My life is in your hands) in 2010, and *Siempre hay una razón para vivir* (There is always a reason to live) in 2011.

Looking Beyond the Return of Religion: The Politicization of Catholicism in the Zapatero Era

If we look closely at the positions taken by the bishops and by the Catholic laity during the transition to democracy, and then compare them with the more recent positions within the hierarchy, we cannot fail to detect a change. The difference is not so much in the overall objectives as in the style and the approach toward negotiations with the government. Nowadays the bishops prefer to ascribe Socialist policies exclusively to the PSOE's anticlerical tradition (still alive but marginalized), refusing to consider them as an attempt to deal with complex phenomena and processes that overlap the religious and the social spheres. I refer here to trends that can be found all over the Western world: from the impact of globalization to multicultural and multireligious societies, which redefine the boundaries of the community, raising questions about how people can live alongside one another. The bishops construct a direct link between what they consider to be a societal crisis (manifested in political corruption, same-sex marriage, divorce, and in many other ways) and the crisis of the church, emphasizing that it will not be possible to emerge from the former until Christianity is placed once again at the center of public life. This link is strengthened by pinpointing the causes of the decadence: they are the result of a deliberate plan on the part of political and social forces who aim to marginalize God and religion in people's lives.[3] This "victimist" view is in contrast to more complex analyses to be found even within the Catholic world. It has led to a pastoral that revives arguments that are typical of an intransigent culture, strengthening them on the basis of conservative thought from the United States.[4] The church views the changes caused by modernization negatively and those brought by secularization pessimistically. For this reason, it adopts reactionary political positions: to address the challenge of multiculturalism and multiple religions, it takes refuge in an exclusionary vision of identity; to the achievements of bioengineering, it reproposes natural law; in the face of demands for a greater local autonomy, it chooses administrative centralism.

The changes in the current positions of the church, however, do not arise exclusively from issues exogenous to the Catholicism; they can also be traced back to endogenous ones: the depletion of the renewal brought by the Second Vatican Council (Miccoli 2007); the return of the Catholicism of presence (more intransigent) vis-à-vis the Catholicism of mediation (more open to dialogue); and the impetus given by church teachings toward emotional religiosity (Aguirre 2005).

The response of the Spanish church may be seen as part of a wider trend of a return to religion (Casanova 1994), but one that has assumed unusual characteristics in Spain since the 1980s (Mardones 1990). In Spain, the hierarchy goes beyond its legitimate position in the public arena and in public debate, moving toward a real politicization of religion.[5] Today some religious feasts, such as the Corpus Christi, Sacred Heart, and Christ the King, are still celebrated with content similar to those held during the Franco regime, giving them strong antilaicist (and almost authoritarian) meaning. Other celebrations such as the Annunciation or the Basque *Virgen Blanca* (White Virgin) are now used to challenge new laws on abortion, while St. Joseph's Day or the Feast of the Holy Family provides an opportunity to put forward an archetypal image of marriage in terms of natural law.

Between "Christian Cultural Roots" and "Sociological Catholicism": Identity and Citizenship after "National Catholicism"

For years Spanish Catholicism had been a key element in defining the identity of the nation and an ethical basis for building citizenship within the state (Botti 1992). This role was questioned by the Second Vatican Council and by the transition. After the acceptance of democracy in the 1970s, the church since the 1980s has changed its strategy, developing a discourse on "Christian roots" (Rouco Varela 1999) and/or "sociological Catholicism" (García de Cortázar 1981). This discourse links religion and identity in a way similar to what happened with national Catholicism before and during the Franco regime (Botti 1992). Today the church does not equate "Catholic" and "Spanish," but for the bishops the Spanish identity (and Spanish citizenship) cannot be separated from Catholicism. The religion is not fused with the idea of the nation, but rather with the culture. This discourse results from the unstoppable process of cultural and religious pluralism. In believers, this pluralism reinforces the privatization of religion (Catholicism à la carte), but it also produces an identity-based reaction (e.g., "we" are Christian and "the others" are Muslims). In the bishops, pluralism produces a peculiar pastoral choice: to conceive of the Catholic religion in a moral and cultural sense (Christianity is the religion of the West, and the West cannot exist without Christianity).

What is the relationship between the "old Spanish nation" and Catholicism in the Zapatero era? The archbishop of Madrid, Cardinal Antonio María Rouco Varela, addressed this question on a number of occasions during the two Socialist mandates. In 2005 in a speech given at the Club Siglo XXI entitled *España y su futuro: La Iglesia Católica* (Spain and its future: the Catholic Church) he underlined the link between the Catholic tradition and Spanish society. Given that "the historical reality [...] of Spain appears [...] unmistakably marked by Catholicism," it is obvious that "it is impossible to neglect the Catholic Church in any analysis of [Spain's] present reality, and even more so of its future horizons."[6] On April 19, 2010, he repeated a similar message in a speech at the opening of the Plenary Assembly of the Episcopal Conference (CEE). There were two main points: "Spanish is not the same as Catholic," but if "the human being is to be truly served" one must remember that "no society can exist without a spiritual soul."[7] Therefore, from this point of view, Catholicism is the spiritual soul of Spain, and by virtue of the relative cultural majority that it has, it must form the basis for the ethics of coexistence—an element that brings Spaniards together and forms the ultimate foundation for Spain's laws. In this sense, Catholicism is reduced to functioning as a civil religion. The CEE document *Moral y sociedad democrática*, drawn up in 1996, had explained this clearly. One section reads as follows:

> [A] civil law that goes beyond the scope of its jurisdiction, contradicting the truth of man, failing to recognize his fundamental rights and even cancelling them out, should not be binding and should not be obeyed; moreover, since it does not strictly bear the features of a law, it forces people with conscience to resist it.[8]

In this sense the hierarchy's opposition to the PSOE's policies represented an attempt to reconsider the relationship not only between believers and politics, but also between citizens and politics, calling for limited autonomy for citizens and believers on ethical issues. The main interlocutors or targets of this were the Socialists, especially those purporting to be believers. But in fact even the PP's leaders were pressured to alter their internal party dynamics and to obtain a commitment from them to adopt positions favorable toward and more in line with the church when deciding on the agenda of future governments. Therefore, it seems clear that during Zapatero's seven-year period in office secularism meant not so much the institutional autonomy of a separation of church and state, but above all competition for the establishment of universal models of coexistence between citizens.

The new civil Catholic religion performs a function analogous to national Catholicism (Álvarez-Bolado 1981, 319). This type of "secularized" national Catholicism may clearly be seen when one analyzes the comments on the Lautsi sentence handed out by the European Court on Human Rights concerning the displaying of crucifixes in state schools. The response of the bishops was to emphasize the cultural value of the icon, thus secularizing its symbolic content but also linking it to an identity from which it cannot be separated. A clear example of this can be found in the CEE's collective statement of June 23, 2010, entitled *Declaración sobre la exposición de símbolos religiosos cristianos en Europa* (Declaration on displaying Christian religious symbols in Europe). The crucifix "is the expression of a tradition recognized by all as of great value." Those who choose to eliminate it

> refute the spiritual and cultural heritage in which they are rooted and they close off the paths of the future. To take a stand against the symbols of values that have shaped the history and culture of a people is to remove the defenses against other cultural values, not always favorable, and to cover up the basic foundations that underpin ethics and rights.[9]

This new convergence between identity and Catholicism, achieved via the discourse on cultural roots, also opened up the opportunity to reactivate a particular type of religiously motivated vote, one that is generated when the question of religion is defined in terms of identity, which also affects the ideological positioning of parties.[10] So this is where an intersection can be found between the CEE's demands and the PP's electoral strategy.

Toward the Right, Beyond the Right?

During the transition, CEE President and Cardinal Vicente Enrique y Tarancón had decided not to support any party that was in any way explicitly linked to Catholicism. This decision took into account the crisis of Christian democratic parties and the new conciliar theology, but it also reflected a clear understanding of the Spanish situation, where the church had been politically overexposed during the dictatorship, and where the serious crisis of Catholic Action in the post-Conciliar period had deprived any possible Catholic party of an organizational base similar to that of other European countries. Finally, the decision to disperse the Catholic vote took into account the widespread left-wing Catholic culture and prevented the polarization of believers and nonbelievers. But having brilliantly overcome the challenges of the transition and the danger of an authoritarian reaction, the combination of the arrival of a new pope and the redefining of Vatican policies brought a different attitude toward the political parties. Between the 1980s and 1990s, Socialist policies of secularization repoliticized Catholicism, pushing the Spanish right to cast itself once again as a Catholic party. This was known as the Wojtylan[11] "correction" to the "neutralist" position of the then CEE president Tarancón. After 1987, the new CEE president, Cardinal Angel Suquía Goicoechea of Madrid, worked alongside Nuncio Mario Tagliaferri to restructure the Spanish right. This provided a post-Franco party, *Alianza Popular* (Popular Alliance), with the opportunity to clean up its own pedigree, to change its name to *Partido Popular* (Popular Party), and to become part of the European party group of the same name. This continued during the Rouco Varela mandate, but with substantial misunderstandings arising, even during the Aznar government. In 2001, first the church did not support the antiterrorist pact put forward by the PP government, thereby provoking strong criticisms from the executive; then it denied rumors coming from the Moncloa executive palace about the imminent excommunication of ETA members. The following year, the joint pastoral letter entitled *Preparar la paz* (Prepare the peace), published by the Basque bishops, caused more hard feelings because it condemned terrorism but not the demands of Basque nationalism[12]; and finally in 2003 Aznar's decision to take part in the preventive war in Iraq provided final confirmation that Spanish *Popularism* could not be linked to the positions adopted by the bishops. Friction then grew when the PP moved from government into the opposition, when the church's less-than-optimal relations with Mariano Rajoy cleared the way for the episcopal leadership to prefer its own direct intervention in politics rather than rely on the mediation of the laity. During the 2004–2008 period, some sections of the episcopate wavered between instrumentally using the laity and attempting to bypass it. An episcopal rejection of the political positions of the sectors of the PP that were more independent of the CEE (and thus an implicit invitation to enhance the Catholic component of the party) came in a speech made by Monsignor Fernando Sebastián, then archbishop of Pamplona-Tudela, in March 2007, and thus shortly before the regional elections in 13 of the 17 autonomous communities. After stating that "the large parties, which guide our social and political lives, are all non-denominational," he went on to remark: "Nowadays in Spain there are some political parties that wish to be totally faithful to the social doctrine of the church, for example, the *Comunión Tradicionalista Católica*, *Alternativa Española*, *Tercio Católico de Acción Política*, and *Falange Española de las JONS*. All these are [...] worthy of consideration and support."[13]

The second Zapatero mandate, however, witnessed less prominent activism on the part of bishops in the public sphere and a church strategy aimed at influencing the PP, instead of simply bypassing it. There were two key moments in this difficult relationship. The first took place in the first half of 2008, beginning just after the PP's electoral defeat and ending with the PP party convention in Valencia in June. The aim of some sectors of Catholicism closest to the episcopate was to get behind the attack that the right wing of the party was waging against Rajoy's leadership. The archdiocese of Madrid was involved in this operation (so much so that the Madrid *Foro Curas* published three strongly worded documents denouncing the close relations between the PP and the diocese), but this initiative to change (or influence) the PP leadership brought no results. Yet the issue of the relationship between the party and the CEE remained open, and a second key stage was reached after the anti-abortion demonstrations of October 17, 2009. Two distinct, but deeply linked, questions came together. On the one hand was the emergence of the "captains of God," composed of Benigno Blanco (*Foro de la Familia*), Alfredo Dagnino (*Asociación Católica Nacional de Propagandistas*), and Ignacio Arsuaga (*Hazte Oír*). On the other hand, rumors circulated that Rouco Varela wanted to start a confessional party based on the movements that had actively worked against the Zapatero government and its leaders.[14] This project was very soon abandoned due to internal dissent, and ultimately proved to be another attempt to push the PP toward the Catholic right. However, it marked a new phase: the hierarchy identified a possible organizational and electoral base for a potential new Catholic party, no longer in Catholic Action and the lay apostolate, but in less structured organizations. This event provided yet more proof of the peculiar relations with the PP, characterized by a tension between proximity and blackmail. Thus, despite statements such as those made by Monsignor Demetrio Fernández (Cordoba) in March 2010 about the need for greater visibility of Christian inspiration in the PP and frequent criticisms aimed at moving the party closer to its positions, the episcopacy consistently appealed for votes for the Popular Party in every round of elections. In effect encouraging a vote for the PP, the *Nota ante las elecciones generales de 2011* (Note regarding the 2011 general elections), which the permanent commission of CEE published on October 21, 2011, closed the cycle, both symbolically and in black and white, that had begun with the same document published for the 2008 elections.

Episcopal Centralism and Theological Conservatism

Between the end of 2009 and the early part of 2010 a process began to redefine the Basque episcopacy. José Ignacio Munilla Aguirre, previously bishop of Palencia, was appointed to the same post in San Sebastián; in

April 2010 Mario Iceta Gavicagogeascoa, ex-auxiliary bishop of Bilbao, was appointed as apostolic administrator of the diocese, officially taking over a few months later. The two appointments marked the convergence of a number of issues: the attempt to promote church figures from a conservative background; the trend to appoint bishops who might strengthen the entourage of Rouco Varela in the CEE; and finally the plan to build a church in the periphery more in line with Madrid. And in reality the Basque priesthood reacted with strong protests, but they did not succeed in influencing events. The most striking events were the collective letter in December 2009, in which 131 priests opposed the appointment of Munilla, and another in June 2010 sent to Nuncio Renzo Fratini by almost 700 believers, urging him to take the local community into consideration when proceeding to appoint the new bishop of Bilbao.

Munilla and Iceta are atypical Basques from a cultural point of view. Both studied outside of the Basque Country; the former studied at the Toledo seminary and in the Faculty of Theology of Spain of the North of Burgos, while the latter is closer to Opus Dei and attended the seminary in Cordoba. The two bishops are not only distant from ETA, a position that the Basque church had already taken in the past, but are also far less supportive of peripheral nationalism in general. Moreover, compared to the previous generation of Basque bishops, Iceta and Munilla represent a church that is more closed, in both theological and pastoral terms, and more traditional; regarding how to respond to secularization and to the PSOE's policies, they are less open to dialogue and more belligerent in tone. Finally, with the appointment of these two figures, the leadership of the Episcopal Conference was trying to avoid another rift between Madrid and the Basque Country similar to the one that had occurred in 2002, with the previously cited joint pastoral letter *Preparar la paz*, and in 2009, with *Purificar la memoria, servir a la verdad, pedir perdón* (Purify memory, serve the truth, ask for forgiveness), on the need to recognize and rehabilitate the priests killed by Francoist repression (Berrettini 2012). This rift that pitted a theologian like José Antonio Pagola against the Episcopal Commission for the Doctrine of the Faith should not be ascribed to the strictly doctrinal question at hand but also to the complex relationship between the center and the periphery. For a number of years, Pagola was vicar general of the San Sebastián diocese under the direction of Bishop Juan María Uriarte. In 2010, the theologian's last work, *Jesús. Aproximación histórica*, was withdrawn from bookstores as a result of pressure from the episcopacy, as it was considered to be heterodox. However, the fact that the book was initially given the all-clear by Uriarte means that CEE rejected the positions of the San Sebastián emeritus. The book's withdrawal also implicitly served as a warning to those prelates that, as Uriarte, intended to mediate between the government and ETA.

Corresponding to the idea that "where nationalism exists, there is more secularization," valid for the Basque Country,[15] there is the idea that "nationalism combined with progressivism has been lethal for the church," which applies in the Catalan context.[16] In 2006, the Plenary Assembly of the CEE issued a pastoral instruction entitled *Orientaciones morales ante la situación actual de España* (Moral guidance regarding the current situation in Spain). The sixth section, dedicated to *Los nacionalismos y sus exigencias morales* (Nationalism and its moral demands), although the result of a long debate between the two blocs within the episcopacy (one of which was more concerned with the issue of historical nationalities, while the other was more focused on Spanish central nationalism), certainly marks the bishops' support for a unitary vision of the Spanish state.[17] The Catalan church, however, had never hid the fact that it supported the special demands made by the region. Two documents published in recent years by the *Conferencia Episcopal Tarraconense* (CET) deserve to be mentioned—*Nota sobre el proyecto de Estatuto de Cataluña* (September 29, 2005) and the *Nota sobre el Estatuto de Cataluña* (April 27, 2006); each gave timid support to the new Catalan statute of autonomy. The Catalan clerics endorsed this autonomist initiative, though they criticized the excessively secular approach, and even though the statute was developed by the parties of the left. This attitude broke with the plan drawn up in Madrid to work side by side with the political right. In January 2011, the Catalan bishops reiterated their position by publishing a document entitled *Al servicio de nuestro pueblo* (At the service of our people; January 2011), which celebrated the twenty-fifth anniversary of another key pastoral letter titled *Arrels cristianes de Catalunya* (Christian roots of Catalonia), and which recognized "Catalonia's personality and unique national characteristics" and defended "the right to demand and promote everything which that implies."[18] In any event, Catalan Catholicism was also undergoing a redefinition: the CEE wanted to break the alliance between religious moderates and Catalan nationalism. From 2008 to 2011 a number of changes could be detected: the COPE network and *Alfa y Omega*, the diocesan periodical in the capital, issued harshly worded attacks on the Catalan statute of autonomy, while in Catalonia the CEE supported (through appointments and promotions) priests who were not linked to Catalan nationalism.

Further signs highlighted the difficult relationship between the hierarchy and theologians. In recent years, a number of cases received the attention of the media, such as those of the previously mentioned Pagola with the CEE; the decision of the Archbishop of Santiago de Compostela Julián Barrio Barrio to distance himself from the Galician forum *Foro Encrucillada*; the request from Bishop Munilla to transfer the Franciscan theologian José Arregui, professor at the University of Deusto (Bilbao), to America, while a group of 200 people protested to show their solidarity in Bilbao, thus allowing the problem to spread throughout the new episcopal leadership in the Basque country. In 2011, Juan José Tamayo, professor of theology and religious sciences at the Carlos III University, was banned from presenting his work, *Otra teología es posible* (A different theology is possible), first by Rouco Varela in Madrid, then by Cardinal Lluís Martínez Sistach in Barcelona. In March 2012 he was the subject of a Note from the Communication Office of the Diocese of Palencia that called him a person who was separated "from the church communion."[19] At the same time Andrés Torres Quieruga, professor of philosophy of religion at the University of Santiago de Compostela, was the subject of a notification by the Commission for the Doctrine of the Faith,[20] and previously the bishops had placed obstacles in the way of his giving lectures.

The church is abandoning its traditional prudence as far as the management of internal pluralism is concerned, while at the Vatican level it was making concessions in order to renew the dialogue with the Lefebvrian fundamentalists of Ecône (Miccoli 2011). This shows that the hierarchy wants to close ranks, strengthen Catholics who are increasingly a minority, and respond to secularization, which is characterized by an ever more personalized religious faith and by the crisis of institutional churches.

Finally, the hierarchy would not tolerate a degree of Catholic autonomy in areas such as education where it was likely to clash with the episcopal strategies. This is shown by examples such as the attacks on the *Federación Española de Religiosos de Enseñanza* (Spanish Federation of Religious Education, FERE) on the issue of *educación para la ciudadanía* (citizenship education). The bishops have always considered this school subject matter, introduced by the Zapatero government in 2006, as a vehicle for laicism, an ideology of gender and statism. They frequently urged parents to use conscientious objection so that their children would be excused from attending these classes. In their own schools, however, FERE turned out to be less than willing to accede to the CEE's demands. In doing so they had to face the repudiation of the hierarchy—from the *Instrucción sobre Educación Para la ciudadania* (Instruction about citizenship education) published by the bishops of Madrid (September

2008) to the statements made by the bishop of Segorbe and president of the Episcopal Commission for Teaching and the Catechism, Casimiro López Llorente (October 2008)—but also harsh criticism from *Alfa y Omega* and from hardline groups that accused FERE of having made secret agreements with Zapatero.

Between Marginalized Moderates and Divided Conservatives: The Future of the Episcopal Conference

The second Socialist legislature began with the "return of the thunderous cardinal"[21] Rouco Varela to the presidency of the CEE. In recent years, the Madrid cardinal, thanks partly to the special relationship he enjoyed with Giovanni Battista Re, the prefect emeritus of the Congregation for Bishops, succeeded in helping move figures close to him toward the position of bishop (from Juan Antonio Martínez Camino, his auxiliary bishop in Madrid, to his nephew Alfonso Carrasco Rouco, the incumbent in Lugo) and in promoting other prelates in important dioceses (e.g., Jesús Sanz Montes to the archdiocese of Oviedo and Carlos Osoro as archbishop of Valencia). But Rouco Varela did not just build an episcopal front in line with his own positions; he has always been very close to church movements (from Communion and Liberation to Neocatechumenal Way); he controls the COPE radio network; he has excellent relations with some leading members of the PP; and he runs a diocese that is at the heart of national politics.

It would, however, be excessive to talk of a "Spanish pope."[22] First of all, the cardinal is constrained by the very elements that give him his strength, particularly the lay ecclesial movements that are in any case not easily accommodated within the traditional structure of the diocese. Second, the last few years have seen the Vatican's greater interest in Spain. The Holy See has intervened more directly, as shown by the numerous visits by the Secretary of State Tarcisio Bertone and by Benedict XVI himself (from the Compostelan Holy Year to the World Youth Day, with the consecration of the Sagrada Familia basilica in Barcelona in between), while it has also made efforts to create a series of alternative power centers by helping prelates with opinions or styles that are different from Rouco Varela's. Certainly, this does not represent a repudiation, but rather a "correction" that is perfectly in line with the traditionally cautious papal approach. In any event, these steps taken by the Vatican had indirect impacts on the relations between the church and the Zapatero government. The greater involvement of the secretary of state made it possible to avoid serious rifts and to strengthen the dialogue with the Socialists due to the collaboration required to organize large religious events. The support given to alternative figures who were not involved in the Rouco administration enabled them to act as a counterweight to the CEE president. In fact, the signals of confidence in Monsignor Ricardo Blázquez (who was appointed archbishop of Valladolid in 2010, later apostolic visitor of the Regnum Christi movement, which had been torn apart by sex scandals) coming from the Vatican caused his stock to rise, and he became the most credible candidate from the moderate camp for the presidency of the CEE once Rouco's term of office comes to an end. If Blázquez were again elected as leader of the episcopate—which is far from certain given that the moderate bishops are in the minority—it would signify a more pluralistic or less centralized management of the CEE and a more flexible attitude toward any government it needed to deal with.

Among the more conservative bishops, however, the main figure to consider is Monsignor Antonio Cañizares, cardinal primate of Spain and currently Vatican prefect of the Congregation for Divine Worship and the Discipline of the Sacraments. His personal closeness to Pope Benedict XVI and his institutional role in the Holy See are key elements that play in his favor when standing as a strong candidate for a future leading role in the Spanish church. An Episcopal Conference "modeled" on Cañizares would be characterized by the expression of hardline positions in the media but a realistic dialogue with politicians on specific issues. In any event, the possibility of Cañizares drawing support from a conservative episcopate remains unlikely. While his views are close to Rouco's, he is separated from him by a generational divide, a greater propensity for dialogue with the PSOE, and because he opposes the current archbishop of Madrid's intention to influence the configuration of the Spanish church after his departure from the scene.

Therefore, while the moderates may be on the margins, the conservatives are divided. Already during Zapatero's second term, every appointment and every replacement in the Assembly of Bishops was a test of its internal equilibrium. There will be various elements at play when the future shape of the assembly is determined, not least of which is who will be the new archbishop of Madrid. Indeed, being appointed to lead the most important diocese in Spain has provided a launching pad for the presidency of the CEE ever since the times of Cardinal Tarancón.

Whoever takes over the episcopacy in the near future, however, it is unlikely that there will be significant changes from the point of view of the pastoral. The approval of the plan entitled *La nueva evangelización desde la Palabra de Dios. "Por tu Palabra, echaré las redes (Lc 5:5)"* by the Plenary Assembly of the CEE in April 2012 set out a path that will be followed until at least 2015. For the bishops "the diagnosis carried out in the latest pastoral plans can be considered valid in its fundamental outlines." They continued therefore to criticize "relativism and laicism," which characterize a culture "that proudly declares its distance from God" and they warned of the dangers of the "internal secularization" of the clergy.[23] These views were confirmed a few months later with the presentation of *La verdad del amor humano. Orientaciones sobre el amor conyugal, la ideología de género y la legislación familiar* (The truth about human love. Guidance on conjugal love, gender ideology, and family law). In this document there was a renewed denunciation of "radical feminism," of the "absolute depersonalization of sexuality" and of the present-day "process of the 'deconstruction' of the individual."[24] These were bombastic expressions used by the bishops to oppose sexual freedom and support a society based on more conservative morals. In the context of a serious economic crisis, the decision of the prelates to avoid a pastoral specifically dedicated to social and work-related problems showed what their true priorities were, and it seemed to be an invitation to the new government to change the legal status of same-sex families.

Conclusions

Of course, the Spanish church is not just the episcopate, but rather a complex organization. The powerful tensions between the "management" and the "base" are symptomatic of the vitality of the nonhierarchical church. Yet the latter remains on the margins, with very little chance of influencing the decisions taken at the top. The divisions that have surfaced between the various sectors of Spanish Catholicism over relations with the world of politics have been deep, and the CEE leaders (or the more conservative sectors) have often made use of anti-Socialist rhetoric to remind believers of their duty to be obedient and disciplined, and to provide a clearly defined model of what the church and society should be. As a matter of fact, in recent years the bishops' decisions have not just been a reaction to the policies pursued by the government, but also an indirect response to a complex series of phenomena (globalization, modernization, and secularization). In doing so the hierarchy has continued along the path begun immediately after the transition, and pursued it in an even more determined way. It is not simply an involution; it is more a case of getting back onto a track that it had only left temporarily during the time when Tarancón was at the helm. Part of the episcopate remains deeply rooted in a vision of a church protected by the state. These bishops do not accept legislative changes that reflect the current religious pluralism, and therefore put Catholicism on an equal status with other religions. These prelates are still influenced by the traditional view of the church as an institutional body of the state, and so they tend to converse with governments as equals or to oppose them when they feel under attack. There is also a strongly rooted tendency to operate on the political stage in the first person, considering the laity more as an instrument of political pressure rather than a player capable of intervening independently of the clergy. It goes without saying that the sense of nostalgia for a church as a pillar of a "well-ordered" society is widespread even among lay people, who are prepared to woo an episcopate that is only too glad to be wooed. To speak of a return to national Catholicism tout court would be wrong. At an episcopal level, a new attitude has been shaped, but it did not go in the direction indicated by the Second Vatican Council, rather it is an adaptation of more traditional positions, a new form of doctrinal purity, that for this reason shows great dynamism. On the one hand, there is still an attempt to define the identity of a community in relation to its religious creed, even though it is done through an indirect process and along cultural lines; on the other, there is still strong resistance to (which at times spills over into a full rejection of) the principle of the law-making autonomy of the community and therefore of the very essence of democracy.

Notes

1. Episcopal Conference (CEE) Plenary Assembly, *Plan Pastoral de la Conferencia Episcopal Española 2006–2010 "Yo soy el pan de vida" (Jn 6:35) Vivir de la Eucaristía*, March 30, 2006, p. 9. All CEE documents are available at: http://www.conferenciaepiscopal.es/documentos.
2. An interesting analysis of the first Socialist mandate may be found in Aguilar (2010). More generally, see Ollero Tassara (2011) and Araujo Cardalda (2012). I would like to warmly thank the author and the editors for allowing me to read the work before it was published.
3. For example, Sebastián (1991).
4. There are some examples of this conservative thinking as well as studies on this issue in Neuhaus (1984) and Berger (1982).
5. For sociological models reference may be made to Manuel et al. (2006) and Gurrutxaga (2008).
6. A. M. Rouco Varela, "España y su futuro. La Iglesia Católica," *Ecclesia*, October 29, 2005, p. 35.
7. A. M. Rouco Varela, "Discurso del presidente de la Conferencia Episcopal en el comienzo de la 95ª reunión de la Asamblea Plenaria," *Alfa y Omega*, April 22, 2010, p. 22.

8. CEE Plenary Assembly, *Moral y sociedad democrática*, February 14, 1996, p. 7.
9. CEE Permanent Committee, *Declaración sobre la exposición de símbolos religiosos cristianos en Europa*, June 23, 2010, p. 1.
10. On the other hand, Calvo and Montero (2002) emphasize the importance of secularization in voting choices.
11. A reference to Pope John Paul II's birth name, Karol Józef Wojtyła.
12. The text is available on the diocese of Bilbao website: http://www.bizkeliza.org.
13. Published later in Sebastián (2008).
14. J. M. Garrido, "Rouco Varela planea crear un partido político católico liderado por 'los capitanes de Dios,'" *El Plural*, October 29, 2009; J. M. Vidal, "Los Propagandistas Católicos ven la 'hora de pasar a la acción' en política," *El Mundo*, October 20, 2009.
15. L. R. Aizpeolea, "Rouco busca nuevos fieles en el País Vasco," *El País*, December 20, 2009.
16. J. Lozano, "El nacionalismo unido al progresismo ha sido letal para la Iglesia en Cataluña," *Libertad Digital*, January 23, 2012.
17. Very briefly: (1) "The historical and cultural unity of Spain can be made manifest and managed in very different ways" but it is still a unity; (2) "[i]n any case, it will always be necessary to respect the will of all the citizens involved, so that the minorities do not suffer any impositions or restrictions on their rights"; and (3) "the nationalists' proposals must be justified with reference to the common good of all of the population that are affected either directly or indirectly." See CEE Plenary Assembly, *Orientaciones morales ante la situación actual de España*, November 23, 2006, pp. 17 and 18.
18. Available at: http://www.tarraconense.cat.
19. Available at: http://www.diocesispalencia.org.
20. Episcopal Commission for the Doctrine of the Faith, *Notificación sobre algunas obras del Prof. Andrés Torres Queiruga*, March 30, 2012.
21. L. Galán, "El retorno del cardenal tronante," *El País*, March 9, 2008.
22. J. M. Vidal, "El 'Papa' español," *El Mundo*, January 6, 2008.
23. CEE Plenary Assembly, *La nueva evangelización desde la Palabra de Dios. "Por tu Palabra, echaré las redes (Lc 5:5)*," April 27, 2012, pp. 3 and 6.
24. CEE Plenary Assembly, *La verdad del amor humano. Orientaciones sobre el amor conyugal, la ideología de género y la legislación familiar*, April 26, 2012, pp. 12 and 13.

WorksC ited

Aguilar, S. 2010. "El activismo político de la Iglesia católica durante el gobierno de Zapatero (2004–2010)." *Papers* 4: 1129–55.
Aguirre, R. 2005. "Gestión de las tradiciones y crisis de la Iglesia." *Zona Abierta* 24: 14–17.
Álvarez-Bolado, A. 1981. "¿Tentación nacionalcatólica en la Iglesia de hoy?" *Iglesia Viva* 94: 317–47.

Araujo Cardalda, L. X. 2012. "La laicidad y sus límites en España. Acción legislativa y bloque católico." In C. Colino and R. Cotarelo, eds., *España en crisis. Balance de la segunda legislatura de Rodríguez Zapatero*. Valencia: Tirant Humanidades, pp. 163–90.

Berger, P. 1982. "From the Crisis of Religion to the Crisis of Secularity." In M. Douglas and S. Tipton, eds., *Religion and America*. Boston: Beacon, pp. 14–24.

Berrettini, M. 2012. "A settant'anni dalla Carta Collettiva dell'Episcopato spagnolo: Jerarquía, martirio, memoria collettiva." In E. Acciai and G. Quaggio, eds., *Un conflitto che non passa. Storia, memoria e rimozioni della Guerra Civile spagnola*. Pistoia: ISRPT, pp. 132–52.

Botti, A. 1992. *Nazionalcattolicesimo e Spagna nuova (1881–1975)*. Milan: Franco Angeli.

———. 2005. "Chiesa e governo socialista in Spagna." *Il Mulino* 2: 353–63.

Calvo, K., and J. R. Montero. 2002. "Cuando ser conservador ya no es un problema: religiosidad, ideología y voto en las elecciones generales de 2000." *Revista Española de Ciencia Política* 6: 17–56.

Casanova, J. 1994. *Public Religions in the Modern World*. Chicago: University of Chicago Press.

García de Cortázar, F. 1981. "Iglesia y sociedad en la España contemporánea." In S. Castillo, ed., *Estudios sobre Historia de España. Homenaje a Manuel Tuñón de Lara*, vol. II. Madrid: Universidad Internacional Menéndez Pelayo, pp. 567–91.

Gurrutxaga, A. 2008. "La institución lobby: la religión en la política. El reencuentro de la religión con la política en contextos múltiples." In A. Pérez-Agote and J. A. Santiago García, eds., *Religión y política en la sociedad actual*. Madrid: Centro de Investigaciones Sociológicas, pp. 67–86.

Manuel, P. C., L. C. Reardon, and C. Wilcox. 2006. *Catholic Church and Nation State. Comparative Perspectives*. Washington: Georgetown University Press.

Mardones, J. M. 1990. "La desprivatización del catolicismo en los años ochenta." *Sistema* 97: 123–36.

Miccoli, G. 2007. *In difesa della fede. La chiesa di Giovanni Paolo II e Benedetto XVI*. Milan: Rizzoli.

———. 2011. *La Chiesa dell'anticoncilio. I tradizionalisti alla riconquista di Roma*. Rome: Laterza.

Neuhaus, J. 1984. *The Naked Public Square. Religion and Democracy in America*. Michigan: Eerdmans Publishing Company.

Ollero Tassara, A. 2011. "La política religiosa de los gobiernos Zapatero." *Razón y fe* 264(1353–1354): 79–89.

Rouco Varela, A. M. 1999. "Avivar las raíces cristianas de España." *Cuenta y Razón* 112: 24–26.

Sebastián, F. 1991. *Nueva evangelización. Cultura y política en la España de hoy*. Madrid: Encuentro.

———. 2008. "Situación actual de la Iglesia, algunas orientaciones prácticas." *Altar Mayor* 1: 143–66.

CHAPTER 10

Gender Equality Policymaking in Spain(2008–11): LosingM omentum

Celia Valiente

In the first term of Socialist prime minister José Luis Rodríguez Zapatero (2004–2008), legislation such as the 2004 gender violence law and the 2007 gender equality law put Spain at the vanguard of gender equality policymaking in the European Union (EU) (Calvo & Martín 2011; León 2011b; Lombardo 2009; Valiente 2008).[1] In contrast, a first glance at his second term (2008–11) would lead us to conclude that there was a more modest, but not negligible, level of innovation in gender equality policy. While the executive continued to appoint a large number of women to positions of political decision-making and parliament passed important legislation, in particular abortion decriminalization and new regulations for domestic workers, in general these measures have not been considered pathbreaking.

However, this chapter argues that if we consider both policy formulation and implementation, the contrast between the Socialist Party's (PSOE) record on gender equality policymaking in Prime Minister Zapatero's first and second terms is less pronounced than a superficial observation would lead us to conclude.[2] Some societal and political factors conducive to proactive women's rights policymaking were present in both terms, including secularization and an (imperfect) separation of church and state, the high presence of women in civil society, the (relative) vitality of the women's movement, interparty consensus on many (but not all) gender equality issues, and consolidated gender equality institutions (Valiente 2008). Nonetheless, in the second term, there was less room for legislative reforms to improve women's status precisely because major legal changes had already passed between 2004 and 2008. These needed to be implemented in the subsequent years. Therefore, policymakers were busy not so much adopting innovative legislation but rather implementing policies passed during the first term. This was a task of monumental proportions because of the ambitious goals to be reached, and would be extremely hard to achieve in any economic context. The economic crisis that marked the second, but not the first, term made their full implementation nearly impossible. When the conservative Popular Party (PP) won an absolute majority of the seats in the November 20, 2011, general elections, the Spanish economy was in deep trouble. It was therefore relatively easy for PP politicians to declare that the implementation of costly policies would simply be paralyzed.

This chapter is organized in four parts. The first part succinctly describes gender equality policymaking during the Zapatero governments, contrasting developments in the first and second terms, and places these developments in historical perspective. The second part explains why the PSOE's record on gender equality policy was more modest in the second term than in the first. The third part addresses what remains to be done in the policy area of women's rights according to different strands of the women's movement. In the fourth part, I evaluate the prospects for gender equality policy under the PP administration that won office in 2011. The research is based on secondary sources, legislation, and newspaper reports, as well as face-to-face semistructured interviews with the general secretary on equality policies between 2004 and 2008, Soledad Murillo,[3] and six leaders of the women's movement.[4]

Central State Gender Equality Policies

The Historical Context

To better understand the policies adopted during Zapatero's two terms in office, it is important to provide some historical perspective on gender policy and women's status. First, there is a sharp contrast between the Socialist policies toward women covered here and the policies of predemocratic Spain. From the mid-1930s until 1975, Spain was governed by a right-wing authoritarian regime, headed by General Francisco Franco, which actively opposed the advancement of women's rights and status. The ideal family was a hierarchical unit, and it was assumed that authority rested with the father, who was supposed to be its sole (or, at least, its main) supporter. Motherhood was defined not only as a woman's main family duty, but also as a women's primary national and societal obligation. The role of mothering was seen to be incompatible with other activities, such as paid work. Between the late 1930s until the late 1950s to early 1960s, the state took measures to prevent women from working outside the home. An example of this was the requirement that married women obtain their husband's permission before signing a labor contract and "engaging in trade." Sex-segregated schools were the norm; boys and girls not only attended different schools but also studied different curricula. Divorce was illegal, and the selling and advertising of contraceptives was criminalized. Abortion was defined as a crime punished by prison. From the late 1950s and early 1960s to 1975, policymakers of the Francoist regime approved some liberalizing measures related to women's status. They abolished some obstacles to paid employment, for instance, the prohibition against women working once married, and also the exclusion of women from some professions in the field of law. Liberalization, however, did not take place regarding the regulation of sexuality or reproduction (Morcillo 2000; Ruiz 2007).

The PSOE politicians who governed Spain between 2004 and 2011, however, were not the first public officials to elaborate gender equality policies in postauthoritarian Spain. While it is not possible to enumerate all of the gender equality policies enacted between 1975 and 2004, let me refer to some examples. The selling and advertising of contraceptives was decriminalized in 1978. Divorce in cases of civil marriage was permitted in 1981. The post-Franco governments encouraged girls and boys to go to school together, and this is now the norm with very few exceptions. A partial decriminalization of abortion took place in 1985 (Blofield 2006). Additionally, since 1975, the central state and later the regional governments have provided an ever-increasing number of free educational programs for children between the ages of three and five (school is mandatory at six years of age). In part as a result of this policy, school attendance rates for three-, four-, and five-year-olds are comparatively high in Spain at 99, 99, and 100 percent, respectively (academic year 2009–10).[5]

The center-right Union of the Democratic Center (UCD) that governed the country between 1977 and 1982 advocated some of the gender equality policies initiated after 1975. Although the PSOE governments between 1982 and 1996 enacted many gender equality policies, the conservative PP governments between 1996 and 2004 maintained some of them. Gender equality therefore was firmly on the political agenda regardless of the ideological color of the party in office. Gender equality policy received an additional push after the electoral victory of the PSOE in the spring of 2004.

Developments during the Zapatero Years

Policymaking on women's rights during Zapatero's first term has often been considered to be in the vanguard. The PSOE's actions also coincided to a substantial degree with the demands of the feminist movement. After the 2004 general elections, the social democratic government quickly initiated a series of proactive gender equality policies. In 2004, the parliament passed the law on the integral protection against gender violence (organic law 1/2004, of December 28, 2004). It contained a full package of prevention, protection, and punishment measures. One of its main innovations is that the punishment for domestic violence is more severe when it is committed by men than by women. The prevention of violence against women has been a priority and a unifying battle for the Spanish feminist movement over the last two decades. Additionally, law 13/2005 of July 1, 2005, the so-called 2005 gay marriage law, permitted same-sex marriage. This law satisfied the demands advanced by part of the feminist movement to provide equal family rights to all people regardless of their sexual orientation. Parliament approved a new law that regulated divorce in 2005 (law 15/2005 of July 8, 2005, hereafter the 2005 divorce law). It permits shared custody only if both parents want it, which was in line with the preferences expressed by many but not all feminist organizations that judges should not grant shared custody in the absence of the parents' agreement.[6] In 2006, parliament also passed a law to promote the personal autonomy and care of dependent people, defined as those who cannot care for themselves (law 39/2006, of December 14, 2006, hereafter the 2006 dependency law). It established the universal right of dependent people to receive care partly or completely financed by the state. For decades, the feminist movement denounced the fact that dependent people were cared for mainly by female relatives on an unpaid basis, and, in turn, they demanded some state responsibility in the provision of care.

Additionally, in 2007, a comprehensive gender equality law was passed (organic law 3/2007, of March 22, 2007). Among other provisions, the law required all companies with more than 250 workers to negotiate firm-level equality plans. It mandated a candidate quota, requiring that 40 percent of candidates on all electoral lists be women, and established 13 days of paternity leave, at full pay. In prior decades, part of the feminist movement had denounced that gender equality policy was comprised of a set of dispersed legal provisions, and recommended the adoption of a general equality act. The feminist movement in general favored state action to force private companies to actively pursue gender equality in the workplace, to compel political parties to adopt quotas for women, and to encourage men to provide care.

Women's access to high political office is also a dimension of gender equality policymaking for at least two reasons. First, a high proportion of women in key decision-making positions sends a clear message to society that the government is seriously committed to giving political power to women. Additionally, research on political elites in Western countries concludes that male and female politicians behave differently in the policy area of women's rights, although differences are small. For instance, studies of female members of parliament (MPs) show that in comparison with their male counterparts female MPs are more interested in feminist issues, such as wage equality between women and men and abortion, and in issues traditionally associated with women, such as family and children's issues (the so-called feminine issues) (Childs 2001). Female MPs from time to time translate their interest in feminist and feminine issues into political behavior, since they at times manage to include both types of issues on the political agenda (Dodson 2001). On feminist and feminine issues, female MPs sometimes vote differently from male MPs, although voting differences by gender are small due to party discipline (Ross 2002). After the spring 2004 elections, Prime Minister Zapatero formed a government with an equal number of female and male ministers. One of the two vice presidents of the government (the functional equivalent of a deputy prime minister) was a woman: María Teresa Fernández de la Vega, a well-known feminist.

The establishment and/or consolidation of institutions dedicated to gender equality is another important dimension of gender equality policymaking because these institutions are in charge of advancing measures that erode gender hierarchies (Stetson & Mazur 1995). The Zapatero government created a highly ranked institution on gender equality in the Ministry of Labor and Social Affairs: the general secretariat on equality policies. A prominent feminist Soledad Murillo, an associate professor of sociology with expertise on gender research, was appointed to the position. Her appointment was backed by most individuals and organizations of the feminist movement. Between 1983 and 2004, the gender equality institution of the highest rank had been the women's institute. After 2004, the women's institute was institutionally linked to the general secretariat on equality policies. The creation of the general secretariat meant the upgrading of the gender equality machinery as it was ranked at a higher institutional level than the women's institute.

During Zapatero's second term, the PSOE continued the trend of forming cabinets with a large number of women. During the first term, all PSOE cabinets except one had the same number of women and men, the exception to this pattern being the cabinet active between July 2007 and April 2008 with seven women and nine men (44 percent women). During the second term, the cabinets had even more women than men (53 percent), the exception to this pattern being the cabinets active between October 2010 and December 2011 where women formed 47 percent of cabinet members.[7] This remarkable presence of women was internationally known in part due to specific appointments. For example, the picture of Minister of Defense Carme Chacón, the first pregnant woman to serve in cabinet in democratic Spain, visiting troops in Afghanistan in April 2008 while in the last term of her pregnancy, immediately reached the global audience of the international mass media. In April 2009, another woman, Elena Salgado, became not only minister of economy and finance but also vice president of the government. However, during both terms, the presence of women in executive ranks below the cabinet level was more modest. The proportion of female secretaries of state, the political position immediately below ministers, fluctuated between 20 and 25 percent between 2006 and 2011, with the exception of 2008 when it reached the highest level at 31 percent. The proportion of women among subsecretaries, the position immediately below secretaries of state, oscillated between 25 and 29 percent between 2006 and 2011.[8] In both terms, the PSOE's record on women's presence among the parliamentarian elite was impressive: the proportion of women among PSOE MPs in the Congress of Deputies, the lower and more significant chamber of parliament, was 43 percent in 2008 and 46 percent in 2004.[9]

Regarding gender equality institutions, the second term started in April 2008 with the creation of the ministry of equality, which was the highest ranked gender equality institution ever established. However, in spite of this, the PSOE's record on institution building related to gender equality was mixed. Thirty-one-year-old Bibiana Aído, the youngest woman to serve in cabinet in democratic Spain, was appointed minister of equality. She had not been formerly known as a gender expert or as a member of the women's movement (Bustelo 2009, 534). She had no previous experience in policymaking at the central state level, and she was not a party heavyweight. In October 2010, the ministry of equality was dismantled. Gender equality became the competence of the newly created state secretariat of equality within the newly created Ministry of Health, Social Policy and Equality. Former minister Aído became state secretary of equality. Thus, institutionally gender equality was demoted because a state secretariat ranks below a ministry.

During the second term, one of the chief legal reforms related to women's rights was the 2010 decriminalization of abortion. Abortion on demand during the first 14 weeks of pregnancy was permitted by organic law 2/2010, of March 3, 2010 (hereafter, the 2010 abortion law).[10] Also, according to the law, girls aged 16 and 17 years do not need parental consent to attain an abortion.[11] Most groups in the Spanish feminist movement have been united in calling for abortion on demand since the 1970s, when Spanish feminists first mobilized in favor of decriminalizing abortion (Prata 2007). On paper, the 2010 abortion law represented a huge departure from previous abortion regulation. Under the prior 1985 abortion law, abortion was a crime punishable under the penal code except on three grounds: when the woman had been raped; when the fetus was deformed; and when pregnancy seriously endangered the physical and mental health of the mother. However, in practice, the 2010 abortion law meant a significant but not immense departure from previous abortion regulation. This is because the mental health clause in the 1985 act was used as an imperfect proxy for abortion on demand (Blofield 2006, 92). Nonetheless, abortion on demand was not permitted by the 1985 law. Therefore, doctors and women were under continuous threat of prosecution, which only a legal reform could remedy (Barreiro 1998, 248–52).

Another major legal reform of the second term could have been the extension of paternity leave, at full pay, from thirteen days to four weeks. Law 9/2009, of October 6, 2009, established that the extension would be implemented in 2011. The law was important because it reflected the PSOE's willingness to provide fathers with incentives to care for their newly born babies. However, at the time of writing, it has not taken effect because the last Socialist cabinet and subsequently the first PP cabinet decided to postpone its implementation due to economic constraints.

Additionally, immediately before the 2011 elections, the last Socialist cabinet approved legislation on domestic workers, the overwhelming majority of whom are women. Royal decree 1620/2011, of November 14, 2011, significantly departed from the prior regulations (royal decree 1424/1985, of August 1, 1985) by improving the labor rights of domestic workers. In order to show the contrast between the 1985 and 2011 regulations, let me highlight several aspects of the law. The 2011 regulation made written contracts obligatory, with some exceptions, and assumed that contracts are indefinite, again with some exceptions, while the 1985 regulation also allowed verbal contracts and assumed that contracts were year-long, again with exceptions. Although both the 1985 and 2011 regulations stipulated that the worker's salary must be equal or above the general minimum wage, the 2011 legislation abolished the employer's right to deduct up to 45 percent of the employee's salary for food and accommodation. The 2011 regulations also raised the amount of the extra pay received twice a year from the equivalent of 15 days of pay to a month's pay. The 2011 legislation increased severance pay, per year worked, from 7 to 12 days' salary. Under the 2011 regulations employers also had to pay social security contributions beginning with the first hour of work. In contrast, under the 1985 regulations, employers did not have to pay social security contributions if they hired domestic workers for less than 20 hours per week (León 2012).

The regulation of domestic work affects a significant number of people. In February 2012, 288,100 domestic workers were included in the social security system.[12] However, this only includes those who work in the formal sector of the economy. Experts estimate that at least the same number of people, if not more, work as domestic workers in the informal sector (León 2010). According to the Household Budget Survey (*Encuesta de Presupuestos Familiares*), in 2010 one out of seven households (14 percent) in Spain hired domestic workers.[13]

In sum, during Prime Minister Zapatero's second term, women's presence in high political office remained considerable. PSOE policymakers made access to abortion easier and at least on paper improved labor conditions for domestic workers. Generally speaking, though with exceptions, academic research and the mass media have not considered these developments to be seminal.

The (Relatively) Modest Record of Gender Equality Policymaking in the Second Term: An Interpretation

What explains the more modest record of legislative innovation on gender equality in the second term? To answer this question, I focus first on the reduced room for pioneering reforms, and, second, on the difficulties of implementing the measures approved during the first term.

Reduced Room for Policy Innovation

The comprehensive character of legislative reforms in the area of gender equality during the first term meant that PSOE politicians in the second term had only a small area in which to formulate policy on women's rights. Nonetheless there were important issues remaining, such as abortion rights. Generally speaking, abortion is a highly controversial issue in most polities and Spain is no exception to this rule. In Spain, abortion and women's quotas are the gender issues on which the positions of the PSOE and PP differ the most.

Abortion decriminalization consumed much of the energy of Socialist women's rights policymakers between 2008 and 2010. The establishment of abortion on demand in 2010 was preceded by acute controversy between political and social actors, and received intense mass media attention. The PP opposed both abortion on demand and 16- and 17-year-old girls' having access to abortion without parental consent. Moreover, the dispute was not settled with the passage of the 2010 abortion law because the PP lodged an appeal with the Constitutional Court arguing that some of its articles were unconstitutional. At the time of writing, the Court has not released a ruling. This was not the first time that the PP lodged an appeal with the Court against a Socialist gender equality measure. In 2002, the party challenged the regional laws that made a 40 percent women's quota mandatory in some subnational elections, and in 2007 regarding the 40 percent mandatory quota for women established for all elections by the 2007 gender equality law. This issue was settled in 2008, when the court ruled that mandatory quotas were constitutional (Verge 2012, 402–404). The severe controversy surrounding abortion is a reminder that gender equality policymaking may be difficult for reasons other than economic constraints.

Difficulties of Policy Implementation

The innovative gender equality policies of the first term also had to be implemented in the subsequent years. Implementation absorbed the attention and energy of PSOE public officials during the second term. The rampant economic crisis made the implementation of any measure a difficult task, but the recession was not the only obstacle. Weak implementation has been a feature of gender-equality policy more generally in democratic Spain (León 2011b; Lombardo 2009; Valiente 2008).

The 2006 dependency law illustrates the difficulties of implementation. Other things being equal, a welfare state that provides extensive care services saves women from having to provide care for others on an unpaid basis. Comparatively speaking, the Spanish welfare state has usually been described as one that offers very few care services. Families (and in practice, mainly women within them) are responsible for the provision of care that dependent people of any age need (Esping-Andersen 1990; León 2011a, 3; Sarasa 2011). The 2006 dependency law departed from the existing situation by establishing some state responsibility for the provision of care needed by dependent people. If implemented correctly, it would liberate many women from having to provide care to relatives on an unpaid basis.

The law envisaged a classification of dependent people according to three degrees of dependency (moderate, severe, and total) and two levels within each degree. Dependency here means the need for assistance to perform daily activities, and dependents would receive benefits according to their degree of dependence. The benefits ranged from monetary transfers to care services, such as in-home help, remote assistance, day care and night care centers, and institutional care. The law also envisaged the full implementation of benefits by 2015, starting gradually with dependents with the highest degree of dependence and finishing with people with the lowest degree (but see the following paragraphs). There is no doubt that the dependency law has provided a significant number of dependent people with monetary transfers and/or care services that enhance their personal autonomy. On March 1, 2012, 1,614,748 people had applied to be considered dependents, and 94 percent of these applications (or 1,515,294 applications) were processed. On the same date, 1,046,515 people were officially classified as dependents and thus entitled to some benefits.[14]

What we now know is that the implementation of the 2006 dependency law was riddled with difficulties from the outset. As León (2011b, 69) synthesized, "Insufficient and unclear financing, tensions between different levels of government and lack of a realistic assessment of available resources have translated into a weak transposition." Although most dependents were to be given access to care services, this is not what has happened. On March 1, 2012, 52 percent of the benefits granted were monetary transfers.[15] Monetary transfers have become much more common than what the law foresaw probably because care services are very costly, and existing care services were underdeveloped (León 2011a, 8–9; Sarasa 2011, 247–51). The implementation of the law was geographically uneven, with some regions making greater advances, such as Andalusia, and others falling behind, such as Valencia and Madrid. This geographical imbalance means that two people with the same level of dependence but living in different regions may be granted different benefits (León 2011a, 8).[16] The economic crisis exacerbated the problems of implementation. After the transfer of governmental power to the PP, the government suspended new applications to be declared dependent in the lowest dependency category for 2012 (royal decree 20/2011, of December 30, 2011).

What Remains to Be Done on Women's Rights

During both terms, the formulation of women's rights policy corresponded with the major legal reforms historically demanded by the feminist movement. However, as shown earlier, the same positive assessment cannot be made of policy implementation. Feminist activists time and again have insisted that what is still pending is the full implementation of the measures adopted between 2004 and 2011.[17] Women's organizations close to the PP, such as the Female Employers and Managers Organization, also argue that the implementation of the legal reforms is one of the pending tasks.[18]

While the PSOE, between 2004 and 2011, fulfilled many of the legislative demands advanced by the feminist movement, prostitution is one main exception. As in many other Western countries, the Spanish feminist movement is sharply divided on the subject of prostitution. A sector of the movement is abolitionist. Abolitionists consider prostitution to be an affront to people's dignity; it is then irrelevant whether prostitutes voluntarily consent to prostitution or not. Abolitionists argue that prostitutes should not be legally defined as criminals; in contrast, people who promote the prostitution of others or benefit from it should be severely punished. They also demand that the state and society make serious efforts to help women leave prostitution.[19]

When the PSOE gained power in 2004, broadly speaking, Spanish legislation was (imperfectly) abolitionist. Prostitutes were not legally defined as criminals, and people who benefitted from the prostitution of others were punished (up to four years in prison). Punishment was higher in the case of the prostitution of minors or of those defined as legally incapacitated, such as the mentally handicapped or disturbed (hereafter "legally incapacitated"). During the Zapatero years, the legislation on prostitution that existed in 2004 remained basically unchanged.

However, the PSOE took measures to combat the trafficking of women for sexual exploitation. For instance, in December 2008, the government approved the "integral plan to fight against trafficking in people with the aim of sexual exploitation." Among other initiatives, this comprehensive set of measures established (or improved) protection and benefits for victims who report their traffickers.[20] A 2010 reform of the penal code punished, with up to eight years of prison, those who trafficked in people with the purpose of sexual exploitation (organic law 5/2010, of June 22, 2010).

However, the Socialists did not satisfy the main demands of the abolitionist sector of the movement, who advocated the criminalization of behaviors surrounding prostitution that the existing penal code does not define as crimes, for instance, promoting the prostitution of others (who are not minors or legally incapacitated). Furthermore, abolitionists wanted the state to take significant proactive steps to help women stop working as prostitutes.[21]

In contrast with abolitionists, other activists from the feminist movement support the regulation of prostitution. According to their view, there are two types of prostitutes; those who engage in prostitution voluntarily and those who are forced into prostitution by others. They argue that the state should actively fight to prevent forced prostitution but not voluntary prostitution. These activists conceptualize voluntary prostitutes as sex workers and demand that the state treats them the same as other workers, for example, by allowing them to contribute to the social security system.[22] The Socialists did not satisfy the chief demands of this sector of the movement either because the PSOE did not regulate free prostitution as a profession (as sex work).

It is important to note that the women's rights legislation developed between 2004 and 2011 did not cover all aspects of gender inequality. Therefore, reforms are still pending and necessary to erode gender hierarchies.[23] Childcare is a case in point. In contemporary Spain, preschool works as a functional, although imperfect, equivalent to childcare services for children of certain ages. As mentioned earlier, Spanish preschool attendance rates are among the highest in the EU for children aged three, four, and five. Conversely, the proportion of Spanish children aged two or younger who are cared for in centers is comparatively low: 8 percent for children younger than one year, 28 percent of children aged one year, and 45 percent for those two years old (academic year 2009–10).[24] However, the policies developed during this period were not aimed at significantly increasing care services for babies, toddlers, or children. The current low level of childcare services is still a primary obstacle for Spanish women to be able to combine work and family.

Future Prospects under Popular Party Rule

The beginning of the new legislative term in late 2011 was marked by a decrease in women's presence in high political office. Although the vice president (and minister of the presidency, and cabinet spokesperson) of the new PP government is a woman, Soraya Sáenz de Santamaría, the proportion of women in the first PP cabinet is 31 percent (four women and nine men). This is significantly lower than the proportion of women in cabinets during the prior Socialist governments: usually 50 percent.

After the 2011 general elections, 36 percent of PP parliamentarians in the Congress of Deputies were women. This is lower than the equivalent PSOE proportions in 2004 and 2008 (46 percent and 43 percent, respectively), but only slightly below the portion of PSOE deputies who were women in 2011 (39 percent).[25] As for gender equality institutions, at the beginning of the legislative term, the policy area of gender equality lost institutional importance. After the disappearance of the Ministry of Equality during the prior Socialist term, the institution with the highest administrative rank in charge of gender equality as its only competence was the state secretariat on equality. After the PP reached power in 2011, the highest ranked institution dedicated exclusively to gender equality was the women's institute. This was the same institutional situation that had existed in the period between 1983 and 2004.

Research on gender equality policymaking in Western countries suggests that conservative parties facilitate the development of gender equality policies to a lesser extent than social democratic parties (Bashevkin 1998; Lovenduski & Norris 1993, 1996; Lovenduski et al. 1994). Nonetheless, studies on gender and politics in the Western part of the world have also acknowledged that conservative parties have at times responded to the demands of women's movements (Lovenduski & Norris 1993, 6–7, 13; 1996, 9; Lovenduski et al. 1994, 611–12). Thus conservative parties have to a limited extent converged with socialist parties. Nevertheless, the general conclusion of the gender and politics literature on postindustrial societies is that parties matter and social democratic parties are usually more active than conservative parties in the search for gender equality.

In Spain, since the 1990s, gender equality has increasingly become an area of electoral competition. In the 1980s, the conservative Popular Party paid little attention to the issue of inequalities between women and men; by the 1990s the conservative party was trying to convince the electorate that its gender equality policies would be as good as the Socialist Party's, or even better. This strategic choice by the conservative party was reflected in a convergence of its discourse with the discourse of the Socialists in some policy areas, for instance, with regard to women's waged employment, and in actual policymaking once in office, for example, with respect to sexual harassment and childcare. Between 1996 and 2004, the PP governments preserved most existing gender equality policies established by the preceding Socialist administrations (Bustelo 2009, 533, 543; Ruiz 2006). Thus, one may argue that after the 2011 general elections, the PP will likely maintain most (but not all) of the gender equality measures passed during the Zapatero years. However, one caveat is necessary here. After 1982, the PSOE was in power for fourteen years (1982–96). This was a sufficiently long period to set the governmental agenda with respect to gender equality. The Socialists were able to set targets, values, and staff in government departments and in the civil service. When the PP gained power in 1996, perhaps dismantling existing programs would have represented too high of an electoral cost for the PP (or any party) to pay. Conversely, in the twenty-first century, the PSOE was in office for seven years (2004–11). The Socialists' legacy on gender equality was probably less consolidated in 2011 than in 1996.

The main exception to the general assumption that the PP will preserve existing women's policies is likely abortion regulation. After the 2011 general election, key PP politicians, including Minister of Justice Alberto Ruiz Gallardón and PP General Secretary Dolores de Cospedal, restated their opposition to both abortion on demand and minors' access to abortion without parental consent. Although PP policymakers have not provided all of the details of the abortion policy they favor, they seemed to indicate that they will restore a policy similar to the 1985 regulation.[26]

Preserving Socialist gender equality policies is not an easy task because these policies have to be implemented. While economic constraints will surely put a brake on the PSOE's gender equality legacy, these are not the only obstacles. The case of the 2011 regulation of the domestic sector illustrates the point. Domestic work is performed in private homes where the labor inspectorate's action is very weak. Many employers may be tempted to hire in the informal sector of the economy in order to escape employers' obligations, which are tougher under the 2011 regulation. Spain in the first quarter of 2012 had the highest unemployment rate in the EU (24 percent).[27] This means that employers are able to find numerous women willing to work in private homes as domestic workers under working conditions that are considerably below the level mandated by the law (León 2012). Weak implementation is likely to continue to characterize the policy area of gender equality in the near future.

Notes

1. In this chapter, the words "social democratic" and "socialist" are used synonymously. Given space constraints, this chapter only deals with policies elaborated by the central state. For policies at the regional level, see Bustelo and Ortbals (2007) and Ortbals et al (2012).
2. For the sake of brevity, I use the expressions "first term" and "second term" to refer to "first PSOE legislative term" and "second PSOE legislative term," respectively.

3. Interview with the author in Salamanca on May 3, 2012.
4. Inmaculada Álvarez, president of Female Employers and Managers Organization (Madrid, May 9, 2012); Rosario Carracedo, spokesperson of the Platform for the Abolition of Prostitution (Madrid, May 8, 2012); Ángela Cerrillos, president of Female Lawyers Association Themis (Madrid, April 16, 2012); Susana Martínez, president of the Commission for the Investigation of Violence against Women (Madrid, May 7, 2012); Lucía Mazarrasa, vice president of Forum of Feminist Politics (Madrid, April 20, 2012); and Justa Montero, member of the Spanish Federation of Feminist Organizations (Madrid, May 12, 2012).
5. Ministerio de Educación, Cultura y Deporte, *Las cifras de la educación en España, curso 2009–2010.*
6. Author interviews with Ángela Cerrillos and Susana Martínez.
7. Author's calculation based on ministerial appointments published in the *Boletín Oficial del Estado.*
8. C. Nogueira, "Solo el 28% de los altos cargos nombrados por Rajoy son mujeres," *El País*, April 10, 2012, p. 32. Instituto de la Mujer, *Mujeres en cifras.* Available at: http://www.inmujer.gob.es/estadisticas/portada/home.htm (last accessed on April 7, 2012).
9. Instituto de la Mujer, *Mujeres en cifras.* See previous note.
10. In cases of grave risks to the mother's life or health, and fetus's grave anomalies, abortion can be performed up to the twenty-second week of pregnancy. After that moment, abortion is permitted on two grounds: when the fetus's anomalies are incompatible with life, and when the fetus has an extremely grave and incurable illness.
11. They must, however, inform at least one parent, except in cases of conflictual households when such news would cause extreme conflict.
12. Ministerio de Empleo y Seguridad Social, *Boletín de estadísticas laborales, actualizado a 8 de marzo de 2012.*
13. Instituto Nacional de Estadística, "Encuesta de presupuestos familiares año 2010," *Notas de prensa*, October 27, 2011. Available at: http://www.ine.es /prensa/np683.pdf.
14. IMSERSO, *Información estadística del sistema para la autonomía y la atención a la dependencia: Situación a 1 de marzo de 2012.* Available at: www .dependencia.imserso.
15. IMSERSO, *Información estadística del sistema para la autonomía y la atención a la dependencia: Situación a 1 de marzo de 2012.* See previous note.
16. C. Morán, "César Antón director del IMSERSO: 'No se atiende igual a la gente con la misma dependencia,'" *El País*, March 19, 2012, p. 34.
17. Author interviews with Ángela Cerrillos, Susana Martínez, and Lucía Mazarrasa.
18. Author interview with Inmaculada Álvarez.
19. Author interviews with Rosario Carracedo, Ángela Cerrillos, and Susana Martínez.

20. Gobierno de España, *Plan integral de lucha contra la trata de seres humanos con fines de explotación sexual*, 2008. Retrieved on May 1, 2012 at: www.inmujer.es.
21. Author interview with Rosario Carracedo.
22. Colectivo en defensa de los derechos de las trabajadoras del sexo Hetaira, *¿Qué es Hetaira?*, last accessed on May 22, 2012 (www.colectivohetaira.com); author interview with Justa Montero.
23. Author interviews with Justa Montero and Soledad Murillo.
24. Ministerio de Educación, Cultura y Deporte, *Las cifras de la educación en España, curso 2009–2010*. See earlier.
25. Instituto de la Mujer, *Mujeres en cifras*. See earlier.
26. F. Garea, "Gallardón anuncia un giro conservador," *El País*, January 26, 2012, pp. 12–14; C. E. Curé and F. Manetto, "Dolores de Cospedal, Secretaria General del PP y presidenta de Castilla-La Mancha: 'En España hay que trabajar más horas,'" *El País*, March 12, 2012, pp. 16–17.
27. Instituto Nacional de Estadística, *Encuesta de población activa*, 2012. Available at: www.ine.es.

WorksC ited

Barreiro, B. 1998. *Democracia y conflicto moral: La política del aborto en Italia y España*. Madrid: Centro de Estudios Avanzados en Ciencias Sociales.

Bashevin, S. 1998. *Women on the Defensive: Living through Conservative Times*. Chicago: University of Chicago Press.

Blofield, M. 2006. *The Politics of Moral Sin: Abortion and Divorce in Spain, Chile and Argentina*. London and New York: Routledge.

Bustelo, M. 2009. "Spain: Intersectionality Faces the Strong Gender Norm." *International Feminist Journal of Politics* 11(4): 530–46.

Bustelo, M., and C. D. Ortbals. 2007. "The Evolution of Spanish State Feminism: A Fragmented Landscape." In J. Outshoorn and J. Kantola, eds., *Changing State Feminism: Women's Policy Agencies Confront Shifting Institutional Terrain*. New York: Palgrave, pp. 201–33.

Calvo, K., and I. Martín. 2011. "Ungrateful Citizens? Women's Rights Policies in Zapatero's Spain." In B. N. Field, ed., *Spain's "Second Transition"? The Socialist Government of José Luis Rodríguez Zapatero*. London: Routledge, pp. 109–24.

Childs, S. 2001. "'Attitudinal Feminist'? The New Labor Women MPs and the Substantive Representation of Women." *Politics* 21(3): 178–85.

Dodson, D. L. 2001. "Acting for Women: Is What Legislators Say, What They Do?" In S. J. Carroll, ed., *The Impact of Women in Public Office*. Bloomington and Indianapolis: Indiana University Press, pp. 225–42.

Esping-Andersen, G. 1990. *The Three Worlds of Welfare Capitalism*. Princeton: Princeton University Press.

León, M. 2010. "Migration and Care Work in Spain: The Domestic Sector Revisited." *Social Policy and Society* 9(3): 409–18.

———. 2011a. "Ideas, políticas y realidad: Análisis crítico de la ley de dependencia." *Papeles de Economía Española* 129: 2–14.

———. 2011b. "The Quest for Gender Equality." In A. M. Guillén and M. León, eds., *The Spanish Welfare State in European Context*. Farnham: Ashgate, pp. 59–74.

———. 2012. "Filling the Gaps: Migrant Women in Spanish Households." Unpublished paper.

Lombardo, E. 2009. "Spanish Policy on Gender Equality: Relevant Current Legislation and Policies." *Briefing Note for the European Parliament*. Brussels: European Parliament.

Lovenduski, J., and P. Norris, eds. 1993. *Gender and Party Politics*. London: Sage.

———. 1996. *Women in Politics*. Oxford: Oxford University Press and The Hansard Society Series in Politics and Government.

Lovenduski, J., P. Norris, and C. Burness. 1994. "The Party and Women." In A. Seldon and S. Ball, eds., *Conservative Century: The Conservative Party since 1900*. Oxford: Oxford University Press, pp. 611–35.

Morcillo, A. G. 2000. *True Catholic Womanhood: Gender Ideology in Franco's Spain*. Dekalb: Northern Illinois University Press.

Ortbals, C. D., M. Rincker, and C. Montoya. 2012. "Politics Close to Home: The Impact of Meso-level Institutions on Women and Politics." *Publius* 42(1): 78–107.

Prata, A. 2007. *Women's Movements, the State, and the Struggle for Abortion Rights: Comparing Spain and Portugal in Times of Democratic Expansion (1974–1988)*. PhD dissertation, University of Minnesota.

Ross, K. 2002. "Women's Place in 'Male' Space: Gender and Effect in Parliamentary Contexts." *Parliamentary Affairs* 55(1): 189–201.

Ruiz, A. M. 2006. *De la necesidad virtud: La transformación "feminista" del Partido Popular en perspectiva comparada*. Madrid: Centro de Estudios Políticos y Constitucionales.

Ruiz, R. 2007. *¿Eternas menores? Las mujeres en el franquismo*. Madrid: Biblioteca Nueva.

Sarasa, S. 2011. "Long-Term Care: The Persistence of Familism." In A. M. Guillén and M. León, eds., *The Spanish Welfare State in European Context*. Farnham: Ashgate, pp. 237–57.

Stetson, D. M., and A. G. Mazur, eds. 1995. *Comparative State Feminism*. Thousand Oaks: Sage.

Valiente, C. 2008. "Spain at the Vanguard in European Gender Equality Policies." In S. Roth, ed., *Gender Politics in the Expanding European Union: Mobilization, Inclusion, Exclusion*. New York: Berghahn, pp. 101–17.

Verge, T. 2012. "Institutionalizing Gender Equality in Spain: Incremental Steps from Party to Electoral Gender Quotas." *West European Politics* 35(2): 395–414.

CHAPTER 11

The Spanish Welfare State from Zapatero to Rajoy: Recalibration to Retrenchment

Eloísa del Pino

The modernization and expansion of Spain's welfare state were largely accomplishments of the Socialist Party (PSOE) governments under Prime Minister Felipe González between 1982 and 1996. However, during those years, social spending was also firmly kept in check by economic policy requirements (del Pino & Ramos 2009; Guillén 2010; Rodríguez-Cabrero 2011). This chapter demonstrates that this assertion is also true for the two terms of Socialist prime minister Rodríguez Zapatero (2004–11). I argue that Zapatero's governments enacted some reform initiatives during his first term and the beginning of his second term aimed at modernizing and adapting the welfare state to the so-called new social risks (immigration, aging, changing family structure, new forms of poverty, among others), what in the comparative literature has been dubbed *recalibration* (Pierson 2001). However, due to the general change of policy direction in response to the economic and sovereign debt crises toward austerity and adjustment requirements, in the latter half of the second term the Socialist government was forced to undo some of these policies and enact measures that represented welfare state retrenchment.

Moreover, the implementation of these measures by a left-wing party, which in principle was supposed to be a defender of the welfare state, set the stage for the enactment of further retrenchment measures by the right-wing Popular Party (PP) government under Prime Minister Mariano Rajoy (December 2011 onward). Until then, previous right-center governments had not dared to take that road for fear of being punished at the polls as antilabor and antiwelfare. Although it is too early to measure the extent of the cuts made by the PP government, it seems that we now face a radical retrenchment of the Spanish welfare state.

This chapter first examines the Spanish welfare state's main achievements and the problems it faced when Prime Minister Zapatero took office in 2008. As we will see, some of these were structural and derive from the incomplete nature of the welfare state in Spain, while others are common to other European welfare systems. The second section provides a brief overview of the main reforms undertaken during Zapatero's two terms and those implemented by the Rajoy government during its first months in office. The final section presents some concluding remarks.

Unsolved Problems and New Challenges Aggravated by the Economic Crisis

The Rapid Development and Incomplete Nature of the Spanish Welfare State

It is undeniable that the "transformation of the Spanish welfare state since the mid-1970s can only be called spectacular" (Guillén & León 2011, 5). Social spending as a percentage of gross domestic product (GDP) doubled from 1960, reaching 24 percent in 1993 (and about 21 percent between 2000 and 2007). Moreover, the total tax-to-GDP ratio in 1965 was 15 percent, which rose to about 37 percent by 2007.[1]

However, although most countries of the European Union-15 (EU-15) tried to contain social spending throughout the 1980s and even cut after 1995, the Spanish welfare state never managed to catch up to their spending levels. In 2007, while social spending in Spain was 21.6 percent, in Italy, Germany, and France it reached 24.9, 25.2, and 28.4 percent, respectively.[2] Gaps in the Spanish social protection system have been covered by the important role played by the family and, especially, women, who have taken care of the children and the elderly, and nowadays also of their grandchildren. About 21 percent of women over 65, some 880,000, take care of their grandchildren regularly (Pérez-Ortiz 2004).

Although there are indications that the weight of the family is in decline in Spain (Moreno & Mari-Klose 2013), it is precisely its role, particularly that of the "Mediterranean superwomen" (Moreno 2004), that has made some researchers question the adequacy of the classic typology of "three worlds" of welfare by Esping-Andersen (1990)—social democratic, liberal, and conservative—to characterize Southern European countries' welfare regimes. A new type has been proposed, the so-called Mediterranean type, to which Spain belongs alongside Italy, Greece, and Portugal (Ferrera 1996). In addition to this familistic feature, these countries have in common belated development and the coexistence of more or less generous universal benefits together with contributory and means-tested benefits. In sum, three distinct approaches coexist in these Mediterranean welfare regimes, the social democratic, liberal, and conservative or Bismarckian (Rodríguez-Cabrero 2011).

Some of the main characteristics of the welfare state in Spain are the following:

- Public pensions in Spain include a contributory scheme that offers a pay-as-you-go financed and earnings-related retirement, permanent disability, and survivors benefits; and a noncontributory scheme, established in 1991 and financed by general tax revenues, that pays a means-tested flat rate benefit for elderly and disabled people who do not fulfill the eligibility conditions for a contributory public pension.
- Since 1986 there is a universal national health service (NHS), which is among the best in the world according to World Health Organization assessments (WHO 2000) and citizen evaluations.[3]
- Since 1985, the education system guarantees the universal right to compulsory basic education for children aged 6–16 years.
- Unemployment protection has several components, one of which is contributory, and plays a basic role in ensuring the well-being of society.
- Family policies, in part because of the stigma of the pronatality policies of the Franco dictatorship, have not received attention until recently. Spending on these policies is clearly insufficient, being well below other EU countries.
- Finally, long-term care was launched only in 2006. Also, generally modest minimum income schemes exist in the autonomous communities (ACs) since 1989. Social welfare services were devolved between 1987 and early 1990 to the regions.

Using data from 2009, the most important components of social spending are retirement pensions (30 percent), health care (30 percent), and unemployment protection (14 percent), compared to 39, 29, and 5 percent, respectively, in the EU-27. Regarding education, which is usually excluded from social spending, Spain spends about 5 percent of GDP on it compared to the 5.5 percent average of the EU-27.[4]

Two additional features are critical for understanding Spain's welfare state. First, welfare policies are in large part decentralized. The decentralization of health care and education to the 17 regions culminated in 2002. While pension policies and passive unemployment programs remain almost entirely in the hands of central government, regional governments also have powers in active employment policy, minimum income, and other social welfare services. Over 70 percent of regional annual budgets are dedicated to regional social policies (health care, education, and social welfare).

Second, the role of Europeanization in Spanish social policies is critical. The EU's concern for social issues has been linked to attaining economic competitiveness and employment objectives. Without a doubt, Europeanization impacts the direction of national social policies.

Structural Problems and the Challenge of New Social Risks

When the PSOE took office in 2004, the welfare state faced several unresolved challenges. On the one hand, there was the still limited level of institutionalization in some policy areas, such as long-term care or family. On the other, there were new problems similar to those faced by other European welfare regimes, those referred to as the new social risks (Taylor-Gooby 2004). The pressures of these challenges were progressively compounded as the international economic crisis evolved.

Regarding structural challenges, Spain is, next to Japan, the country with the oldest population in the world. Although the birth rate had grown to 1.46 children per woman of childbearing age in 2008, this trend began to reverse again in 2009 declining to 1.39 (and 1.38 in 2010 and 2011), far, for instance, from the French rate of 2 children.[5] Similarly, life expectancy increased significantly to 81.8 years in 2010, higher than the EU-27 average of 79.4 years.[6] This situation strains the sustainability of the existing pension system, since social security expenditure is expected to rise from 7.4 percent of GDP in 2007 to 15.5 percent in 2050 (OECD 2011b). This also represents a serious challenge for providing care for a large number of elderly dependents, who will become the majority of the population when the large baby-boom generation retires after 2030.

Concerning health care, one of the main problems of the Spanish NHS is its sustainability, derived not only from the aging population and growing number of chronically ill patients, but also due to other challenges such as the incorporation of new diagnostic technologies (Moreno Fuentes 2013). Regarding education, Spain performs well with regard to equity of access to education, being among the top countries in the OECD (Bertelsmann Foundation 2011); however, the results in terms of educational performance are not good (OECD 2012). Among the main challenges, some suggested by EU reports, are: to lower the proportion of 15-year-olds who do not attain a minimum level of basic learning skills; reduce student course failures and dropout rates; increase schooling for children aged 0–2; and increase the number of graduates with technical and engineering degrees (CES 2012).

In 2008, unemployment affected 11 percent of the active population (in 2012 it reached 25 percent) and was the highest in the EU-27. The rate of temporary employment was 32.5 percent compared to an EU-15 average of 13.5. These problems particularly affect the elderly, women, and young people. For young people, unemployment soared after 2008, especially among low-skilled men, from less than 8 percent in 2007 to almost 19 percent in 2008. In 2012 it was over 50 percent. This is the result of the bursting of the housing bubble; the construction sector shed a tremendous number of jobs, particularly impacting young low-skilled men. These are no doubt worrying figures, since the percentage of young people who have dropped out of school without a high-school degree is more than double the EU-27 average (28.4 versus 14.1 percent in 2010) and they will find it very difficult to get jobs due to their lack of qualifications. A generation has appeared that has been dubbed the "neither-nor" (*ni-ni*) generation since they do not study or work.

In addition, they will be particularly affected at the end of their working lives when they realize that they have not contributed enough to qualify for certain benefits. High unemployment and job insecurity also bring about the late emancipation of young people and delay motherhood. While in Finland the average age to leave home is 22.5 years; in Spain it is 28.8 (Moreno & Gentile 2011). An additional problem is the enormous cost of housing, unaffordable for certain social groups. This occurs despite the fact that Spain built more houses in one year than the United Kingdom and Germany combined, countries with nearly twice as many inhabitants as Spain, where there are more than three million empty homes (CES 2012).

Despite economic growth and the substantial expansion of antipoverty policies in terms of both expenditures and recipients, the poverty rate increased between 1991 and 2008, and was especially high among children (23.2 percent) and the elderly (23.3 percent). In 2008, there was more poverty in Spain (over 20 percent of the population) than in most European countries (EU-25 average of about 15 percent). Estimates in 2011 showed new increases (Ayala 2011).

Of the new social risks, one of the challenges of the Spanish social protection system is derived from the accelerated incorporation of women into the workforce. In terms of the female employment rate, that is, the number of employed women aged 15–64 years divided by the total female population, Spain was still 6 points below the EU-27 average in 2009. But, in 15 years it had grown almost 25 percentage points to around 53 percent in 2009.[7] Likewise, new types of families, such as single-parent families, have emerged in Spain, which pose new challenges for designing family policies.

Additionally, in just ten years immigrants in Spain reached 12 percent of the population, greater than in other European countries with long histories as receptor countries. Although the net balance between what immigrants contribute and consume regarding public services is positive for the country (Dolado & Vázquez 2008), their arrival raised a number of challenges for the welfare state, such as increased pressure on public services and its necessary adaptation to a diverse population. Also, immigration has raised the suspicion of citizens who, for example, assess public education and health more negatively in those regions where there are more immigrants (Díaz-Pulido et al. 2012). In the future, the system will have to deal simultaneously with the fiscal pressure of retirement benefits for immigrants and baby-boomers.

From Zapatero to Rajoy: Recalibration to Retrenchment of the Spanish Welfare State (2004–12)

The Political Parties' Visions of the Welfare State

The Spanish Socialists were not satisfied with the modernization of the "puny" social policies of the Franco regime (Moreno & Sarasa 1993). The González governments (1982–96) pushed for universal health care, which the main opposition center-right Popular Alliance (later Popular Party) opposed, and education, the establishment of new retirement benefits and a progressive tax system. However, the difficult economic situation during the transition to democracy and the desire to show that Spain was a safe country for foreign investment led the Socialist governments to pursue some orthodox fiscal policies and to forego much of the expansionist agenda in social policy. The González governments also implemented some adjustment reforms, such as the streamlining of the pension system in 1985 and some cutbacks in unemployment benefits in the early 1990s. Also, beginning in 1993, with the PSOE still in power, the increase in social spending began to slow and the gap began to increase between the Spanish and the average expenditure of the EU-15 (Navarro 2009). Socialist governments have often been accused of being too cautious or "austere" with social spending. This criticism was not necessarily unpleasant for certain sectors of the PSOE, who wanted to show that, as a former González minister expressed, "the left-wing also 'knows' economics" (del Pino & Ramos 2009).

Regarding the Popular Party (PP), the different ideological families within it have adopted a pragmatic stance on the welfare state, focused on expanding the PP's electoral base, since one of the PSOE's main and successful accusations during the years that the PP (and formerly the Popular Alliance) was in opposition was that the party wanted to put an end to the achievements in social policy. However, at least during its time in opposition and during its first term in office between 1996 and 2000, the PP avoided an attack on welfare policies. Although with some internal resistance, the PP signed the Pact of Toledo, committing itself to preserve a public pension system; it maintained the level of fiscal pressure and its socioeconomic policies were directed at cost-containment rather than social-spending cutbacks. One should also acknowledge the PP's inclusion of family policies on the political agenda, which had not received much attention until 2000. However, there is major internal dissent about the direction the party should take in relation to the state's role in the economy.[8] Moreover, the gap between social spending in Spain and the EU-15 kept rising, and there were some initiatives in Aznar's second term (2000–2004), such as the attempt to tighten access to unemployment benefits in 2002, that signified a questioning of the welfare state; and some PP-led regional governments, such as the region of Madrid, enacted outright neoliberal policies in the fields of education and health.

Finally, due to their significance in relation to welfare reforms one should refer to social partners, namely, the two most representative trade unions, the General Workers Union (UGT) and the Workers Commissions (CC.OO.), which have traditionally been linked to the left. The main organization of employers is the Spanish Confederation of Employers' Organizations (CEOE). While communication between the government and the social actors came to a halt at certain points during the late 1980s and early 1990s, the years immediately before the 2008 crisis displayed a new climate of agreement about social policy reforms under the label of "social dialogue." Also important for understanding the logic of social policy reform is the strong support of citizens for the welfare state. Spanish citizens believe that there is still room for the improvement of social policies in terms of taxes and benefits when they compare these policies to their counterparts in other neighboring countries, such as the Nordic countries or France (Calzada & del Pino 2011). Although during the crisis, the support for cuts in policy areas such as the environment and public safety has grown, about 97 percent of citizens oppose the cutbacks in health, education, and public pensions (del Pino et al. 2011).

The Welfare State Trajectory between 2004 and 2012

As argued by Sánchez-Cuenca (2012, 20), the well-known inspiration in the ideas of republicanism (Pettit 1999) of some of the Zapatero policies (2004–11) did not extend to the economy. Policy proposals in that realm had more to do with the orthodox and liberal tenets of the Third Way (Giddens 1998). This author recalls Zapatero's very questionable statement while still in opposition declaring that "lowering taxes is also leftist." In this sense, although Zapatero's social policies between 2004 and 2009 attempted to rectify some of the problems of the welfare state and had some modernizing ambitions, they were always self-restrained. This was so despite the spectacular growth and a budget surplus that Spain maintained until 2008, even though poverty and inequality rates clearly above the EU average posed a clear challenge for a social democratic government.

When in 2008, in the wake of the international economic crisis and the credit crash, Spain's economic outlook deteriorated, Zapatero, in a desperate attempt to maintain employment, applied some Keynesian stimulus policies between 2008 and 2009. However, they were not able to contain the crisis (Molina 2012). Headlines such as "The end of the Spanish miracle" or the "Spanish hangover" began to appear in the international business press. After having been reluctant for some time to acknowledge the real extent of the crisis, even refusing to mention the word "crisis," and having sought to implement a socially and economically progressive response to the crisis, late 2009 saw a clear change toward austerity policies. In the spring of 2010, the Zapatero government radically reversed its expansionist policies. After returning from the EU summit on May 9, under pressure from the International Monetary Fund (IMF), and after having received personal calls from Barack Obama, Angela Merkel, and Hu Jianto, Zapatero presented a comprehensive plan for deficit reduction that included a 5 percent cut in public employees' wages and, as we shall see later, severe cuts in social spending. Without any public debate, the government ruled out a strategy based on increasing state revenues and opted for a reduction of public spending, which would especially penalize recipients of welfare state benefits and services (Fernández-Albertos

2012). The government thereby chose to abandon alternative anticrisis measures more in line with social democracy and the left in general, espousing the austerity path advocated by the German government and the European Commission.

Despite their harshness, the Spanish sovereign debt problems continued. In the summer of 2011, the European Central Bank sent letters to the prime ministers of Spain and Italy, suggesting, at least in the case of Spain, eight new reform items. As a result of the letter, Zapatero, without most of his ministers being aware, announced the reform of the constitution in parliament on August 23 to strictly limit the structural budget deficits and borrowing at all levels of administration in Spain. Among other serious consequences, this definitely affects the scope of the Spanish welfare state since its sustainability will be conditioned by the ability to obtain revenues, which in turn depend on unpopular fiscal policies and general economic conditions. A few months later, the PSOE experienced its worst election result in recent history. Upon the return of the PP to government in December 2011 with Prime Minister Rajoy, and in a context of severe crisis, all areas of social policy were cut, with the exception of pensions. None of these cuts has been debated in parliament and as a deputy of the opposition said, "The parliament has become a simple rubberstamp."

Health Care

Although most Spaniards would have said that the health system (NHS) provided universal coverage, the fact is that universal coverage was not reached until July 2011 with the general law of public health, passed by the Zapatero government. The law extended health care protection to the 200,000 people (about 0.5 percent of the population) who still lacked it, including the unemployed without benefits and the self-employed. However, this seems to have been the last piece of good news in this policy area.

In 2010, the PSOE government tried to contain pharmaceutical expenditures, which are among the highest in the world (OECD 2011a), with various measures such as the obligation to issue medicine prescriptions by active ingredient and the imposition of price cuts on pharmaceuticals. These measures, with a predicted savings of 5,000 million euros, were not fully implemented due to the enormous pressure from the pharmaceutical industry on the government, according to the Federation of Associations for the Defense of Public Health.[9]

Unlike the PSOE's electoral manifesto, the PP's manifesto for the 2011 elections did not present any concrete proposals to ensure the sustainability of the health care system. Nonetheless, the Rajoy government approved new regulations to save 7,000 million euros. Regarding pharmaceutical spending, the government increased the drug copayment for all employed workers (between 40 and 60 percent depending on their income), introduced a copayment for pensioners (between 8 and 60 euros per month depending on income), stopped funding 456 medicines and other pharmaceuticals such as prostheses, dietary products, and even ambulance transport for nonurgent cases. By some estimates drug costs paid by patients will double, from 6 to 12 percent (Sanfélix-Gimeno et al. 2012). Public spending on pharmaceuticals has strong redistributive effects (Gimeno-Ullastres 2000, 321) and therefore the reductions will have significant social implications.

The PP regulations also excluded the irregular immigrant population over 18 years from publicly provided health care, allowing access only in emergencies due to serious illness or accident, and care during pregnancy, childbirth, and postpartum. The government had to rectify the exclusion of some specific groups from the health care system that the new regulations left without protection (such as those over 26 who have not yet contributed and could not demonstrate a lack of resources). As a result, everyone who resides legally in Spain has access to public health care except those who have not contributed before and have incomes above 100,000 euros.

Some regions, like the Basque Country, announced their opposition to these measures and their intention to guarantee the coverage of all people residing within their borders, including illegal immigrants. Some regions have also refused to apply pharmaceutical copayments and medication exclusions. But most regional governments have enacted all sorts of cuts (staff, benefits, hours of operation, and coverage), fees (e.g., for renewal or loss of health cards) and payments (e.g., the so-called health care penny, a sales-tax of a few cents per liter of fuel purchased, which is used for health care spending purposes), and major privatizations, which may disguise the extent of public debt at first but increase health spending in the medium term.

In practice, the cuts in this policy area altered the principle of universality, represent a paradigm shift, and will quite certainly lead to a variety of health care models, creating differences not only between citizens of different regions but also between social groups with different income levels, reducing the redistributive capacity of health spending. This may bring about the deterioration of both the objective and perceived quality of the Spanish health care system.

Long-Term Care
Both the PP and the PSOE included in their 2004 electoral manifestos the implementation of a long-term care system for dependents, in line with other European countries, to correct the problems of the existing fragmented and very inadequate one. The PP government (2000–2004) had created a commission to study the issue but did not enact an initiative in that legislative term for budgetary reasons. With the PSOE in government, the dependency law was passed in 2006, which led to the universal right to public benefits for all dependent people, regardless of ability to pay.

As a result of this law, 760,000 people and their caregivers have improved their quality of life (Rodríguez-Cabrero & Marbán 2013). However, its implementation has been problematic and the situation has worsened steadily with the crisis and the new budget cuts. One of the main problems was that the initial estimate of the number of dependent people fell short. The evaluation of potential beneficiaries is still incomplete and has slowed down. The involvement of different levels of government in its implementation has led to a real war of figures regarding which level of government contributes more and who is responsible for the delays. It has also been criticized for disparities in the level of protection across regions. Finally, contrary to what was proposed in the law itself, monetary benefits have prevailed over the provision of services, largely due to the scarcity of the latter and the long tradition of home care in Spain (Sarasa 2011).

Long-term care had suffered cuts during the Zapatero government. In 2010, under the antideficit plan, the arrears on the long-term care benefits of those with recognized rights were eliminated. The 2011 PP electoral program (p. 116) committed to making the 2006 law sustainable, which Rajoy himself described as "non-viable" during the election campaign. After winning the election, the government extended the waiting period between the filing of a claim and the provision of the benefit and reduced the money that dependents receive for in-home care by a minimum of 15 percent. In addition, family caregivers, mostly women, are now obliged to pay their own contributions to social security, which were previously paid by the government. Finally, the inclusion into the system of those in the moderately dependent category was delayed until 2015, a year later than planned. According to experts, these cuts represent a "covert repeal" of the law, with "heartless and cruel measures" involving a reversion back to the situation prior to adoption of the dependency law.[10]

Education

In addition to initiatives related to early childhood education that will be discussed in the section on family policies, the main contribution of the PSOE government to education was to increase scholarships and programs to try to curb the high dropout rate. The Socialist government doubled the amount spent on scholarships from 2004 to 2010 (from 739 to 1,529 million euros). Already in the wake of the crisis and the new austerity context, it passed several other measures intended to boost vocational training to compensate for its traditional weakness in Spain. However, between 2009 and 2011, education budgets decreased about 1.6 percent even though the number of students, especially those in public schools, increased (CES 2012).

In May 2011, the Rajoy government approved a series of emergency measures to rationalize education spending, in turn affecting the regions, including a 20 percent increase in the number of students per classroom, an increase in teaching hours per teacher, and other measures that postponed or cancelled commitments contained in different organic laws. Most regions made cuts in 2012 ranging from teacher layoffs and pay cuts, suspending the construction of new infrastructure and improvement of the existing infrastructure, to the reduction of schools' daily operating budgets. Some grant programs for the purchase of books, aid for school meals, and scholarships for certain groups of students have disappeared. Many of these measures also apply to university.

Education policy is extremely controversial in Spain, where party alternation in government usually produces a change of the basic features of educational policies. The PP government is currently seeking to move forward the date by which students choose between high school and vocational training, that is, modify the comprehensiveness of education despite the recommendations of the OECD (2012), according to which one should avoid early separation from school and defer students' choice until upper secondary education in order to prevent inequality.

All of these measures led to great public protest and the so-called green tide—in reference to the protesters' use of the color green in the protests, including for their t-shirts—in defense of "public school." Some measures have been challenged before the Constitutional Court for violating the educational powers of regional governments. In late July 2012 the appeal lodged by the region of Navarre was admitted by the court. Some have argued that there is some room for spending cuts and that the amount of public spending is less important than the way it is spent. However, Spain has serious challenges to confront; other countries with similar expenditure levels responded to these long ago. So, the challenge in this policy area is whether more or the same can be accomplished with less money and an unmotivated and decimated teaching staff and/or whether this would imply undoing the progress already achieved regarding equity.

Family and Gender Policies
Zapatero's governments utilized the three main instruments of public policy in this area (programs for early childhood care and education, parental leaves, and cash benefits) over the two legislative terms. As argued by León and Salido (2013), one of the main challenges for Spain, both in terms of the employment of mothers and equal opportunities for children, is the level of education from zero to three years. This is an area dominated by the private sector and whose coverage levels are still very low. As was pledged in the PSOE's electoral manifesto, the government approved the plan to enhance early childhood education 0–3 (Educa3) with the aim of creating 300,000 additional child slots between 2008 and 2012. In 2009 the number of slots had increased by 101 percent and the enrollment rate among children under three years of age was up nearly 24 percent. However, the nearly 80,000 slots created by 2010 are still insufficient and the rate varies greatly across regions (between 52 and less than 15 percent) and is well below the target of 30 percent set by the EU (CES 2012).

However, the Educa3 program was criticized by the current PP minister of education, stating that it was "more an assisted-care program than an educational program" (León & Salido 2013) when he announced the termination of the program despite the PP having made a similar pledge as the PSOE in its 2011 election manifesto (pp. 83–86). The program's suppression can also be criticized because of the scientific evidence showing that early schooling improves intellectual development, especially among the economically disadvantaged, and is negatively correlated with school dropouts and positively with the avoidance of poverty.

On the other hand, regulations in 2007 and 2009 extended paternity leave from 2 to 13 days, which is now an individual and nontransferable leave right for fathers, as planned in the PSOE's electoral program. This measure was at times conceived of as a step to promote natality and at others as an instrument aimed at increasing equality between men and women (Bernadi & Sarasa 2009). The PSOE government also introduced leaves both during a high-risk pregnancy and for the lactation period. Paternity and maternity leaves doubled between 2004 and 2011, reaching more than 647,000. However, no progress was made beyond the framework of the European directives (16 weeks of maternity leave), nor has the goal of extending paternity leave to 4 weeks by 2011, as was pledged in the PSOE's electoral manifesto in 2004, been achieved (León & Salido 2013). Its potential contribution to increasing natality and reaching a family-work balance has been questioned, although its role in promoting gender equality has been recognized (Bernardi & Sarasa 2009).

In 2007, the Zapatero government introduced a program that was strongly criticized for being electorally motivated and improvised. It consisted of a universal cash benefit of 2,500 euros for the birth or adoption of a child. Although this baby allowance was not in the PSOE's electoral manifesto, some documents with similar proposals indeed existed (Bernadi & Sarasa 2009). The PP, which deemed the amount of the benefit, popularly known as the "baby-bonus," insufficient, had also proposed a similar measure. The Zapatero government was also criticized for the program's high cost and universal character, and, most importantly, for its lack of effectiveness in relation to increasing birthrates. The "baby-bonus" was suspended by the Zapatero government in early 2011. Despite the criticisms, this allowance was found to have helped reduce child poverty by 6.5 percent, a quarter of the total (Marí-Klose & Marí-Klose 2012).

Pensions and Social Transfers

During Zapatero's first term and in accordance with the PSOE's electoral manifesto, the government approved an increase of the national minimum wage. Moreover, between 2004 and 2008, minimum pensions increased by between 12 and 19 percent in real terms (OECD 2011b). While its impact on the reduction of poverty among the elderly has been minimal, it somewhat improved the purchasing power of employees and retirees with fewer resources (Bernardi & Sarasa 2009).

In early 2010, Prime Minister Zapatero announced a substantial pension reform consisting of a progressive increase of the retirement age from 65 to 67 and the extension of the period used to calculate the pension amount from 15 to 25 years. These measures will contribute to the financial sustainability of the Spanish pension system because they will reduce pension spending by the equivalent of 3.5 percent of GDP in the long term (OECD 2011b). However, it will also represent a substantial cut of more than 15 percent in the pensions of citizens. The reform also tightened the conditions to access early retirement. This reform was approved in parliament in July 2011 with only the support of the governing party and one regional party. It was negotiated with the unions, who managed to soften some of the original goals and obtained some advantages for groups such as women and young people (Rubio 2012).

In May 2010, Zapatero also announced the freezing of pensions in 2011, excluding noncontributory ones, arguing that the average pension had grown 16 percent since 2004 and 27 percent in the case of minimum pensions. He did not attain any support in parliament.

Although Spain faces worrying demographic trends, Spanish governments have implemented constant but only modest reforms to curb pension costs due to strong public support for the pension system and the concomitant political fear of being punished at the polls (del Pino & Ramos 2009). Although the problem of an aging population and the sustainability of the pension system clearly had to be addressed at some point (Chulia 2011), the budgetary impact of this reform will occur in the very long term, more than a decade after its enactment. It seems clear that the reform was intended to demonstrate the government's reformist will to international economic institutions and markets, and to take advantage of the weakness of social actors (Sánchez-Cuenca 2012).

At the time of writing, the Rajoy government has not touched pensions. However, the labor minister stated that an aging population requires "a change of the regulatory framework" to ensure the sustainability of the system. Still, many different measures are being discussed, from formulas that encourage working until an older age, to those proposed by the European Commission to accelerate the implementation of retirement at age 67, and even to cut back benefits and further increase the retirement age. Finally, one of the issues systematically lacking in the debate on pension reform is what its impact will be on other social problems associated with an aging population. For instance, who will take care of dependents and grandchildren if more women work longer and the pensions of their own dependents are less generous? How will it affect the employment of the young? What will happen to those numerous households in Spain that survive thanks to the pensions of grandparents?

Both Zapatero and Rajoy carried out important reforms that were opposed by the unions. However, in regard to unemployment protection, the dramatic rise in unemployment and its persistence encouraged Zapatero to introduce in August 2009 a new benefit of 426 euros for the unemployed who have exhausted their contributory or noncontributory unemployment benefits. This measure was replaced in February 2011 by a temporary retraining program (Prepara), which included a 400 euro stipend. The government extended this new program in August 2011. The Rajoy government approved a second extension of six months in December 2011. At the time of writing, it is uncertain if the government will eliminate the program. The government considered the program's performance to be poor, since only 6 percent of the unemployed found jobs (CES 2012), but, at the same time, abolishing it would leave about 100,000 families in a critical situation.

The PP government's economic adjustments enacted in July 2012 included a reduction of the amount of the unemployed benefit (the base unemployment benefit reduced from 60 to 50 percent from the sixth month onward for new recipients) and other measures that impede access to benefits for specific groups, such as the middle-aged and elderly unemployed. Rajoy justified the initiative by stating that it was intended to encourage people to get back to work, which is paradoxical in a country where 24 percent of the population is unemployed, and desperation among the unemployed is visible every day in news and in which the government eliminated many of the active employment policies in the 2012 budget, precisely those that are aimed at facilitating a return to the labor market. Also, in July 2012, access to the active insertion income, an extraordinary benefit for people with great difficulty finding a job, has been tightened. All of this occurs in a context in which two worrying trends are observed: a decline in the rate of benefit coverage, which will increase social vulnerability, and the intensification of the process of what has been called the "assistentialization" of unemployment protection, that is, the tendency to rely on noncontributory and means-tested benefits, as a result of long-term unemployment and the tightening of the conditions to receive contributory, and therefore more generous, benefits (CES 2012).

The Zapatero government also launched the basic income for emancipation in 2007 for young people between 22 and 30 years of age and living in rented accommodation. However, in December 2011, the Rajoy government eliminated this benefit for new applicants and reduced the monthly benefit amount for existing recipients to 210 euros (CES 2012). The Zapatero government abolished in 2010 a traditional subsidy for home purchases, and reduced the amount of some of the remaining assistance for home buying. Finally, other plans such as the National Action Plan for Social Inclusion 2011–13 are still pending or in the case of the strategic plan to help integrate immigrants (2011–14) have seen their budget allocation reduced, in this case to 800 million euros (from 2,000 in 2007–10). To these cuts, we must add widespread wage cuts, tax increases, at times of more regressive taxes, and the rising prices for other goods and basic services such as gas and electricity.

Conclusions

Structural problems, new social risks, and economic crisis have created a complex and variegated set of challenges for the Spanish welfare state.

The Socialist government sought to meet some of these challenges with the more or less successful modernization of social policies in its first term and in the first half of the second one. However, at the end of its mandate, beset by crisis, without any public or internal debate, it adopted harsh adjustment measures focused on reducing public spending, in particular social spending and, therefore, with serious consequences for equality. Zapatero's government ruled out other measures, for example, an adjustment via increasing revenues that a priori would seem more characteristic of a social democratic government.

The perception of the Socialist government's inefficient, clumsy, and unjust management of the crisis led to the PSOE's worst electoral defeat in recent democratic history. The victory of the political right was facilitated by the fact that a left-wing government, supposedly the defender of the welfare state, presented its welfare cuts as inevitable. When in December 2011, the PP took office with a vague electoral program, including only blurred proposals to reach the fuzzy aim of the country's sustainability, more aggressive cuts were implemented, again without a public debate. These cuts dismantled the modernizing reforms undertaken by Zapatero in the first term and even called into question some basic pillars of the Spanish welfare state. It remains to be seen what the consequences of these cuts will be in terms of social cohesion, democratic legitimacy, and political disaffection.

Notes

1. Eurostat data. Available at: http://epp.eurostat.ec.europa.eu/portal/page/portal/eurostat/home/.
2. Eurostat data.
3. Eurobarometer, European Commission, *Health and Long-Term Care in the European Union*, December 2007. Available at: http://ec.europa.eu/public_opinion/archives/ebs/ebs_283_en.pdf.
4. Eurostat data.
5. Instituto Nacional de Estadística (INE) data. Available at: http://www.ine.es/.
6. Eurostat data.
7. Eurostat data.
8. J. M. Lasalle, "Liberalismo antipático," *El País*, April 21, 2008.
9. Federation of Associations for the Defense of Public Health, untitled document. Available at: http://www.fadsp.org/pdf/RETIRADA%20DE%20MEDICAMENTOS%20DE%20LA%20FINANCIACION%20PUBLICA.doc (last accessed on October 5, 2012).
10. State Association of Managers and Directors of Social Services Spain, *Derogación encubierta de la Ley de dependencia*, July 16, 2012. Available

at: http://www.directoressociales.com/prensa/103-derogaci%C3%B3n-enc
ubierta-de-la-ley-de-dependencia.html.

WorksC ited

Ayala, L. 2011. "Tackling Poverty." In A. M. Guillén and M. León, eds., *The Spanish Welfare State in European Context*. Farnham: Ashgate, pp. 259–84.

Bernardi, F., and S. Sarasa. 2009. "Las nuevas políticas sociales del Gobierno Zapatero." In A. Bosco and I. Sánchez-Cuenca, eds., *La España de Zapatero. Años de cambios*. Madrid: Fundación Pablo Iglesias, pp. 227–48.

Bertelsmann Foundation. 2011. *Sustainable Governance Indicators 2011*. Berlin: Bertelsmann Foundation.

Calzada, I., and E. del Pino. 2011. "Are Spaniards Different? European Convergence and Regional Divergence in the Evaluation of the Welfare State." In Guillén and León, eds., *The Spanish Welfare State*, pp. 139–65.

CES (Consejo Económico y Social). 2012. *Memoria sobre la situación socioeconómica y laboral de España 2011*. Madrid: CES. Available at: www.ces.es.

Chulia, E. 2011. "Consolidation and Reluctant Reform of the Pension System." In Guillén and León, eds., *The Spanish Welfare State*, pp. 285–312.

Del Pino, E., and J. Ramos. 2009. "Las reformas de las políticas de bienestar en España." In L. Moreno, ed., *Reformas de las políticas de bienestar en España*. Madrid: Siglo XXI, pp. 337–62.

Del Pino, E., J. Díaz-Pulido, and P. Palop. 2011. *La administración publica a juicio de los ciudadanos*. Madrid: AEVAL.

Díaz-Pulido, J., E. del Pino, and P. Palop. 2012. "Los determinantes de la satisfacción con las políticas de bienestar del Estado autonómico." *Revista Española de Investigaciones Sociológicas* 139: 45–84.

Dolado, J. J., and P. Vázquez. 2008. *Ensayos sobre los efectos económicos de la inmigración en España*. Madrid: Fedea.

Esping-Andersen, G. 1990. *The Three Worlds of Welfare Capitalism*. Cambridge: Polity Press.

Fernández-Albertos, J. 2012. *Democracia intervenida. Políticas económicas en la gran recesión*. Madrid: Catarata.

Ferrera, M. 1996. "The Southern Model of Welfare in Social Europe." *Journal of European Social Policy* 6(1): 17–37.

Giddens, A. 1998. *The Third Way: The Renewal of Social Democracy*. Oxford: Blackwell.

Gimeno-Ullastres, J. 2000. "La incidencia redistributiva del gasto público en España." In R. Muñoz de Bustillo, ed., *El Estado de Bienestar en el cambio de siglo*. Madrid: Alianza Ensayo, pp. 279–322.

Guillén, A. M. 2010. "Defrosting the Spanish Welfare State: The Weight of Conservative Components." In B. Palier, ed., *A Long Goodbye to Bismarck. The Politics of Welfare Reform in Continental Europe*. Amsterdam: Amsterdam University Press, pp. 183–206.

Guillén, A. M., and M. León eds. 2011. "Introduction." In Guillén and León, eds., *The Spanish Welfare State*, pp. 1–14.

Léon, M., and O. Salido. 2013. "Las políticas de protección a las familias en perspectiva comparada: divergencias nacionales frente a desafíos compartidos." In E. del Pino and M. J. Rubio, eds., *Los Estados de Bienestar en la encrucijada. Políticas sociales en perspectiva comparada.* Madrid: Tecnos, pp. 291–309.

Marí-Klose, P., and M. Marí-Klose. 2012. "Edad, vulnerabilidad económica y Estado de Bienestar. La protección social contra la pobreza de niños y personas mayores." *Panorama social* 15: 1–19.

Molina, I. 2012. "Gobierno y desgobierno de la economía: las políticas de respuesta a la crisis." In C. Colino and R. Cotarelo, eds., *España en Crisis. Balance de la Segunda Legislatura de Rodríguez Zapatero.* Madrid: Tirant Humanidades, pp. 49–72.

Moreno Fuentes, F. J. 2013. "Políticas sanitarias en perspectiva comparada. Descentralización, mercados y nuevas formas de gestión en el ámbito sanitario." In del Pino and Rubio, eds., *Los Estados de Bienestar en la encrucijada*, pp. 169–88.

Moreno, L. 2004. "Spain's Transition to New Welfare: A Farewell to Superwomen." In P. Taylor-Gooby, ed., *New Risks, New Welfare: The Transformation of the European Welfare.* New York: Oxford University Press, pp. 133–57.

Moreno, L., and S. Sarasa. 1993. "Génesis y desarrollo del Estado de Bienestar en España." *Revista Internacional de Sociología* 6: 27–69.

Moreno, L., and P. Mari-Klose. 2013. "Bienestar Mediterráneo: trayectorias y retos de un régimen en transición." In del Pino and Rubio, eds., *Los Estados de Bienestar en la encrucijada*, pp. 126–46.

Moreno-Mínguez, A., and A. Gentile. 2011. "I giovani-adulti spagnoli tra lavoro e famiglia. Conciliazione di emancipazione in una prospettiva comparata e di genere." *Rivista delle Politiche Sociali* 3: 251–70.

Navarro, V. 2009. *La situación social de España.* Madrid: Biblioteca Nueva.

OECD. 2011a. *Health at a Glance.* Paris: OECD.

———. 2011b. *Pensions at a Glance: Retirement-Income Systems in OECD and G20 Countries.* Paris: OECD.

———. 2012. *Equity and Quality in Education.* Paris: OECD.

Pérez-Ortiz, L. 2004. "Envejecer en femenino. Perfiles y tendencias." In *Boletín sobre el envejecimiento 9.* Madrid: IMSERSO.

Pettit, P. 1999. *Republicanism: A Theory of Freedom and Government.* New York: Oxford University Press.

Pierson, P. 2001. "Coping with Permanent Austerity. Welfare State Restructuring in Affluent Democracies." In P. Pierson, ed., *The New Politics of the Welfare State.* Oxford: Oxford University Press, pp. 410–56.

Rodríguez-Cabrero, G. 2011. "The Consolidation of the Spanish Welfare State (1975–2010)." In Guillén and León, eds., *The Spanish Welfare State*, pp. 17–38.

Rodríguez-Cabrero, G., and V. Marbán. 2013. "La atención a la dependencia desde una perspectiva europea: de la asistencialización a la cuasi-universalización." In del Pino and Rubio, eds., *Los Estados de Bienestar en la encrucijada*, pp. 237–61.

Rubio, M. J. 2012. "Los avatares del Estado de Bienestar: Mercados, Política y Reforma de las Pensiones de Jubilación en España." In Colino and Cotarelo, eds., *España en Crisis*, pp. 383–410.

Sánchez-Cuenca, I. 2012. *Años de cambios, años de crisis. Ocho años de gobiernos socialistas 2004–2011*. Madrid: Catarata.

Sanfélix-Gimeno, G., S. Peiró, and R. Meneu. 2012. "La prescripción farmacéutica en atención primaria." *Gaceta Sanitaria* 26: 41–45.

Sarasa, S. 2011. "Long-Term Care: The Persistence of Familialism." In Guillén and León, eds., *The Spanish Welfare State*, pp. 237–58.

Taylor-Gooby, P. 2004. *New Risks, New Welfare*. Oxford: Oxford University Press.

WHO (World Health Organization). 2000. *World Health Report 2000*. Geneva: World Health Organization.

CHAPTER 12

Conclusions

Alfonso Botti and Bonnie N. Field

After a an extensive review of the second term of Prime Minister José Luis Rodríguez Zapatero and the initial months of the Popular Party (PP) government led by Mariano Rajoy, the contributors to this volume agree on some points, as do a number of other analysts, political scientists, historians, sociologists, and economists that have engaged elsewhere in their own analyses in the still sparse international academic literature on the subject (Colino & Cotarelo 2012; Sánchez-Cuenca 2012).

The first is the view that Zapatero's first term in office was highly innovative regarding the extension of rights, particularly welfare and women's rights. The reforms and changes of the first term, though they were in some cases attacked for being too radical, received the support of the citizens of the Iberian country in the general elections of 2008. Another interpretive convergence is one that highlights the significant difference between the first and the second terms—the second term marked by the outbreak of the financial and later international economic crisis—and underlines the Socialist leader's lack of effective judgment, and his underestimation of the gravity of the crisis with the resulting delay in the adoption of polices able to counteract it effectively. Most of the contributors also agree that the principal causes of the Socialist Party (PSOE) defeat in the November 2011 general elections were precisely this delay and the nature of the policies adopted, and moreover that the disillusionment of the Socialist electorate was the reason for the extraordinary triumph of Mariano Rajoy's Popular Party. They also tend to share the view that the results of the November 2011 elections represented a defeat of the Socialists more than a triumph of the Popular

Party. Along the way, there were other interpretive convergences that are still provisional and require more time and research to be conclusive. This is particularly true of those that relate to the new political phase that began with the inauguration of the Rajoy government, which had yet to complete a year in office when this book went to press.

Like his predecessor after 2008, Rajoy enjoys very little decision-making autonomy in the face of European authorities' directives due to the extraordinary magnitude of the economic crisis. For this reason, Rajoy also continued along the same path of more adjustments and even deeper cuts, to which he added an increase of value added taxes (VAT), which will affect consumption, demonstrating very little sensitivity for the conditions of the popular classes. On the other hand, along with the policies that signify a retrenchment of the welfare state, which will disproportionally impact women—and that the government has attempted to justify as necessary for reducing government spending—the new government has also brought back ideological attitudes characteristic of the political right. Examples include: the announced reform of the abortion law that if enacted would mean a return to the legislation that existed prior to 1985; little demonstrated willingness to date to facilitate the definitive dissolution of ETA (Basque Homeland and Freedome) (possibly through moving prisoners closer to home, aiding their reintegration into civilian life, and so forth); the suppression of public health care for undocumented immigrants, which unleashed the protests of hundreds of doctors. Moreover, it is now clear that the Rajoy government's actions do not fulfill the promises made during the election campaign and that the PP's votes opposing the Zapatero government's policies to confront the crisis were political in nature.

Despite the limited autonomy mentioned previously, Rajoy is reproached by much of the public for not being able to take advantage of the autonomy he does have. He is criticized for bypassing parliamentary debate, not communicating with the public, and, in the end, for the same calming attitude in political communication that was used by his predecessor. An example of this is his refusal to use the word *rescate* (rescue) when referring the financial bailout of the banking sector. This assistance was negotiated with the Eurogroup in the summer of 2012 and provides up to 100,000 million euros to recapitalize banking institutions such as Bankia, whose debt exposure (especially due to the rate of unpaid mortgages) was estimated to be, at worst, 270,000 million euros.[1] In the short term, the Spanish government set the necessary amount at 62,000 million euros to confront the emergency.

Data provided by *Centro de Investigaciones Sociológicas* (CIS) for July 2012 reveal that: 68.9 percent of those surveyed viewed the country's political situation negatively or very negatively; 56.1 percent viewed the actions of the government in the same way; and those who indicate that they have "a lot" or "sufficient" (*bastante*) confidence in Mariano Rajoy amounts to only 19.9 percent of those surveyed, compared to 77.9 percent that indicate they have "little" or "no" confidence in the current prime minister.[2]

There are two additional conclusions that clearly emerge from various book chapters. The first underlines the structural dimensions of the Spanish economic crisis, finding its roots in the economic model of the Iberian country. This interpretation, on the one hand, reduces the responsibility of the two Socialist Party governments of Prime Minister Zapatero and implicates the prior Popular Party administrations of José María Aznar, and, on the other, it makes the two principal parties co-responsible in a longer-term perspective due to their lethargy in changing the economic model, a model that is too dependent on real estate and tourism, *ladrillo y sombrilla*[3]; an industrial system marked by low productivity indexes, poor export capacity, poor workforce specialization, insufficient investment in research and innovation, and belated and inadequate attention to energy problems and alternative and renewable energy sources. An economic model moreover that is based on the excessive power of banks and, more generally, on the idea that economic growth would never end, and in a culture of easy enrichment thanks to risky financial operations (implanted in Spain in the second half of the 1980s during the period of economic expansion under the Socialist administration). A culture shared by the middle and large sections of the working classes who far from saving have become indebted not only to purchase their homes, but also their cars and various consumer goods to order to attain a certain standard of living.

In the face of unemployment, government spending cuts, the impoverishment of the so-called middle class, and the falling living standards of a vast majority of Spaniards—one in four of which lives in poverty—it would be easy to conclude that the country as a whole has euphorically lived above it possibilities. However, this would only be a half-truth because a judgment of this nature would leave out that it has been precisely Spain's lifestyle, with its *fiestas* and even excesses included, the extraordinary processes of modernization of infrastructure and of its collective mindset, and the continuous generational change at the summit of political power, that, beginning with its transition to democracy, converted Spain into one of the most vital, dynamic, and energetic countries of the *viejo continente* (old world).

The second shared conclusion is that the crisis the country is experiencing is not only economic in nature but also social, cultural, and political. In fact various factors indicate that the economic crisis coincided with, or led to, or simply joined a political and systemic crisis that could lead to the end of a period that began in 1975–78 and with it the need for a "second transition." A real second transition and not the one Prime Minister Aznar announced with electoral motivations in the mid-1990s (Aznar 1994). Sectors of the political left and some peripheral nationalists before and during Prime Minister Zapatero's first term also expressed their desire for a second transition in Spain that would expand, correct, or improve, from their perspectives, some of the limitations of the transition from the dictatorship to democracy and of the current democracy, but their expectations were frustrated (Field 2011). It is the opinion of the authors that many important political changes have indeed occurred, with Aznar and later with Zapatero, but not a deep reconfiguration of democracy in Spain that is perhaps necessary.

The symptoms of this social, cultural, and political crisis are quite clear. To begin with, the loss of citizen confidence in Spain's political class that we mentioned in the introduction to this volume is clear. Spain's political class is numerically bloated with more politicians per capita than any other country in Europe—300,000 more than in Germany and double the number in France and Italy.[4] The perception of corruption is another symptom. The tensions that have ridden society, upon which the indignant movement acted, are still another indication. The criticisms of the electoral system, which appears to be locked into a closed alternation between two parties that together represent only 49.9 percent of the electorate and 73.4 percent of those who cast a vote,[5] point to an additional problem. The territorial organization of the state and the multilevel administrative system, which including municipalities, provinces, autonomous communities, and the central-state administration, need reform, perhaps structural, that without jeopardizing the level of political-administrative decentralization would prevent the exponential increase of the bureaucracy (and its corresponding costs) and contribute to better managing the distinct identities in Spain and their coexistence.

We must not forget that it has been precisely during times of crisis, whether of vision for the future or economic, that the social and political fabric and the identity of the Iberian country have cracked or even broken. This is what happened after the crisis of 1898 when some regionalisms were converted to nationalisms, often anti-Spanish. And despite the distance that separates us from that time, there are indications that lead one to think about a future in which the so-called peripheral nationalisms may again determine the political agenda of the Iberian country.[6] This is the case of Catalonia, which in the summer of 2012 saw the radicalization of sovereignty (self-determination) demands, which for the first time were explicitly adopted by Convergence and Union (CiU). This is a development that, if strengthened, could end up creating a crisis for Spain's peculiar condition of plural and in large part shared identities (Botti 2007).

Moving from society and politics to the institutions—even the monarchy finds itself on less solid ground than before. On May 13, 2009, in the Mastalla stadium in Valencia, with King Juan Carlos present, the soccer fans of the two teams competing in the *Copa del Rey* (King's Cup), Atletic Bilbao and Barcelona's Barça, booed and hissed during the playing of Spain's national anthem. The state television censored the protest, which with the presence of the sovereign signified its antimonarchical as well as anti-Spanish significance. The royal family has also been tainted by the scandals associated with Princess Cristina's husband Iñaki Urdangarín, allegedly involved in illicit financial dealings that have been under investigation since November 2011. On April 12, 2012, King Juan Carlos himself broke a hip while in Botswana for a safari. The carefree living of the sovereign while his subjects were suffering the economic crisis did not go unnoticed by public opinion. This time the media did not keep it quiet, and for the first time, setting an important precedent, the media broke the curtain of respectful silence that had protected the crown since the night of February 23, 1981, when the king was instrumental in frustrating the attempted military coup led by Coronel Tejero. The king had to publicly apologize. Under the circumstances some even suggested the king abdicate in favor of his son Prince Felipe, whose marriage to Letizia is also not free from rumors. In constitutional monarchies the private lives of the royal family form part of the public debate; however, Spain had never experienced what in the United Kingdom is commonplace. This is a turning point in terms of public attitudes that any honest researcher cannot help but note and report.

For the same reason it would not be appropriate to disregard two features, this time positive, that the Spain of recent years and concretely Zapatero's two terms have left as a legacy. The first refers to the end of ETA's (Basque Homeland and Freedom) terrorist activity. Independent of Zapatero's willingness to dialogue that led to ETA's announcement of a ceasefire on March 22, 2006, the police investigations and the state apparatus' fight against terrorism never ceased during the prime minister's two terms. Proof of this is the captures of ETA's political leader Mikel Albizu along with his companion Soledad Iparragirre on October 3, 2004, of the reputed top leader of ETA, Javier López Peña, on May 20, 2008, in

France, and, also in France, of Aitor Elizaran Aguilar on October 19, 2009, considered to be the organization's ideological leader.

Several factors led to ETA's announcement in October 2011 of the definitive end of armed conflict. Without implying a rank order, we must mention: the weakening of the terrorist organization itself due to the police activity just mentioned (that naturally extends to include the two terms of Prime Minister Aznar); the banning of *Batasuna* under the political parties law that was supported by the PP and the PSOE on June 27, 2002; pressure from radical nationalists who came to conclude that an exclusive commitment to political activity was more productive; a change of the domestic and international climate with the threat and concrete activity of Islamist terrorism; and ETA's lack of a strategic direction after the failure of the strategies of insurrection, of attrition, and of the nationalist front (Botti 2003; Sánchez-Cuenca 2009).

The second positive feature relates to immigration and Spanish society's overall attitude toward it. By March 31, 2012, non-European Union (EU) foreign, legal residents amounted to 2,730,907 (29.8 percent of which are from Morocco), to which we must add 2,563,803 EU citizens (35.3 percent or 903,964 of which come from Romania) that are also resident in Spain, which totals 5,294,710 foreigners and represents an increase of 0.83 percent over the prior trimester. In both cases the age group most represented is 20- to 54-year-olds, who are therefore of working age; 68 percent of non-EU foreign residents live in four autonomous communities, specifically Catalonia (781,881), Madrid (507,420), Andalusia (286,956), and Valencia (278,980), for a total of 1,855,237 people.[7] To these numbers we would need to add the unknown number of clandestine or undocumented immigrants.

The migration flows began to affect the demographic structure of the Iberian country in the second half of the 1990s; the presence of immigrants consistently increased from 2 percent in 2000 and reached 12 percent of the total resident population in 2012, according to recent data from the Spanish National Statistics Institute (INE).[8] Even considering the slight decrease in the presence of foreigners during the past year, due to the economic crisis, it is relevant to note that along with the demographic structure Spain's human landscape has changed.

During the last decade immigration has been a contentious subject of public debate, used instrumentally, especially by the political right, for electoral ends, not very differently than what has occurred in the rest of the European Union. Spain has certainly experienced episodes of high tension, confrontations in which force was used to keep immigrants out (such as occurred between September and October 2005 on the border between Morocco and Melilla, a Spanish city in north Africa), and frequent appeals to European authorities to enact common measures within the framework of a EU policy on immigration.

Yet, and considering the high rate of unemployment, it must be seen as a positive that in Spain, despite some episodes of racism, the right has not experienced a xenophobic turn, nor have xenophobic populist movements arisen, with one exception that will be discussed here, as has occurred in other European countries: in France with the National Front of Le Pen, father and daughter (13.6 percent of the vote, 2012 first-round legislative elections); in Italy with the Northern League of Umberto Bossi and Mario Borghezio (8.3 percent, 2008 parliamentary elections); in Switzerland with the Swiss People's Party of Christoph Blocher (26.6 percent, 2011 federal elections); in Austria with the Freedom Party and Alliance for the Future of Austria (17.5 and 10.7 percent, respectively, 2008 legislative elections); in the Netherlands with the Freedom Party of Geert Wilders (15.5 percent, 2010 legislative elections); in Belgium with Flemish Interest (7.8 percent, 2010 parliamentary elections); in Hungary with *Jobbik*, the Movement for a Better Hungary (16.7 percent, 2010 parliamentary elections); in Romania with the Greater Romania Party (8.6 percent, 2009 European elections); in Bulgaria with the *Ataka* party (9.4 percent, 2009 parliamentary elections); in Sweden with Sweden Democrats (5.7 percent, 2010 parliamentary elections); in Norway with the Progress Party (22.9 percent, 2009 parliamentary elections); in Denmark with the Danish People's Party (12.3 percent, 2011 parliamentary elections); in Finland with True Finns (19 percent, 2011 parliamentary elections); and last in Greece with the neo-Nazi Golden Dawn (7 percent, June 2012 parliamentary elections), not to mention in Germany with the German Republican Party, the National Democratic Party, and the German People's Union.

In Spain, specifically in Catalonia, which is the autonomous community with the greatest presence of immigrants, the movement Platform for Catalonia (PxC) led by Josep Anglada has been active since 2001. Anglada is a Francoism nostalgic who belonged to the extreme right-wing organization *Fuerza Nueva* (New Force) of Blas Piñar, for which he was a candidate in the European elections of 1989. In the Catalan regional elections of 2010 PxC won approximately 75,000 votes (2.4 percent of the vote) and did not obtain any seats. Similar movements have also appeared in the autonomous communities of Valencia and Madrid, but with little or no success.

Various factors may help explain why populist, xenophobic, and even neo-Nazi parties in Spain have not been successful: a Catholicism that in its distinct forms, from the most traditional to the postconciliar and more progressive, has never supported racially exclusive discourse; anti-Francoist exile and the memory of it; an electoral system that does not favor the formation of new political parties; and finally the reaction since the transition to democracy against the prior intolerance have all made Spain one of the most tolerant countries in Europe. Even in an era of uncertainty like we are now experiencing, not everything that comes from the other side of the Pyrenees is cause for worry.

Notes

1. "Las consultoras cifran las pérdidas esperadas hasta 270.000 millones," *El País*, June 22, 2012.
2. Centro de Investigaciones Sociológicas (CIS) study 2951 (July 2012). Available at: www.cis.es.
3. Translation: brick and beach umbrella.
4. This is according to a study carried out by three advisors of the Presidency of the Government. See: "España tiene más políticos que policías, médicos y bomberos juntos," *Financiero Digital*, May 21, 2012.
5. Data from the 2011 elections. The latter statistic is calculated based on the total number of valid votes.
6. This is echoed in some of the contributions collected in "La Spagna non è l'Uganda," *Limes*, 2012, n. 4.
7. Official data of the Spanish government. Available at: http://extranjeros.empleo.gob.es/es/Estadisticas/operaciones/con-certificado/201203/Principales_resultados_31032012.pdf. Also see: "Bad New Days," *The Economist*, February 4, 2010.
8. Data available at: http://www.ine.es/prensa/np710.pdf.

WorksC ited

Aznar, J. M. 1994. *España: Una segunda transición*. Madrid: Espasa Calpe.

Botti, A. 2003. *La questione basca*. Milan: Bruno Mondadori.

———, ed. 2007. *Le patrie degli spagnoli. Spagna democratica e questioni nazionali (1975–2005)*. Milan: Bruno Mondadori.

Colino, C., and R. Cotarelo, eds. 2012. *España en crisis: Balance de la segunda legislatura de Rodríguez Zapatero*. Valencia: Tirant Humanidades.

Field, B. N., ed. 2011. *Spain's "Second Transition"? The Socialist Government of José Luis Rodríguez Zapatero*. New York: Routledge.

Sánchez-Cuenca, I. 2009. "ETA: del proceso de paz al regreso de la violencia." In A. Bosco and I. Sánchez-Cuenca, eds., *La España de Zapatero: Años de cambios, 2004–2008*. Madrid: Editorial Pablo Iglesias, pp. 129–52.

———. 2012. *Años de cambios, años de crisis: Ocho años de gobiernos Socialistas, 2004–2011*. Madrid: Catarata.

Index